Landgartha

Landgartha.

A Tragie-Comedy, as it was presented in the new Theater in *Dublin*,
with good applause, being
an Ancient story,

✿✿✿✿✿✿✿✿✿✿✿✿✿✿✿✿✿✿✿✿✿✿✿✿✿✿✿✿✿

VVritten by H. B.

✿✿✿✿✿✿✿✿✿✿✿✿✿✿✿✿✿✿✿✿✿✿✿✿✿✿✿✿✿

HORAT.
Hunc socci cepere pedem, grandesq; cothurni.

Printed at *Dublin* Anno 1641.

LANDGARTHA
A Tragie-Comedy

HENRY BURNELL

edited with an introduction and notes by
Deana Rankin

FOUR COURTS PRESS

Set in 10.5 pt on 12.5 pt Bembo for
FOUR COURTS PRESS
7 Malpas Street, Dublin 8, Ireland
www.fourcourtspress.ie
and in North America for
FOUR COURTS PRESS
c/o ISBS, 920 N.E. 58th Avenue, Suite 300, Portland, OR 97213.

A catalogue record for this title
is available from the British Library.

ISBN 978–1–84682–339–8

Printed in England
by Antony Rowe Ltd, Chippenham, Wilts.

Contents

The Literature of Early Modern Ireland series

Also in the series:
Faithful Teate, *Ter Tria*, ed. Angelina Lynch (2007)
Henry Burkhead, *Cola's Furie*, ed. Angelina Lynch and Patricia Coughlan (2009)
Richard Nugent, *Cynthia*, ed. Angelina Lynch and Anne Fogarty (2010)
William Dunkin, *The Parson's Revels*, ed. Catherine Skeen (2010)

Early Irish Fiction, *c.*1680–1820

Titles in the series
[Anon.] *Virtue Rewarded; or, the Irish Princess* (1693), ed. Ian Campbell Ross and Anne Markey (2010)
Sarah Butler, *Irish Tales* (1716), ed. Ian Campbell Ross, Aileen Douglas, and Anne Markey (2010)
Henry Brooke, Margaret King Moore, John Carey, *Children's Fiction, 1765–1808*, ed. Anne Markey (2011)
Thomas Amory, *The Life of John Buncle, Esq.* (1756), ed. Moyra Haslett (2011)
Elizabeth Sheridan, *The Triumph of Prudence over Passion* (1781), ed. Aileen Douglas and Ian Campbell Ross (2011)
William Chaigneau, *The History of Jack Connor* (1752), ed. Ian Campbell Ross (2013)

Forthcoming title in the series
Charles Johnstone, *The History of Arsaces, Prince of Betlis* (1774), ed. Daniel Sanjiv Roberts (2014)

Preface

This series of editions of English-language texts from seventeenth- and eighteenth-century Ireland was begun in 2007, under the general editorship of Professor Andrew Carpenter of University College Dublin, in the belief that the study of Early Modern Ireland was in a new and exciting phase. With thousands of web-based images of English-language texts from Early Modern Ireland increasingly available to scholars and students – notably through Early English Books Online (EEBO) and Eighteenth Century Collections Online (ECCO) – the necessity for critical editions of key texts was, and remains, acute. The intervening years have confirmed the high levels of interest in Early Modern Ireland and the series continues to offer authoritative editions of texts, edited to the highest standards and set in context by scholars of international standing, at a time when the very need for such critical editions is increasingly little understood outside of departments of English and related disciplines.

The Literature of Early Modern Ireland series runs in tandem with the Early Irish Fiction, *c*.1680–1820 series of prose fictions, under the general editorship of Professor Aileen Douglas of Trinity College Dublin, Professor Moyra Haslett of Queen's University Belfast, and the present General Editor. The series now includes six titles, offering works published between 1693 and 1808, with a further title scheduled for 2014 and other titles under active discussion.

Ian Campbell Ross
General Editor
Dublin, July 2013

[7]

Acknowledgments

I acknowledge with thanks grants from the Royal Holloway, University of London Research Fund and the Department of English, Royal Holloway, towards the costs of publication. The frontispiece illustration of the title-page of *Landgartha* (1641) is from Malone 203 (2) and is reproduced by kind permission of the Bodleian Libraries, University of Oxford.

Work on this edition has benefitted enormously from conversations with colleagues in Girton College, Cambridge, Royal Holloway, NUI Galway and in many other places. My thanks are especially due to Toby Barnard, Sarah Broom, Colin Burrow, Nicholas Canny, Daniel Carey, Jean Chothia, Patricia Coughlan, Juliet Dusinberre, Sinéad Garrigan Mattar, Ed Gaughan, Selina Guinness, John Kerrigan, David Norbrook, Jane Ohlmeyer, Patricia Palmer, Will Poole, Kiernan Ryan, Elizabeth Schafer, Anne Varty and Nick Whitfield. Thanks also to the staff of the Bodleian Library, Boston Public Library, British Library, Harvard University Library, Henry E. Huntington Library, National Library of Ireland, Trinity College Dublin Library. As editors for this series, Andrew Carpenter and Ian Campbell Ross have given both inspiration and endless, patient support. Thanks are also due to Martin Fanning and the staff of Four Courts Press. Finally, as ever, thanks to Wes Williams – my best and most demanding reader – to T.J., and to Elsie Mae, my Amazon.

Deana Rankin
Oxford, July 2013

Introduction

Deana Rankin

Originally dedicated '*To all faire, indifferent faire, vertuous, that are not faire and magnanimous Ladies*', Henry Burnell's *Landgartha: A Tragie-comedy* (Dublin, 1640) dramatizes the epic adventures of a Norwegian Amazon, her loyal followers and her royal neighbours – Frollo, King of Sweden and Reyner, King of Denmark.[1] Burnell is far from alone in reworking this Amazon heroine's tale: from tragi-comedy, through historical drama, to ballet, and most recently a television series, hers is a story that has been subject to a number of distinct, compelling re-imaginings. On each occasion, she has served to inaugurate, or authorize, a new mode of dramatic representation: Burnell's *Landgartha* is the first play by an Irish-born writer to be both staged and published in Dublin.[2] Performed at the first purpose-built theatre in Ireland, the published text also takes pride in presenting an English-language definition of its chosen genre, tragicomedy, unique for the early modern period.

Landgartha also has the distinction of being one of just two major characters from the canon of early modern plays in English who can be said to trace their origins back to Saxo Grammaticus' twelfth-century *Gesta Danorum* or *The History of the Danes*; the other is Hamlet.[3] While Shakespeare's *Hamlet* (*c.*1599–1601) is generally held to be one of the most performed plays of all time, *Landgartha*, so far as I can ascertain, has been performed just once, on St Patrick's

---

1 *Landgartha*, 'The Epistle Dedicatorie' (p. 73). All subsequent references are to this present edition and are given in parentheses in the text.

2 The figure of Landgartha/Lathgertha inspired the tragic heroine of the historical drama *Lagertha* (1789) by Christen Pram, one of the leading Norwegian-Danish writers of his day and the first ballet based on Nordic History *Lagertha* (1801), composed for the Royal Danish Ballet, was adapted by Vincenza Galeotti from Pram's play. More recently, Lagertha and her husband Ragnar Lothbrok have co-starred in the acclaimed Irish-Canadian TV series *The Vikings,* dir. Michael Hirst (Octagon Films and Take 5 Productions for the History Channel, 2013–). She was also central to Joshua Barnes' unperformed masque 'Landgartha, or the Amazon Queen of Denmark and Norway' (1683), see note 89 below.

3 On *Hamlet* see Israel Gollancz, *The Sources of Hamlet* (London: H. Milford, 1926); William F. Hansen, *Saxo Grammaticus and the Life of Hamlet* (Lincoln, NE: University of Nebraska Press, 1983).

Day, 17 March 1640, at the Werburgh Street Theatre, Dublin.⁴ We know of this performance only because Burnell himself records the date in the published version of the play, which appeared, also in Dublin, some months after the event, prefaced by four celebratory poems – in Latin and in English – and the dedication '*To all faire, indifferent faire, vertuous, that are not faire and magnanimous Ladies*' noted above. If Burnell's *Landgartha* now appears, in a second Dublin edition, complete with liminary materials, more than 370 years after its first appearance, then it does so in the hope of reaching a wider audience among those interested in any or all of the diverse fields across which Landgartha's adventures take her: early modern literature in English; theatre and performance; Irish history; women's studies, and the reception of Scandinavian literature.

Given its Scandinavian subject, Burnell's play might, at first sight, appear less than likely to engage its original Dublin audience. In fact, *Landgartha* speaks to immediately contemporary events and lends itself readily to an allegorical reading. The three Scandinavian kingdoms of Norway, Denmark and Sweden can be mapped neatly on to the British kingdoms of Ireland, England and Scotland. In the immediate context of early 1640, as tensions across the Three Kingdoms escalated, and as Charles I looked to Ireland for both financial and military help in the battle against Scotland, Burnell's Scandinavian drama, far from being received as oddly exotic, was most likely recognized by its contemporary audience as a locally engaged piece of political theatre. The Norwegians, chiefly Landgartha and the Amazons, stand for the Irish; Reyner and the Danes are Charles I and the English in allegorical disguise; and Frollo, Vraca and the Swedes represent the Scots.

When the printed version appears in the year following the performance, its title-page proudly advertises the 'good applause' *Landgartha* received. Acknowledging that his experiment was not an unqualified success, Burnell also regretfully admits, on the final page of his text, that 'Some (but not of best judgements) were offended at the Conclusion of this Play'. Beyond this, we know nothing about the reception of the play's one and only performance. *Landgartha* enjoyed little in the way of serious critical attention over the centuries that followed. Its modern reception begins with Ethel Seaton's memorable characterization of it as '[a]n absurd play of no merit.'⁵ Chastizing Burnell for the ill-informed application of his apparently little learning, Seaton, whose book remains the standard scholarly study of early modern links between Scandinavia

---

4 Unless otherwise indicated, dates given follow the Gregorian calendar with the first day of the year being 1 January.

5 Ethel Seaton, *Literary Relations of England and Scandinavia in the Seventeenth Century* (Oxford: Clarendon Press, 1935), p. 320.

and England, is scathing in her criticism. Pursuing a realist reading, she closes in on inaccurate character names as an example of 'the limits of Burnell's knowledge and the barrenness of his invention, Scania and Elsinora unsuitably applied to two Norwegian ladies!'[6] Seaton's comments may appear dated, but more recent critics – the present writer included – have also been rather dismissive of *Landgartha*.[7] Christopher Murray, in his introduction to early Irish drama for *The Field Day Anthology*, calls it, in terms clearly not intended as complimentary, 'a gallimaufray of the most extraordinary kind'. The repeated accusation is not only that the author has little control over his material, but also that the local contexts of the play are imperfectly managed. Referring to the scene in which the Irish Amazon Marfisa dances at Landgartha's wedding, Murray speculates that a frustrated John Ogilby – Master of Revels and manager of Dublin's Werburgh Street Theatre – must have intervened from behind the scenes to make at least some local sense of the exotic action: 'One may infer that Ogilby, a dancing master after all, thought to win Dublin audiences by interpolating Irish dances and a dash of spectacle into quite foreign material'.[8]

Both Seaton and Murray usefully draw attention to the question of the play's geographical and generic complexity, but both, also, miss the point. For Burnell is striving neither for authenticity nor for locally accented realism: *Landgartha*'s unique qualities lie rather elsewhere. Murray rightly acknowledges the importance of the Werburgh Street Theatre, and its manager Ogilby, but misses the significance of the performance of Burnell's play on this particular stage at this particular time.[9] For *Landgartha* captures the evanescent cultural energy of a particular ethnic group

6 Ibid., 321. In 1640 Scania (now in Sweden) and Elsinore (Helsingør) were both part of Denmark.

7 This edition expands, updates and corrects my previous writings on *Landgartha*, see Deana Rankin, 'Burnell, Henry (*fl.* 1640–1654)' *ODNB* (Oxford: Oxford University Press, 2004); *Between Spenser and Swift: English Writing in Seventeenth-century Ireland* (Cambridge: Cambridge University Press, 2005), pp 75–116; '"Betwixt Both": Sketching the Borders of Seventeenth-Century Tragicomedy' in Raphael Lyne and Subha Mukherji (eds), *Early Modern Tragicomedy* (Woodbridge: D.S. Brewer, 2007), pp 193–208; 'Kinds of Irishness: Henry Burnell and Richard Head', in Julia M. Wright (ed.), *The Blackwell Companion to Irish Literature* (Oxford: Wiley-Blackwell, 2010), I, pp 108–24.

8 Christopher Murray in A. Bourke, A. Carpenter, S. Deane et al. (eds), *The Field Day Anthology of Irish Writing*, 5 vols (Derry: Field Day, 1991–2002), I, p. 501. This scene is discussed further below pp 56–64. For an informed and nuanced contextualization of the play, see Anne Fogarty, 'Literature in English, 1550–1690' in Margaret Kelleher and Philip O'Leary (eds), *The Cambridge History of Irish Literature*, 2 vols (Cambridge: Cambridge University Press, 2006), I, pp 140–90 (165–6).

9 John Ogilby, first Master of Revels in Ireland, established the Werburgh Street Theatre *c.*1637; it closed in 1641. A successful translator, publisher and geographer, Ogilby returned to Dublin after the Restoration in 1662 to establish the Smock Alley Theatre, see K. van Eerde, *John Ogilby and the Taste of his Times* (Folkestone: Dawson, 1976).

at a crucial moment in its history: the Old English in Dublin on the verge of war and political upheaval across the Three Kingdoms. Even the singularity of the 'one night only' performance can, when seen from this perspective, be argued as a source of strength. *Landgartha*'s staging of marital and military contracts, its tracing of a sorry tale of fidelity and betrayal, was a piece of early modern performance art: a time-based installation, designed not simply as entertainment for St Patrick's Day, but for one particular St Patrick's Day: the eve of the opening of the first session of business for Charles I's second Irish parliament.[10]

As Patricia Coughlan has eloquently argued in her introduction to Henry Burkhead's 1646 Kilkenny play, *Cola's Furie*, the study of early modern Irish plays has benefited greatly in recent years from renewed scholarly interest in the broader political contexts of drama of the Caroline and Republican periods, *c*.1630–60.[11] In the case of *Landgartha*, Catherine Shaw was one of the first to relocate the play in its particular moment and to explore the resonances of contemporary political crisis which animate the drama. Others swiftly followed, inscribing the play's presence in a pre-history of modern Irish drama.[12] As *Landgartha* began to establish itself as part of a small but growing canon of Irish literature in English, the first printed edition of the play since 1641 appeared as part of a larger editorial project on early modern Irish drama.[13]

A number of recent critical studies have helped to correct certain misconceptions concerning the significance of the play in its peculiar political moment. In so doing, they draw on what we might call the folk memory of the single

10 The second Irish parliament opened on 16 March, was recalled for 18 March and then – because Wentworth had only just landed from England – was prorogued until 20 March, when business began, see Viscount Mountnorris, *The History of the Principal Transactions of the Irish Parliament, from the Year 1634 to 1666*, 2 vols (London, 1792), I, pp 333–4.

11 Angelina Lynch (ed.) *Henry Burkhead, A Tragedy of Cola's Furie; or, Lirenda's Miserie* (Dublin: Four Courts Press, 2009), pp 9–32 (10–12). See, for example, Martin Butler, *Theatre and Crisis, 1632–1642* (Cambridge: Cambridge University Press, 1984), though he does not include discussion of the Dublin stage; Sue Wiseman, *Drama and Politics in the English Civil War* (Cambridge: Cambridge University Press, 1998); Dale B.J. Randall, *Winter Fruit: English Drama, 1642–1660* (Lexington: University Press of Kentucky, 1995); Janet Clare, *Drama of the English Republic, 1649–60* (Manchester: Manchester University Press, 2002).

12 Catherine M. Shaw, 'Landgartha and the Irish Dilemma', *Eire-Ireland*, 13 (Spring 1978), 26–34. See also Alan Fletcher's seminal study *Drama, Performance, and Polity in Pre-Cromwellian Ireland* (Toronto: University of Toronto Press, 2000), pp 261–80 and his *Drama and the Performing Arts in Pre-Cromwellian Ireland, sources and documents from the Earliest Times until c.1642* (Woodbridge: D.S. Brewer, 2001), pp 450–2, 488; Christopher Morash, *A History of Irish Theatre, 1601–2000* (Cambridge: Cambridge University Press, 2002), pp 8–10.

13 Christopher Wheatley and Kevin Donovan (eds), *Irish Drama of the Seventeenth and Eighteenth Centuries*, 2 vols (Bristol: Thoemmes, 2003), I, pp 1–79. This edition omits the Latin liminary material. The brief introduction and notes provide a valuable supplement to the un-annotated online versions which were also becoming available at the time. See also Margaret Marran (ed.), 'Landgartha: a tragie-comedy, [An edition]' (MA Thesis, Trinity College Dublin, 1988).

performance of *Landgartha,* a memory which survived for many years only by way of play catalogues and theatre histories, each of which carried their own particular political charge. The original edition of the play is listed for sale in two surviving publishers' lists of the 1650s, in both cases appearing alongside Shirley's *St Patrick for Ireland* and *The Constant Maid.*[14] It is also listed in three library sale catalogues from the late-eighteenth century, the auction price rising from 2*s.* and 6*d.* in 1787 to 7*s.* in 1797.[15] In 1691, the drama collector and historian Gerard Langbaine published the brief account of the play and its author which formed the basis of further, minimal, mentions across the eighteenth century and beyond.[16] Of these, it is worth singling out three early comments that exemplify developing critical perspectives on a specifically Irish theatre. W.R. Chetwood, the English-Irish theatre practitioner and historian, gives *Landgartha*'s singular performance and the subsequent outbreak of the 1641 Rebellion brief but equal attention in a substantial footnote; Thomas Wilkes is the first theatre historian to integrate the play within a larger narrative concerning the history of the Irish stage; he is followed in this by Robert Hitchcock, who adds the (wholly unsubstantiated) claim that 'This piece was for several years in possession of the stage'.[17] Even as the play goes on to be included in the major drama reference works of the nineteenth and early-twentieth centuries, very little new evidence or interpretation is introduced: Alfred Harbage, for instance, suggests that the two missing Irish plays *The Toy* and *The Irish Gentleman* are 'Possibly Burnell H.'. Gerald Eades Bentley for his part reports this suggestion, before concluding that there is no evidence for the attribution.[18]

14 See 'These Books following are to be sold by Joshua Kirton, at the Kings Arms in Pauls Church-yard' in Hugo Grotius, *Of the authority of the highest powers about sacred things. Or, The right of the state in the Church... Put into English by C.B. M.A.* (London, 1651), separately paginated list at end of volume, B2v; William London, *A catalogue of the most vendible books in England...: all to be sold by the author at his shop in New-Castle* (London, 1657), F2r.

15 Thomas and John Egerton, *A catalogue of the library of Richard Wright, M.D. Fellow of the Royal Society (deceased.)* [London, 1787], Item 1666, ms note '2' 6d', p. 57; *Bibliotheca Pearsoniana. A catalogue of the library of Thomas Pearson, Esq. (deceased)* [London, 1788], Item 3575, p. 347; Leigh and Sotheby, *A catalogue of the very curious and valuable library of the late Mr. James William Dodd, Of the Theatre Royal, Drury-Lane.* [London, 1797], Item 1242, ms note '7s', p. 47.

16 Gerard Langbaine, *An account of the English dramatick poets ...* (Oxford, 1691), p. 42. Langbaine had previously noted *Landgartha* in *Momus triumphans: or, The plagiaries of the English stage expos'd...* (London, 1687) as 'written' by Burnell – a rare accolade given Langbaine's intention in the expanded title to expose 'from whence most of them have stole their plots.'

17 W.R Chetwood, *A General History of the Stage* (London and Dublin, 1749), p. 52; Thomas Wilkes, *A General View of the Stage* (London, 1759), p. 306; Robert Hitchcock, *An Historical View of the Irish Stage,* 2 vols (Dublin, 1788–94), I, pp 12–13 (12).

18 Alfred Harbage, rev. by S. Wagonheim, *Annals of the English Drama, 975–1700,* 3rd ed. (London: Routledge, 1989), p. 142; Gerald E. Bentley, *The Jacobean and Caroline Stage,* 7 vols (Oxford: Clarendon Press, 1941–68), III, pp 96–8 (97). Bentley makes the rather odd comment that 'the

It is in Ireland itself, in a series of studies of Irish theatre published just before and after the Second World War, that a more distinctive interest in *Landgartha* slowly emerges, and begins to crystallize around certain points. G.C. Duggan mentions in his brief discussion of the Werburgh Street Theatre that 'A lost play "Langartha" [sic] on Danish history by an Irish writer, Henry Burnell, was also produced' but then omits it from the chronological list of Irish plays which supplements his narrative account.[19] Shortly afterwards, Duggan is corrected by the American theatre scholar La Tourette Stockwell who, stressing that *Landgartha* is not so much lost as forgotten, includes a fairly full plot summary and brief discussion of its characters, especially the Irish Amazon Marfisa, in her study of early Dublin theatre.[20] Stockwell's careful historical contextualization, however, seems lost on the patriot theatre historian Peter Kavanagh for whom both *Landgartha* and its author are deeply disappointing: 'One would expect', he writes, 'a more nationalistic play from one whose ancestors had fought violently against the English'.[21] It is left to W.S. Clark to redress the balance in his 1955 study of early Irish theatre when, following Stockwell and countering Kavanagh, he extends the discussion of Marfisa further: 'The Irish-costumed Amazon, though in no way essential to the plot, gives *Landgartha* the distinction of being the first play written by an Irishman with Irish local colour'.[22] For the subsequent generation of critics, more concerned with the colonial 'Othering' of Ireland, and thus with English representations of Ireland, than with an Irishman's account of an old Norwegian tale, *Landgartha* remained largely unexplored.

The present edition does not simply seek to affirm *Landgartha*'s position as an 'Irish' play. For as scholarly debate between historians of the Three Kingdoms and literary critics of English continues to explore the complexities of the cul-

effeminate tone of the play is often ludicrously in contrast with the chronicle material on which it is based' (ibid). See also W. Greg, *A Bibliography of English Printed Drama to the Restoration*, 4 vols (London: Bibliographical Society, 1939–59), II, p. 738.

19 G.C. Duggan, *The Stage Irishman* (Dublin: Talbot Press, 1937), pp 178, 318. The opportunity to consider Marfisa is thus sadly lost; the first example of a stage Irish woman discussed is much later: Sally Shamrock in Samuel James Arnold's 1796 comic opera *The Shipwreck*, see pp 268–70.

20 M.E. La Tourette Stockwell, *Dublin Theatres and Theatre Customs, 1637–1820* (Kingsport TN: Kingsport Press, 1938), pp 5, 17–22. She further notes that the published version of *Landgartha* includes the first record of an allowance by the Master of Revels in Ireland, p. 309. The book develops an earlier article, '*Landgartha*: a forgotten Irish Drama', *The Dublin Magazine* 9:3 (July–September 1934), 32–6.

21 Peter Kavanagh, *The Irish Theatre* (Tralee: the Kerryman Ltd, 1946), p. 24, see also pp 40–5, 267. James Shirley, by contrast, is hailed as a hero. Kavanagh fondly and utterly improbably imagines that had Shirley stayed in Ireland, 'he would have written a series of historical plays on Irish subjects and perhaps founded a school of Nationalistic Drama', p. 20.

22 W.S. Clark, *The Early Irish Stage: the Beginnings to 1720* (Oxford: Clarendon Press, 1955), pp 37–9 (39).

tural and political history of the seventeenth century, it is clear that the interest of Burnell's play is much more than 'local'. When, as readers and audiences, we fuse the sophistication of post-colonial theory with the contextualization of the historicist, we generate insights which create a new map of early modern culture. As John Kerrigan has argued in his nuanced and visionary study *Archipelagic English* (2008), such insights challenge the very foundations of English Literature as an academic discipline: 'the subject', he concludes, 'can neither be defined, nor Anglophone literature be historically understood, along purely national lines'.[23] *Landgartha* stands as a persistent reminder of the need to reassess the writing of this period in relation to its articulation of the patterns of allegiance, both political and cultural, across national borders. Even as Burnell's kings and Amazons criss-cross ninth-century Norway, Sweden and Denmark, so too they conjure for the Dublin stage both contemporary and enduring tensions along the contested borders between Ireland, England, Scotland – and beyond.

THE AUTHOR IN CONTEXT

Identifying 'H.B': 'Though thou England *never saw'st'*
(Jo. Bermingham 'To … Henry Burnell', l.19.)
We know very little about the 'H.B.' of the title-page. The intrigue of the initials is only short-lived, since it is clear from the liminary materials that the author of *Landgartha* was one Henry Burnell. The prologue to the Dublin edition further suggests that Burnell had written an earlier play – not well received – also produced at the Werburgh Street Theatre; but this unnamed work, if it ever existed, is no longer extant. Beyond the text, little information about its author survives. Records show that he was the son of Christopher Burnell of Castleknock near Dublin and was married to Frances Dillon, daughter of Sir James Dillon, first earl of Roscommon, with whom he had six children. This marriage connected Burnell to the wider Dillon family circle, including the Viceroy, Thomas Wentworth.[24] We also know that as war broke out across the Three Kingdoms, Burnell joined the Catholic Confederation,

23 John Kerrigan, *Archipelagic English: Literature History and Politics, 1603–1707* (Oxford: Oxford University Press, 2008), p. 411. I am indebted to Kerrigan's reading of *Landgartha* in the broader context of the drama of Caroline Ireland, pp 169–94.

24 Dublin, Genealogical Office MS 72, p. 55 and MS 172, p. 78, cited Fletcher, *Drama and the Performing Arts*, p. 447, see also pp 275–7. Their children are referred to, though two remain nameless, in the funeral entry for Frances Dillon, 1640 (National Library of Ireland, G.O. MS 72). James Dillon, third earl of Roscommon, was married to Wentworth's sister, Elizabeth; their son, the poet Wentworth Dillon, was born in Dublin in 1637. For an invaluable survey of the playwright's family and its archive, see Nessa Malone, 'The social, cultural and intellectual milieu of the Burnell family of Dublin, 1562–1660' (PhD Thesis, NUI Maynooth, 2008).

established in Kilkenny in 1642.[25] We catch glimpses of him here and there in correspondence from the period: two orders that he be paid £25 'for the Army of Leinster' in late 1645 and early 1646, then in 1647, an order to Ormond's rent agents for payment of 'a competent subsistence unto Henry Burnell and his father'.[26] A letter from Sir Robert Talbot to Thomas Preston, dated Kilkenny 3 September 1646, reports that when the Confederation split along native Irish and Old English lines, Henry's cousin Michael Burnell sided not with the native Irish O'Neill and the papal nuncio Giovanni Battista Rinuccini, but with Ormond and the predominantly Old English Royalists.[27] We might reasonably infer that Henry did the same. These several brief mentions do more than simply inform us about who 'H.B.' might have been; they also suggest that *Landgartha* is (among other things) an enquiry into what it means to be Old English in 1640s Ireland.

The date and cause of Burnell's death are unrecorded. The final resonant mention of him while still alive is in a 1654 petition to the Cromwellian administration requesting a dispensation from the order to transplant to Connaught: 'Henry Burnell, for his tedious and languishing sickness, sought time till 1st June next, by which time it was probable he might recover his strength, and be able to travel on foot to Connaught'.[28] This prospect of an enforced, defeated trek to the West of Ireland would have been a bleak one. For Henry Burnell was a Dublin Palesman through and through. He was of Old English descent: that is

---

25 See the 'Oath of Association of Irish Confederation' and its signatories in J.T. Gilbert (ed.), *History of the Irish Confederation and the War in Ireland 1641–[1649] containing a Narrative of Affairs in Ireland* [by Richard Bellings], 7 vols (Dublin, 1882–91), II, pp 210–19.

26 R.P. Mahaffy (ed.), *Calendar of State Papers relating to Ireland of the Reign of Charles I, 1633–1647* (London: HMSO, 1901), pp 643, 713–14.

27 'Verum mea sententia Burnellum esse honestum' in Stanislaus Kavanagh et al. (eds), *Commentarius Runuccinianus de sedis apostoliciae legatione ad Foederatos Hiberniae catholicos per annos 1645–1649*, 6 vols (Dublin: Irish Manuscripts Commission, 1932–49), II, p. 362. See also the late 1646 'List of the Forces of the Confederate Catholic Army, showing how it is divided amongst the various Counties for Winter Quarter', *CSP Ire., 1633–1647*, pp 572–3. The 'Burnell Book', a manuscript collection of family documents and notes, belonged to Captain Michael Burnell's grandfather, Robert Burnell (NIA Townley-Hall MSS 95, 96).

28 J.P. Prendergast, *The Cromwellian Settlement of Ireland* (London, 1865), p. 41. Malone mentions a Carrickfergus clerk named Henry Burnell accused of embezzlement in 1664 and the very unlikely attribution to Burnell of the late seventeenth-century 'The Fingallian Travestie' (BL MS Sloane 800), but also admits that no Burnell seeks to challenge the fact that both Henry and his son Christopher are outlawed by the Armagh Court of Claims in 1662 'presumably because both were dead', 'Burnell family of Dublin', pp 243–5, 249. There are intriguing references on various genealogy websites to a 1656 Virginian settler named Henry Burnell; the British Library persists in attributing *The Worlds Idol, Plutus A Comedy Written in Greek by Aristophanes: Translated by H.H.B.* (London, 1659) to Henry Burnell, but I have found no evidence to connect the playwright to any of these later appearances.

to say, he could trace his ancestry back to the aftermath of the twelfth-century 'annexing' of Ireland by Henry II. Indeed – like many of the ancient and influential families of the Dublin Pale – he was Anglo-Norman and could trace his origins to the invasion of England in 1066: the name Burnell appears on the Magna Carta list of Knights rewarded for services to William I. The Burnell connection with Ireland in general and with the Dublin Pale in particular began around 1265 when the young Robert Burnell – soon to be Chancellor to Edward I and a driving force behind the King's reformation of English Common Law – travelled to Ireland as a Judge of Assizes and acquired property in Balgriffin near Dublin. This signalled the start of a long and distinguished family history of legal and administrative service in Ireland.[29] The Burnells remained staunchly Catholic, even when, in the wake of the Reformation, successive plantations of New English Protestant settlers (commonly known as the New English) began to erode Old English powers in Ireland.

For well over a century prior to the appearance of *Landgartha*, then, the Burnells had played a key role in defending the Old English, Catholic right to full participation in Irish civic life. As a result, the family's relations with the crown had grown increasingly turbulent: in 1500, Henry VII made Robert Burnell of Balgriffen Sheriff, entrusting him with the custody of the whole county of Dublin; by 1545 the Balgriffen lands had fallen forfeit to Henry VIII because John Burnell, Robert's son, had been executed at Tyburn for playing a leading role in the Kildare Rebellion of 1534–5. John's son, Henry Burnell (*c.*1540–1614), grandfather to the playwright, made the law (rather than arms) his weapon of choice. In 1561, he entered Lincoln's Inn – where a number of recusant lawyers from Ireland were trained – and quickly became involved in Old English protests against plans to raise a cess tax in the Pale.[30] In 1577, alongside Richard Netterville, Patrick Bermingham and Barnaby Scurlough, he led a

---

29 Robert Burnell served as Chancellor (1274–92) and as Bishop of Bath and Wells (1275–92), see F. Elrington Ball, *The Judges in Ireland, 1221–1921*, 2 vols (London: J. Murray, 1926), I, pp 18–21; Ball also notes: Robert Burnell, lord of Balgriffin, appointed second baron of the Exchequer for Ireland in 1388, who married Mathilda, sister and co-heiress of Robert Tyrell, baron of Castleknock (167); John Burnell of Balgriffin, a descendant of Robert's, who became second baron of the Exchequer in 1478 (185); Patrick Burnell, baron of the Exchequer (109) and Henry Burnell the playwright's grandfather (223). Two women of the family – Elizabeth Burnell and Alice Burnell – are mentioned as married to other influential families of the Dublin Pale (204, 208). Robin Frame lists a Robert Burnell appointed Commission of the Peace in 1461 in 'Commissions of the Peace in Ireland, 1302–1461', *Analecta Hibernica* , 35 (1992), 3–43 (13). See also John D'Alton, *The History of the County of Dublin* (Dublin, 1838), pp 226–9, J.T. Gilbert, *A History of the City of Dublin*, 3 vols (Dublin 1854–9) I, pp 296–7.

30 His signature appears in 'The Book comprehending the miserable estate of the English Pale' (National Archives. London State Papers 63/54/5f. 136). See also D. Cregan, 'Irish Catholic Admissions to the Inns of Court', *Irish Jurist*, 5 (1970), 107–13.

deputation to London to petition Elizabeth for support against the Viceroy Sir Henry Sidney's plans to introduce another tax on Old English Palesmen.[31] He was initially imprisoned in the Tower but then released and returned to Dublin, where he continued to hold Crown appointments even as he waged legal and political war against the increasing demands of the English administration. At some point, Burnell also married not an Old English wife, but a daughter of the O'Reillys of Briefne, County Cavan, a powerful Old Irish family; they had three children: Joan, Elizabeth and Christopher (born c.1582), father to the playwright. As a member of the 1585 Dublin parliament, Burnell tussled with Sidney's successor, Sir John Perrot, advocating the repeal of Poynings' Law (which laid down the conditions under which the Irish Parliament operated under the authority of the English Parliament) in order to defeat the Viceroy's reform plans, and in 1605 he was a key figure in Old English resistance to the Penal Laws which required Sunday attendance at a Protestant service.[32] As Sir John Davies prepared to present revised plans for the repeal of Poynings' Law to the 1613–14 parliament, Burnell once again played a prominent role in organizing Pale opposition. This time, however, he did not join the Old English delegation to the King in London; the elder Henry Burnell died at Castleknock in 1614.

Of Christopher Burnell, the playwright's father, we catch only a few intriguing glimpses. In 1616, shortly after he inherited his father's estates, he was '34 and married'; in 1625, he is mentioned along with five other Pale landowners, in a legal pardon 'for having alienated the manor and lands of Mulhussey, Portane, and other lands, in the county of Meath, without licence of the Crown July 28'.[33] This coincides with his involvement in 1625–6 with an Old English scheme instigated by Richard Hadsor to raise armed and trained bands for local defence. We might reasonably deduce even from such scant information that, in his own quieter way, Christopher Burnell too regarded Old English rights in Ireland as sacrosanct. The younger Henry Burnell's ancestry was, then, both resistant and engaged. As we shall see in more detail, his ostensibly Norwegian play registers the impact of this contested history; Landgartha effectively stages a

---

31 See Ciaran Brady, The Chief Governors: the Rise and Fall of Reform Government in Tudor Ireland, 1536–1588 (Cambridge: Cambridge University Press, 1994), p. 240, and (ed.) Sir Henry Sidney, A Viceroy's Vindication? Sir Henry Sidney's Memoir of Service in Ireland, 1556–1572 (Cork: Cork University Press, 2002), p. 95.

32 D'Alton notes that he served as Recorder (1573) and Justice of King's Bench (1590), History of the County of Dublin, I, pp 227–8. He acted as council for the Kildare family in the 1580s, a fact which later returned to haunt him when he was found guilty of forgery in 1608, see Ball, The Judges in Ireland, I, p. 223.

33 Pardon cited in James Morrin, Calendar of the Patent and Close Rolls of Chancery in Ireland, of the Reign of King Charles I: First to Eighth year inclusive (Dublin, 1863), p.15. See also A. Clarke, The Old English in Ireland, 1625–42 (London: Macgibbon and Kee, 1966), pp 32–4 and Malone, 'Burnell Family of Dublin', chapter 5.

live and animated contribution to the debate concerning kin and kind, alliances and allegiance both in – and far beyond – early modern Ireland.

An 'Irish' Army: 'Valiant and Strong to purchase what's your birth-right' (1. 224)
While we may know little of the detail of Henry Burnell the playwright's life, we can usefully situate him in relation to a younger generation of Old English Catholic intellectuals and lawyers: Royalists who anticipated the accession of Charles I with optimism. For them the 1620s and 30s offered a series of opportunities to exploit England's shifting relations with France and Spain in order to gain the kind of full participation in civil and military life at home in Ireland which the last fifty years of conquest had denied them. In 1622, for instance, Richard Hadsor – the only Old English member of the Irish commission – had made the controversial suggestion that 'only British or approved Irish of the English descent' should be included in the military. The apparent modesty of the proposal is belied by that 'or'; for Hadsor is here suggesting that the loyal Catholic Old English should now be allowed to join the armed forces.[34] It took a decade or more for his vision to be realized, but his sense of timing was impeccable. In the same year, soon after the recently appointed Lord Deputy, Viscount Falkland, elaborated plans for the enforcement of anti-Catholic legislation in Ireland, James I instigated negotiations for the marriage of his son Charles to the Spanish Infanta.[35] Falkland found himself obliged to curtail his plans for silencing the Old English of their priests; they looked likely to gain a powerful advocate close to the throne.

The Old English were also regaining what we might call cultural confidence. In 1624, the poet and historian Richard Bellings – a peer of Burnell's – published in Dublin a slim quarto volume of poems together with a continuation of Sir Philip Sidney's popular romance, *Arcadia*.[36] The collection was in effect an Old English response to the at once cultural and political legacy of the Sidney dynasty in Ireland. Several signs suggested that full participation in the civil, military and cultural life of Ireland might soon be a very real possibility.

The Spanish marriage plans swiftly fell apart, but Old English hopes soon revived when, in 1625, Charles married Henrietta Maria of France. Not only did

34 Cited George O'Brien (ed.), *Advertisements for Ireland: being a Description of the State of Ireland in the Reign of James I contained in a Manuscript in the Library of Trinity College, Dublin* (Dublin: Royal Society of Antiquaries of Ireland, 1923), p. 50.

35 V. Treadwell, *Buckingham and Ireland, 1616–1628: A Study in Anglo-Irish Politics* (Dublin: Four Courts, 1998), pp 193–4.

36 R.B. Esq, *A Sixth Booke to The Countess of Pembrokes Arcadia* (Dublin, 1624). From 1627 onwards, Bellings' continuation was routinely incorporated into seventeenth-century editions of Sidney's text. See Rankin, *Between Spenser and Swift*, pp 191–229 and Gavin Alexander, *Writing after Sidney: The Literary Response to Sir Philip Sidney, 1586–1640* (Oxford: Oxford University Press, 2006), pp 262–82.

this marriage resuscitate the promise of a close hearing for the Catholic cause, it also – in shifting England's alliance from Spain to France – gave Ireland the added 'advantage' of sudden strategic importance on the stage of the European Thirty Years War. Ever since the Battle of Kinsale (1601) the spectre of Spanish invasion by way of Ireland had haunted England; with war between England and Spain now more likely, Ireland's defence became crucial to England's safety. The Old English response to the crisis – to them an opportunity – combined political pragmatism with considerable financial power. In 1625, they offered to both assemble and finance their own Irish defence forces in return for twenty-six 'matters of grace and bounty'. Faced with strong protests from Lord Deputy Falkland and the New English settlers, the Old English entered direct negotiations with Whitehall. The strategy worked: in return for 'The Graces' they had petitioned for, they were required to come up with three annual payments of £40,000 to ensure that Ireland did not become a drain on the English purse during the war years. They were also, crucially, themselves allowed to enrol in the increased army – for the protection of Ireland from invasion. Hadsor's dream of military participation became a reality.

When Thomas Wentworth, future earl of Strafford, arrived in Dublin in July 1633 to replace Falkland as Lord Deputy, this same group of young Old English gentlemen still entertained high hopes of participating in the English civic administration in Dublin. Initially welcomed, Wentworth seemed set to be the trusted representative of a sympathetic king who had previously shown himself well-disposed towards Irish Catholics. Moreover, the financial subsidy arrangements for the army were up for renegotiation, and Charles I stood in need of continuing assistance. Reopening negotiations, the Old English sought once again to ensure that their contributions would smooth the path to still fuller participation in both the military and civil government of Ireland.[37] For the beneficiaries of 'The Graces' – the generation to which Henry Burnell belonged – trained in the skills of both pen and sword, the 1630s also appeared to offer golden cultural opportunities. For Wentworth clearly had plans to put Dublin on the cultural map of the Three Kingdoms, pursuing what David Howarth has termed 'a sustained programme and exposition of visual splendour'.[38] If not

37 See A. Clarke, *The Old English in Ireland: The Graces, 1625–42* (Dundalk: Dundalgan Press, 1968); 'Ireland and the General Crisis', *Past & Present*, 48 (1970), 79–99; H. Kearney, *Strafford in Ireland, 1633–1641: A Study in Absolutism* (Cambridge: Cambridge University Press, [1959] 1989), pp 187–9.

38 David Howarth, *Images of Rule: Art and Politics in the English Renaissance, 1485–1649* (Basingstoke: Macmillan, 1997), pp 191–216 (216). See also, for example, T. Barnard, 'The Viceregal Court in later seventeenth-century Ireland' in E. Cruickshanks (ed.), *The Stuart Courts* (Stroud: Sutton, 2000), pp 256–65; M. Craig, 'New Light on Jigginstown', *Ulster Journal of Archaeology*, 38 (1970), 107–30; O. Millar, 'Strafford and Van Dyck' in R. Ollard and P. Tudor-Craig (eds), *For Veronica Wedgwood These: Studies in Seventeenth-century History* (London: Collins, 1986), pp 109–23.

exactly a cultural policy, Wentworth had at least strong cultural aspirations for the 'Englishing' of Ireland. His support for John Ogilby's establishment of the Werburgh Street Theatre (where *Landgartha* would be performed) and for the residency of James Shirley (against whom *Landgartha* was in some measure written) was part and parcel of this viceregal ambition.

But if the hopes of Burnell's generation were initially embodied in the new Lord Deputy, whose cultural ambitions would set the scene for the 1640 St Patrick's Day production of *Landgartha*, Wentworth's trial and execution within just over a year of the performance signalled the end of Old English aspirations for participation in the English – that is to say colonial – administration of Ireland. And in truth, even as Wentworth had sailed into Dublin, he harboured private plans for the government of Ireland which ran counter to the public pronouncements which had fostered Old English belief in him. '[T]he Truth' about Ireland, he had written, back in 1633, 'is [that] we must there bow and govern the Native by the Planter, and the Planter by the Native'.[39] Perhaps the clearest index of this theory of 'government' in practice was Wentworth's relentless pursuit of English land claims in Ireland, the policy which came to be known as 'thorough'. Prosecuted across the decade against all sections of Irish society, whether Native Irish, Old or New English, this proved to be a textbook example for, to coin Nicholas Canny's phrase, 'Making Ireland British'.[40]

The question of Old English participation in the Irish army is similarly vexed in respect of Wentworth's Lord Deputyship. For the six months prior to the opening of the Dublin parliament (and to the performance of *Landgartha*), Wentworth had been away from Dublin serving as close advisor to Charles I on the Scottish crisis. Recently invested with the rank of Lord Lieutenant (rather than Deputy), he was returning from London to Ireland in triumphant mood – and with plans, sanctioned by the King, to raise a new Irish army. Wentworth was confident that the Irish parliament, with its comfortable Protestant majority, would support the King's needs.[41] He was, moreover, confident that Ireland would prove a template, that the English parliament would follow the Irish example, and that both would support the campaign against Scotland. But he severely underestimated

---

39 Wentworth to Coke, 31 January 1633 in W. Knowler (ed.), *The Letters and Dispatches of the Earl of Strafforde with an Essay towards his Life by Sir George Radcliffe*, 2 vols (London, 1739), I, p. 199.

40 Nicholas Canny, *Making Ireland British, 1580–1650* (Oxford: Oxford University Press, 2001). On Wentworth's Spenserian dislike for the Old English, see pp 279–88.

41 In March 1640 the Irish commons was composed of 161 Protestant and 74 Catholic members. Its composition shifted radically over the next year to a large Catholic majority. See Bríd McGrath, 'A biographical dictionary of the membership of the Irish House of Commons, 1640–41' (PhD Thesis, Trinity College Dublin, 1995) and 'The Irish elections of 1640–41' in Ciaran Brady and Jane Ohlmeyer (eds), *British Interventions in Early Modern Ireland* (Cambridge: Cambridge University Press, 2005), pp 186–206.

Irish parliamentary resistance to the Old English cause. Unlike in the 1620s, this was not to be an 'Irish Army' raised to defend Ireland against foreign invasion; this time it was proposed that, under the King's command, armed Catholics were to have a military mandate throughout the Three Kingdoms. Whilst this might conceivably have represented the summit of Old English pan-Royalist military ambitions, it ran counter to the wishes of the Irish Parliament.

Parliament did eventually agree, in March 1640, to provide four subsidies of £45,000 each to finance an army of 9,000 men, but only after much bullying from Wentworth. A bill was passed stipulating that this new force, to be made up of mainly Catholic soldiers commanded by mainly Protestant officers, should be deployed in Scotland by the end of June 1640. On the ground, resistance meant that the force never actually took part in the Bishops' Wars. Recruitment had been slow, transport proved impossible, and the translation of policy into practice proved frustrating both to Wentworth and to those amongst the Old English who had allied themselves with the king's cause.

From the perspective of London, the mere existence of Wentworth's hybrid army was enough to fuel fears and rumours of a 'popish' conspiracy led by the king. The vexed question of the Irish Army proved, furthermore, to be the catalyst for Wentworth's downfall as the peers of Ireland and England – exceptionally – joined together in a devastating personal campaign against the man they termed the 'tyrant' advisor. And included amongst the many charges levelled against him was the claim that, on 5 May 1640, he had advised Charles I to use this Irish army against his English subjects. In many respects, then, Wentworth's Irish adventures can be said to have escalated tensions across the Three Kingdoms in the run up to the Civil Wars. Indeed his trial and execution have been read as a kind of rehearsal for the later proceedings against King Charles I.

Having alienated all sections of Irish society, the Lord Lieutenant left Ireland for the last time in April 1640 – a month or so after the performance of *Landgartha*. After a brief period fighting in the northern borders campaign, Wentworth found himself imprisoned in the Tower in November of the same year. Members of the Irish parliament played a significant part both in engineering his recall to London, and in the subsequent pursuit of his impeachment, trial and execution. During the course of the trial which opened in London in March 1641 – the earliest likely date for the Dublin publication of Burnell's play – Wentworth found that Irish peers of all backgrounds were ready to line up to testify against him.[42] After much legal wrangling, and an abandoned promise by

42 See the 1641 'Queries' compiled against Wentworth for the Irish judges, *CSP Ire., 1633–47*, pp 261–3. For a succinct account of Irish influence in his downfall see Jane Ohlmeyer, 'The Irish peers, political power and parliament, 1640–41' in Brady and Ohlmeyer (eds), *British Interventions*, pp 161–85, and her *Making Ireland English: The Irish Aristocracy in the Seventeenth*

the king that he would arrange the release of his faithful Lieutenant, Wentworth was beheaded on 12 May 1641.

While it may be fanciful to read *Landgartha* as in any strict sense prophetic, it is clear that embodied in the play are the many and complex tensions surrounding governance, military alliances, kinship and kingship in early modern Ireland, tensions which would soon develop into bitter conflict. From an Old English perspective the story of Wentworth's Irish rule is one of expectations raised, only to be disappointed; of political negotiation, military ambition, legal accommodation, and financial brokering all coming to nought. From the more specific perspective of Burnell, it is striking that the period which signals the downfall of the king's Lord Lieutenant in Ireland also marks a reflective pause between the performance and publication of his play. Whether they had seen the performance or not, his readers would – as Burnell was well aware – find the significant moments, characters and themes of recent history transposed into *Landgartha*.

LANDGARTHA FROM STAGE TO PAGE

The Performance: 'presented in the new Theater in Dublin, with good applause'
(Title-page)
The moment of *Landgartha*'s original and only performance is carefully and dutifully detailed a year or so later on the closing page of the published version of the text: 'This Play was first Acted on S. *Patricks* day, 1639. with the allowance of the Master of the Revels.'[43] The 'allowance' granted by John Ogilby reminds us that during the Lent period, theatres would normally be closed; it signals the fact that the performance was an exceptional event. The sense of occasion registered here is in fact, two-fold: not only is it (as the title-page states) St Patrick's Day, but it is also – as noted above – the eve of the opening of the much anticipated first session of Charles I's second Irish parliament. Although this second point is not mentioned explicitly by Burnell (or his publisher), we glimpse, perhaps, the pressure of meeting such an important deadline in the admission in the epilogue that:

> This Tragie-Comedy with the expence
> Of lesse then two Months time he pen'd: For he
> 's not too ambitious of the dignitie
> Of a prime Poet; (Epilogue 11–14).

Century (New Haven and London: Yale University Press, 2012), pp 232–49. See also Kearney, *Strafford in Ireland*, pp 185–208; Canny, *Making Ireland British*, pp 301–89, and P. Little, 'The Earl of Cork and the fall of the Earl of Strafford, 1638–41', *Historical Journal*, 39 (1996), 619–35.
43 i.e. 1640 in the Gregorian calendar, see note 4 above.

The sacrifice of poetic accomplishment proved more than worthwhile, since the 'expence' of the performance reaped significant dividends. *Landgartha* was precisely timed to send a clear political message to Wentworth and the parliament. But the timing also sends a sharp response to the Werburgh Street Theatre's most celebrated playwright, James Shirley. It seems highly likely, given his choice of Norwegian subject, that Burnell is challenging the Machiavellian version of Norwegian statecraft found in Shirley's *The Politician* (London, 1655), believed to have been written around 1639.[44] Whether Burnell is responding to an as yet undiscovered performance or to rumours about (or fragments of) Shirley's play circulating around Werburgh Street, his honest Irish Amazon Marfisa is clearly a counterpart to Shirley's scheming Norwegian Queen, Marpisa. More acutely, however, given the date of performance, Burnell is offering a riposte to Shirley's *St Patrick for Ireland,* performed in Dublin the previous year, in which he had painted a very English portrait of the controversial Irish saint. The apparent modesty in the poet's self-description as 'not too ambitious' belies, then, the strength of the claim which *Landgartha* asserts on the cultural possession of St Patrick's Day by Burnell, on behalf of the Old English community to which he belonged.

It seems that Wentworth missed both the performance of *Landgartha* and the opening of parliament: proceedings were adjourned until the Lord Lieutenant, delayed in London on the king's business, made it across the water. Whether or not Shirley was in the audience that night remains a matter of speculation; given that the evidence indicates that he did not leave Dublin until April 1640, accompanying Wentworth and his entourage on their final exit, it is certainly possible.[45] But what of the rest of the audience? What, in particular, of those MPs enjoying some city entertainment with their families before taking their seats in parliament the next day? What sense did they make of this Northern tale as they watched it unfold on the Werburgh Street stage?

Landgartha is, as we have seen, a play which speaks to contemporary events and permits a straightforward allegorical reading. Norway, Denmark and Sweden represent the three British kingdoms of Ireland, England and Scotland; as a consequence, the Norwegians, chiefly Landgartha and her multi-ethnic Amazons, can be read as standing for the Irish. If Landgartha herself might be seen as Old English, the Amazons around her serve to represent the many and varied kinds of early modern Irishness. Charles I and the English find their coun-

---

44 See R. Fehernbach, *A Critical Edition of THE POLITICIAN by James Shirley* (New York and London: Garland, 1980), pp vi–vii, lii–lviii.

45 Allan Stevenson dates Shirley's arrival in Chester as *c*.16 April 1641; he also suggests that Shirley's *Rosania* was played at Werburgh Street during the previous month, see 'Shirley's Years in Ireland', *The Review of English Studies*, 20 (1944), 19–28; 'Shirley's Dedications and the Date of his Return to England', *Modern Language Notes*, 61 (1946), 79–83.

terparts in Reyner and the Danes, while Frollo, Vraca and the Swedes are rather monstrous representations of the New English/Scots. In respect of the plot, rather than the characters, it is clear that the wars and complex negotiations in the play read as transpositions both of the escalating situation in the so-called 'Bishops' Wars', and – as discussed in the previous section – of the efforts made by Wentworth and others to secure Irish financial and military support for the king. The focus of this section will be on the ways in which the contemporary resonances of Burnell's play might have been even more acutely attuned to the moment of performance. For as the St Patrick's Day audience watched the tale of *Landgartha* unfold – as peoples and nations negotiated political and military contracts and alliances; as kings and Amazons fell in and out of love and marriage – they could not fail to be reminded of the coming parliamentary session. Not only was the subvention of Wentworth's controversial 'Irish Army' up for debate; also on the agenda, also subject to Wentworth's keen attention, was the Act for the Repealing of the Statute of Bigamy.[46]

Irish bigamy – or more accurately what English courts perceived to be 'bigamy' – had long been a fraught issue. The marriage and family practices of the native Irish and Old English had consistently been vilified by New English settlers. Spenser famously regarded intermarriage, fostering and the failure to distinguish between legitimate and illegitimate children as key factors in the 'degeneracy' of the English in Ireland.[47] The real affront to English dignity presented by the intermarriage of elite native Irish and Old English families, however, concerned not the bedroom, but the courtroom. For, underscoring the professed concerns about moral and sexual degeneracy was the question of property rights. Complex alliances, strategically negotiated between influential Catholic Irish families, and sealed with clandestine ceremonies by priests oper-

---

46 Despite being high on the agenda for this parliament, the first reading of the bill was in fact delayed until October, *The Journals of the House of Commons of the Kingdom of Ireland*, 19 vols (Dublin, 1796–1800), I, pp 127, 160. See also Fletcher, *Drama, Performance and Polity*, pp 275–6; Kerrigan, *Archipelagic English*, pp 175–7.

47 'Other great houses there bee of the *English* in *Ireland*, which thorough licentious conversing with the *Irish*, or marrying, or fostering with them, or lacke of meete nurture, or other such unhappy occasions, have degenerated from their auncient dignities, and are now growne as *Irish*, as *O. Hanlons breech*, as the proverbe there is', Edmund Spenser, 'A View of the State of Ireland' in Sir James Ware (ed.), *The Historie of Ireland, collected by three learned authors viz. Meredith Hanmer Doctor of Divinitie: Edmund Campion sometime fellow of St John's Colledge in Oxford: and Edmund Spenser Esq.* (Dublin, 1633), p. 47. Unless otherwise stated, all subsequent references are to this edition, the 'View's first appearance in print. See also Gillian Kenny, 'Anglo-Irish and Gaelic marriage laws and traditions in late medieval Ireland', *Journal of Medieval History*, 32:1 (2006), 27–42; Jane Ohlmeyer, *Making Ireland English*, pp 169–209; D. Jackson, *Intermarriage in Ireland, 1550–1650* (Montreal, Minneapolis: Cultural and Educational Productions, 1970).

ating in defiance of official state religion, already posed a threat to New English ambitions to dominate the ownership of Irish land. When such powerful dynasties further invoked the intricacies of Brehon law – a system which protected female property rights, and allowed for matrilineal influence, adoption and female inheritance – it became virtually impossible to determine Irish property ownership in ways recognized by English law. Burnell, of course, had intimate experience of such practices: the marriage alliance made by his grandfather with the O'Reilly's had been an influential one. Now Wentworth had resolved to tackle the problem by strengthening the regulation of the marriage contract under English law and extending this law to Ireland; the native Irish and Old English were determined to resist. Burnell's play, the pre-parliamentary entertainment, may be read as part of that resistance.

For all that *Landgartha* may have been 'Acted ... with the allowance of the Master of Revels', the play does not quite toe the official line on the 'bigamy' of the Irish. Rather, it is the Irish figures in the play who are firmly identified as the proponents of true chastity and commitment, within the marriage contract or without. On the one hand, the 'Irish' Amazon Marfisa simply refuses to break her vow of chastity, in spite of all her suitor Hubba's pleading. On the other, Landgartha, having made the decision to marry, is determined to honour the contractual consequences of having done so; she is, above all, absolutely clear as to what constitutes 'bigamy'. When she marries Reyner, the contractual as well as the personal commitments she makes are irreversible; without her consent to a divorce, Reyner's second 'marriage' has no validity. As Landgartha spits forth at Vraca:

> Your clayme is nothing: and your
> Possession is but meere intrusion
> On what's anothers due, if she were pleas'd
> To challenge it; (5. 534–7)

The first and final clauses here echo each other: so determined is Landgartha of the rightness of her case that she feels it is beyond argument. Not only is her female legal agency here shown to be unassailable; it is also made crystal clear that she occupies the moral high-ground.

In making the Norwegian/Irish figures the advocates of fidelity, Burnell is both encouraging the kind of allegorical mapping of the play outlined above and putting it under considerable strain. For if we add the particularity of the imminent parliamentary debate on bigamy to the more general background noise of the contemporary tensions between Ireland, England and Scotland, the allegorical reading of *Landgartha* quickly becomes very uncomfortable. This is particularly true when, in respect of the relationship between Reyner (Charles I) and Landgartha (the Old English), questions of political duty are interwoven with questions of marital fidelity. Reyner certainly cuts a fine and kingly military hero in Act 1. Pursuing a noble and just war, he negotiates honourably with his Amazon allies in peace as in war; but what of the love-sick invalid he has become by the start of Act 2? All at once the king proves not only unfit to govern, he is also fundamentally uninterested in government. No longer the martial hero, he is reconfigured as an impetuous bully, who forces his former ally, now his subject, Landgartha into marriage, against her better and very eloquently expressed judgment. To compound the insult, in Act 4, for exactly the reasons that Landgartha had foreseen, the king abandons his wife and 'marries' the daughter of her worst enemy. When in Act 5 Reyner faces ruin and rebellion, it is the extraordinarily faithful and dutiful Landgartha who once again mobilizes her forces, and in so doing saves her treacherous husband. Having pointed out the error of his bigamous ways, she leaves him to contemplate the lonely possibility of a future without her.

The message is clear: it is Reyner who is the bigamist here. In the face of such treachery, Landgartha's loyalty, her at once contractual and personal fidelity to the king, her husband, is remarkable but, as her final exit makes plain, loyalty may also have its limits. It is, the play maintains, the treacherous actions of rulers and lawmakers that undermine the private structures of fidelity which strengthen civil life. Burnell might hope that the audience would profitably carry the lessons of the night's entertainment into the next few weeks of parliamentary proceedings. The Old English will fight and will win the king's battles with and alongside him, but only if the king in turn both recognizes and honours the inviolable private rights enshrined within their alliance. Wentworth won parliamentary subvention for the Irish army; perhaps the price he paid was to delay discussion of, and thus effectively lose his battle against, Irish so-called bigamy.

The Book: 'Printed at Dublin *Anno 1641' (Title-page)*
The performance of *Landgartha* stands as evidence that in Dublin in 1640 the institutions of parliament and playhouse were in conversation. Yet it is also a sharp reminder of the ephemeral nature of occasional theatre. If the printed text did not survive, it would be impossible to recreate the moment: there are, as noted above, no external sources mentioning the performance. Nor does anything beyond the text itself indicate why Burnell chose to publish *Landgartha*, and to do so in Dublin. What we have referred to as Wentworth's cultural policy, John Ogilby's establishment of the Werburgh Street Theatre, and the presence of the celebrated James Shirley in the city had all made the publishing – or, more accurately, the reading – of plays produced there a viable proposition. Shirley's Werburgh Street plays, although they were actually printed in London, were sold in a Dublin edition through the distribution partnership of

Crooke and Crooke.[48] Burnell's is not the first play to be published in Dublin itself; that honour goes to Thomas Randolph's *Aristippus or the Joviall Philiosopher* (Dublin, 1635).[49] But *Landgartha* is the first Dublin-produced play to be also published in the city. Burnell (and his publisher) must have believed his piece had a contribution to make to civil conversation which extended beyond those who had assembled to watch the show itself, and – perhaps – beyond the confines of local and immediate allegory. We can only speculate as to the motive behind this new venture, a partnership between the playwright and, as Wheatley and Donovan suggest, William Bladon, a relatively recent arrival on the scene.[50] But it seems likely that following Shirley's departure for London and the closure of the Werburgh Street Theatre, Burnell and Bladon decided to supplement for the absence of performances, by seizing the opportunity to celebrate a home-grown Irish laureate and create a local market for his plays. Indeed the inclusion of Latin verse suggests that their ambitions stretched further: writing in the language which continued to serve as a pan-European medium for intellectual discussion – perhaps particularly for Irish Catholic scholars exiled in Europe – Burnell's daughter Eleonora voices not only her own conviction, but also wider ambitions for the success of her father's work:

> *Terra tuas certum est exhauriet extera laudes;*
> *clarescet scriptis insula nostra tuis* (74).

[Sure it is that a foreign land will drink up your praises, and our island will become illustrious through your writings].

If this is the aim, then the venture was a risky one. In McClintock Dix's meticulous catalogue of Dublin publications for 1641, *Landgartha* is second on the list, sandwiched between on the one hand the Earl of Ormonde's *Lawes and Orders of Warre* and on the other Gerard and Arnold Boate's *Philosophia Naturalis Reformata*, the first publication of the Hartlib circle to appear in Ireland. Of the

---

48 Allan Stevenson, 'Shirley's Publishers: The Partnership of Crooke and Cooke', *The Library*, 4th Series, 25 (1944–5), 140–61. See also R. Gillespie, *Reading Ireland: Print, Reading and Social Change in Early Modern Ireland* (Manchester: Manchester University Press, 2005), pp 65–74; Christopher Morash, 'Theatre and Print, 1550–1800' in R. Gillespie and A. Hadfield (eds), *The Oxford History of the Irish Book Volume III: The Irish Book in English, 1550–1800* (Oxford: Oxford University Press, 2006), pp 319–35.

49 A university play about excessive drinking and philosophizing, *Aristippus* was first performed in Trinity College, Cambridge, 1626 and was published in London in 1630. Its author had been 'adopted' as a 'son' of Ben Jonson and the play became associated with the defence of theatre from puritan attack.

50 William Bladon bought the printing stock of the Dublin Society of Stationers in 1638 but did not start printing under his own name until later in 1641, see Wheatley and Donovan (eds), *Irish Drama*, I, p. 69.

remaining publications for the year, the vast majority are proclamations of the Dublin 'parliament' or of the 'Lord Justices and Councell', their urgency escalating towards October and the 'Irish rebellion'.[51] As the Three Kingdoms move towards war, as Ireland moves irrevocably towards the formation of the Catholic Confederation, as the New English colonial reformers develop both resources and strategies for whole-scale reform of a 'conquered' Ireland, *Landgartha* already reads – just a year on from its singular performance – as a relic of a lost age.

Like the performance itself, the published version of *Landgartha* was exceptional. The volume demonstrates ambitions beyond the preservation of the play-text itself. We suggested above that as *Landgartha* shifts from ephemeral (lost) prompt-script to printed text, so too do the fortunes of the Old English to which Burnell belonged change. As we shall see now, these changes, along with the historical reception of the play, and the aspirations of its author are inscribed in the paratextual materials accompanying the 1641 edition. Burnell supplements the five-act script with the customary list of 'The persons of the Play'; to this he adds an 'Epistle Dedicatorie' addressed *'To all faire, indifferent faire, virtuous, that are not faire and magnanimous Ladies'*, and four commendatory verses – two in Latin by Burnell's daughter Eleanora, one in English by 'Jo Bermingham', who calls himself Burnell's cousin, and the fourth and last in Latin by one 'Philippus Patricius', who addresses Burnell as his 'friend'.[52] These poems are themselves followed by a Prologue 'delivered by an Amazon with a Battle-Axe in her hand'; this prologue was presumably (though not necessarily) delivered at the performance, but, as we shall see, it also serves as part of the paratextual argument pursued from title-page to epilogue. Indeed, following the five acts of the play proper, the reader is offered an afterword, in the author's own voice, consisting of a brief but spirited defence both of this particular play and of the genre

---

51 E.R. McClintock Dix, *Catalogue of early Dublin-printed books, 1601–1700*. With intro. and notes by C.W. Dugan. (Dublin, 1898–1912), Part II, pp 73–5 (74). While it is difficult to pin down the date of publication with certainty, the position in the list suggests at least early April. The next play to be printed in Dublin is Katherine Philips, *Pompey: A Tragoedy* (Dublin, 1663).

52 Little is known of John Bermingham/Birmingham. Considering Patrick Bermingham, ally of Henry Burnell senior in 1577, C. Brady suggests that this Anglo-Norman family is descended from Peter de Birmingham who owned estates in Birmingham, Warwickshire and Oxfordshire, *The Chief Governors: The Rise and Fall of Reform Government in Tudor Ireland, 1536–1588* (Cambridge: Cambridge University Press, 1984), p. 240. His eldest son, John, came to Ireland with Henry II, served as earl of Louth (1290–1309) and acquired property near the Burnell estates in Offaly and Kildare, and also in Galway (*ODNB*). The *Landgartha* poet, it seems, is involved in attempts – stopped by the Lord Justices – to ship soldiers from the disbanded Irish army to Spain in 1641, see 'Petition of Colonel John Bermingham to the Lord Justices and Council', 27 August 1641, *CSP Ire., 1633–47*, pp 339–40. He later serves as a treasurer of Confederate funds and is signatory to the 'Order and Resolutions of the Provincial Committee for the Army of Leinster and of other Confederate Catholic Bodies' in 1645–7, ibid., pp 399, 640.

of tragicomedy in general.[53] The whole is then signed off with details of the Master of Revels' 'Allowance' and the performance itself.

If we omit, as many readers and editors of *Landgartha* have done, the Latin verse with its overt claims to classical scholarship and education, to international standards of writerly decorum and skill; if we read only the English liminary materials, then the striking, dominant tone as they usher Burnell's 'poore braine borne Infant' into the coveted 'light' of publication appears defensive. One senses that this defensiveness is motivated by more than a standard deployment of the humility *topos* common to early modern prefaces; but the question then arises as to why the author did not put more time and effort into revising his play. Why did he not claim with more confidence the 'dignitie/Of a prime poet' (Epilogue, 13–14)? I have elsewhere considered the publication of *Landgartha* as a late sally in the contest to replace Ben Jonson as poet laureate, a contest which extended to Irish shores.[54] The story involves, once again, the combative figure of James Shirley, but it also reaches back into the longer history of English writing in Ireland. It is worth revisiting and revising certain aspects of that story here, for doing so should allow us to discern something other than defensiveness in Burnell's tone: an Apology both for this kind of theatre, and for his Old English kin.

It was as Wentworth's Master of Revels that John Ogilby set up and managed the Werburgh Street Theatre; his luring of Shirley, an old university friend, to Dublin during an outbreak of plague in London in 1636 had been a major coup, and proved instrumental to the theatre's success. Shirley had already established himself as a prolific playwright both at the Cockpit Theatre, London, and as part of Queen Henrietta Maria's court circle. He had been drawn to the attention of Ogilby's paymaster, Wentworth, in a letter praising Shirley's *Triumph of Peace*, a pageant staged in collaboration with Inigo Jones, by the Inns of Court in 1633–34 in order to distance the institution from the attack on theatre by one of their wayward members, William Prynne.[55] Shirley came recommended, then, as an able apologist for the theatre, and as a vigorous defender of the queen, whom Prynne's volume implicitly attacked for her own appearances on the private court stage. Of further and particular interest to his Irish audience was the fact that Shirley had embarked on his career as playwright after giving up his position at St Alban's Grammar School, apparently because of a religious conversion; Dublin's first English playwright in residence was, it was rumoured, not simply one of the Queen's Men, he was also himself a Catholic.

53 For discussion of this epilogue, see below, pp 64–6.

54 Rankin, *Between Spenser and Swift*, pp 75–116.

55 William Prynne, *Histrio-mastix: The players scourge, or, actors tragaedie* (London, 1632). Prynne's attack on the theatre in general and actresses in particular was deemed critical of Henrietta Maria's court performances; he was tried and famously sentenced to lose both ears.

Shortly after his arrival, Shirley published *The royall master* (London and Dublin, 1638). It was in effect, a manifesto: the recent death of Ben Jonson, literary relic of the Elizabethan age, inheritor of Edmund Spenser's unofficial laureateship and salary, had left a vacancy, which Shirley hoped to fill. His bid is of interest in this context in that the lavish volume – available, exceptionally, in both a London and a Dublin edition – is calculated to show Shirley's Irish connections off to best advantage. Dedicated to Shirley's patron, George Fitzgerald, earl of Kildare, it announces a play 'Acted in the new Theater [...] And Before the Right Honourable the Lord Deputie of *Ireland*, in the Castle.'[56] *The royall master*'s liminary material, laced with references to Irish dignitaries, and celebrating a talented and appreciative literary coterie, paints a fine picture of courtly Ireland. Among the dedicatory poems, that of 'Dru. Cooper' in particular gives the volume a distinctively Irish twist. It begins 'When Spencer reign'd sole Prince of Poets here', and goes on to place Shirley in a tradition of Irish cultural service to the English crown:

> Shirley *stand forth and put thy Lawrell on*
> Phoebus *next heire, now* Ben *is dead and gone*
> *Truly legitimate* Ireland *is so just*
> *To say, you rise the Phenix of his dust.*[57]

Shirley's ambitions are made plain in Cooper's poem: he is seeking both to make a name for himself in Dublin and to raise his cultural capital back home. His aim is to return to London doubly legitimate: successor to both Spenser and Jonson.

Shirley's campaign was unsuccessful, but it left its mark on Dublin literary culture. Three years later, long after the laureateship was granted to Sir William Davenant in December 1638, we find a response to Cooper's poem in a corresponding liminary dedication: John Bermingham's poem in praise of *Landgartha*. Bermingham turns Cooper's defense of Shirley against itself; he echoes Cooper's terms, so as to set all thoughts of the failed would-be laureate aside, and to stake, instead, the literary claims of his own candidate: his cousin and confederate comrade-in-arms, Henry Burnell, whom he addresses directly as follows:

> And though thou *England* never saw'st: Yet, this
> (Let others boast of there owne faculties,

---

56 James Shirley, *The royall master* (London and Dublin, 1638), A2v. On the extensive liminary material see S. Burner, *James Shirley: A Study of Literary Coteries and Patronage in Seventeenth Century England* (Lanham and London: University Press of America, 1988), pp 124–7; Justine Williams, 'The Irish Plays of James Shirley, 1636–1640' (PhD Thesis, University of Warwick, 2010) and Deana Rankin (ed.), 'The royall master' in Eugene Giddens, Teresa Grant and Barbara Ravelhofer (eds), *The Complete Works of James Shirley*, 10 vols (Oxford: Oxford University Press, forthcoming 2013–).

57 Shirley, *The royall master*, A3v–A4r. Richard Bellings also contributes a poem.

Or being Sonne to *Johnson*) I dare say,
That thou art farre more like to *Ben*: then they
That lay clayme as heires to him, wrongfully:
For he survives now only, but in thee
And his owne lines; the rest degenerate.

(Jo. Bermingham 'To ... Henry Burnell', 19–25).

Bermingham's words are well-chosen and well-placed: he banishes the 'boasting' upstart Shirley to that punning parentheses – by now he has not only lost the poet laureateship, he has also abandoned the Irish stage. With Shirley dismissed, Bermingham takes on – by way of the final clause quoted above – a far more significant opponent: Edmund Spenser. For though Bermingham never mentions the poet by name, the figure whom Cooper had invoked as 'sole Prince of Poets here' is clearly recalled in the powerful Spenserian term: 'degenerate'. This was the word Spenser had famously used in his 'A View of the Present State of Ireland' (*c.*1590) to describe and damn the Old English: those English who 'turn native' when they take up residence in Ireland. In the 1630s, as the 'View of the State of Ireland' found a new generation of readers, the term, despite the attempts of Spenser's judicious editor James Ware to remove its sting, risked gaining currency among the New English.[58] In this context, then, Bermingham's use of the word in his poem represents an attempt to reverse the effects of a potent curse. Amplifying a vocabulary of 'heirs' and 'lines', poetry and blood, he articulates Old English claims to legitimacy. It is Burnell who emerges triumphant from the unseemly wrangles about Jonson's inheritance; and it is the Old English who 'survive' as the true inheritors of the Elizabethan literary legacy.

Landgartha is, as Bermingham's poem makes plain, a play both in thrall to and at war with James Shirley, and, through him, with the theatrical legacy of Jonson. Moving further through the paratextual materials, we see that Burnell's own direct response to Jonson can be said to be framed by the very opening of the play, with that prologue 'deliver'd by an Amazon with a Battle-Axe in her Hand'. For his Dublin audience, Burnell's Amazon would carry strong echoes of the elite masque culture of Henrietta Maria's circle to which Shirley had been attached; she may further invoke the cultural links between the Catholic circles of London and Dublin, and voice the shared sense of the need for appropriate military action in support of the king and the emerging Royalist cause. But the 'Battle-Axe in her hand', a weapon inherited by the Irish from the fierce North, also gives the stage image a distinct edge. For as well as generating contemporary

---

58 On James Ware's alterations to Spenser's 1596 manuscript see A. Hadfield and W. Maley (eds), *A View of the State of Ireland: from the first printed edition (1633)* (Oxford: Oxford University Press, 1997).

court resonances, it also calls to mind Jonson's famously 'arm'd prologue' in the *Poetaster*, his combative sally in the late Elizabethan 'War of the Theatres', waged in London in 1601. Indeed that very Jonsonian 'armed Prologue', this time delivered by one of his 'Sonnes' – and 'arm'd with arts' – introduced *Aristippus*, the first play to be printed in Dublin.[59] Burnell's battle-axe then sets down a further marker: this play – the Prologue suggests – is not simply an allegorically charged moment of political drama; it is also a raising of the stakes in a series of long-standing struggles concerning literary, and more broadly cultural, succession.

The 'arm'd Prologue' is not the only Jonsonian memory evoked by *Landgartha*. A more powerfully resonant image is that left by events which occurred at the end of 1613 – just a few months before Burnell's grandfather died at Castleknock – when, as part of the celebration of the controversial marriage of Frances Howard and Robert Carr, Jonson staged *The Irish Masque at Court*.[60] In London at the time was a delegation of Old English lawyers who had travelled from Ireland to protest against the perceived gerrymandering which had greatly increased New English presence in the 1613 Dublin parliament. Their journey was, in some senses, a re-enactment of Burnell and Birmingham seniors' 1577 delegation to Elizabeth; this time, however, the delegation were not imprisoned, but granted a Royal Commission to address their queries. The resulting adjudication of April 1614 went against them, but even as they waited on its deliberations, the group found themselves subjected to the caustic pen of Jonson. In his much-debated masque, four comic Irish footmen rush in to apologize to the King for the delayed arrival of 'a doshen of our besht maishters' for the wedding, 'for te villanous vild Irish sheas have casht away all ter fine cloysh' (57–61). The footmen loudly protest their loyalty to 'King Yamish' (4–5): Dennis, one of these four 'good shubshects of Ireland' insists with pride that 'I mine one shelfe vash born in te English pale, an't pleash Ty Majesty' (43–46). They present the court with exuberant displays of Irish music and dance, only to be silenced when the real gentleman 'imbasheters' (9, 56) eventually arrive. These Gentlemen first 'dance forth a dance in their Irish mantles to a solemn music of harps' (113–114). This, we might assume, could be 'ti *Phip a Dunboyne*' (68) promised by Dermocke, another of their comic servants. Finally 'a civil GENTLEMAN of the nation, who brings in a BARD' steps in to banish the 'anti-masquers' (125) and silence any further disorder. Civility is restored with a

59 Randolph, *Aristippus*, Prologue, 4.
60 'The Irish Masque at Court (1613)' in D. Bevington, M. Butler, I. Donaldson (eds), *The Cambridge Edition of the Works of Ben Jonson*, 7 vols (Cambridge: Cambridge University Press, 2012), 4, pp 239–50. References to line numbers are given in the text. See also D. Lindley, 'Embarrassing Ben: The Masques for Frances Howard', *English Literary Renaissance*, 16 (1986), 343–59 and J. Smith, 'Effaced History: Facing the colonial contexts of Ben Jonson's *An Irish Masque at Court*', *English Literary History*, 65 (1998), 297–321.

speech and a song, during which 'the Masquers let fall their mantles and discover their masquing apparel, then dance forth' (156–7). Courtly dignity is restored; the Palesmen are pushed from the stage.

I have argued that the lapse of time between the 1640 performance and the 1641 publication of *Landgartha* presented Burnell with the opportunity for a reflective pause. As we have seen, these were turbulent months, marking significant changes in English-Irish political relations. The period encompassed begins with Wentworth's confident return to Ireland to preside over the Irish parliament of 1640, with hopes of supervising the raising of an Irish Army for Charles I; it witnesses the beheading of that same Wentworth for treason in May 1641; and it ends in October 1641 with the outbreak of the so-called 'Irish Rebellion'. Set against this background, the Burnell family genealogy traced in part one of this introduction becomes ever more important. For it should be clear that a strong sense of Old English inheritance – political, financial and cultural – inscribes itself on Burnell's play. In the published version, Old English allegiances are quite literally inscribed on the page: John Bermingham's dedication to his cousin Henry Burnell both replicates and reasserts the alliance of their grandfathers in 1577 as they travelled to London to protest at Sidney's imposition of unjust taxes. Burnell the would-be Irish laureate counters both Jonson's early silencing of the Old English in his *Irish Masque*, and the more recent taming of the colony proposed by Shirley's staging of St Patrick 'for Ireland'. His *Landgartha* gives voice to the claims, the arguments and the enduring loyalty of the king's faithful allies.

SOURCES AND ANALOGUES

If the first two sections of this introduction have focused on the dynastic inheritance and contemporary historical contexts for the production and publication of *Landgartha*, then what follows shifts our attention to the literary sources, inspirations and resonances of the play. Burnell himself tells us only that his play tells 'an Ancient story': he gives no list of sources, no bibliography of works consulted. This deracination has led some critics to dismiss the subject of the play as 'foreign material' – to refuse to admit both the contextual sense of the drama and the possibility that Burnell might have knowingly reshaped this 'Ancient story' to give it a contemporary tragicomic form. The closer we read however, the more it becomes apparent that Burnell's choice both of subject matter and of literary form is deliberate. *Landgartha* is carefully positioned to respond to a number of contemporary debates occupying both Britain and Europe: on ethnicity, on historiography, on the challenges facing the writer who seeks to recount, and account for, their origins. If *Landgartha* is a tragicomedy about Ireland, then it is an Ireland which imagines itself not only in relation to

England, nor even just as part of the 'Three Kingdoms' who were soon to go to war. Rather, against the pan-European background of the Thirty Years War, and in the wake of the remarkable career of the 'Lion of the North', King Gustavus Adolphus of Sweden, Burnell has sought out both a story and a form which can do justice to the complexities – literary, historical and political – of his world.

Belleforest's Histoires Tragiques*: 'Being an Ancient story' (Title-page)*
Burnell did not go directly to Saxo Grammaticus for his source material. *Landgartha* – like *Hamlet* – comes to us (most probably) by way of François de Belleforest's *Histoires Tragiques.* Initiated by Pierre Boaistuau, this voluminous and hugely popular late sixteenth-century French anthology was composed of tales translated and adapted for the most part from the Italian original by Matteo Bandello. However, Belleforest both extended the collection far beyond Boiastuau's original six tales in translation and also interpolated his own discoveries and inventions. One of these – the eightieth tale in the collection – is the story of Landgartha: 'Amour de Regner Roy de Norvege, & comme il espousa Landgerthe, & puis la repudia & des faits louables d'icelle Princesse'. One of five tales derived from Saxo Grammaticus which Belleforest first included in the fourth volume of *Histoires Tragiques* published in Turin in 1571, it is also the last story in this particular volume.[61] As the narrator's prefatory commentary testifies, it is so positioned by editorial design. For 'Landgerthe' represents, Belleforest suggests, one of those '[s]ainctes impressions de vertu qui doyuent estre comme naturalisees en nostre ame' ['saintly examples of virtue which should be imprinted as it were by nature on our souls'] (875). Her story, an exemplary tale

---

61 'The love of Regner, king of Norway and how he married Landgartha and then cast her off and the valliant deeds of that princess' in François de Belleforest, *Le Quatriesme Tome des Histoires Tragiques: Partie extraictes des oeuvres Italiennes de Bandel, & partie de l'invention de l'Autheur Francois* (Turin, 1571), LXXX, pp 838–75. Page references are given in parentheses in the text, translations are my own. See also Kerrigan, *Archipelagic English*, p. 177. The earliest version in English of Belleforest's tale appears to be 'The Story of Landgartha, Queen of Norway', a retelling of the plot, but without the moralizing framework of the narrator, serialized in *The European Magazine,* March 1815, 209–12; April 1815, 309–13. The introduction tells how the anonymous contributor, 'a British Soldier', reads it in a northern inn while having his boots mended. The publication (silently) coincides with Norway's declaration of independence from Denmark in 1814. By 1640, Belleforest's *Histoires Tragiques* – which eventually comprised seven volumes (1564–82) – already had strong Irish connections: Sir Geoffrey Fenton, principal Secretary of State in Ireland in the 1580s, translated a selection of the tales – including a possible source for Shakespeare's *Othello* – and dedicated them to Lady Mary Sidney, wife of the then Lord Deputy Henry Sidney, *Certaine tragicall Discourses* (London, 1567). Barnaby Rich, the prolific soldier-commentator on early modern Ireland, also drew on Belleforest for *Rich, his Farewell to Militarie Profession* (London, 1581). *Landgartha*'s 'Epistle Dedicatorie' recalls Rich's dedication to the 'Gentlewomen both of England and Ireland'. Neither Fenton nor Rich include the story of Landgerthe in their anthologies.

of Northern female virtue, serves as moralizing counterpoint to the Italian excesses of Bandello's heroines.

Burnell does not cite Belleforest directly as a source but Belleforest's account would have been accessible to him. It also makes good sense as a source, not least because of a number of important differences in the shape and texture of Burnell's play and Belleforest's narrative. These differences, taken together with other alterations made to other possible additional sources, all suggest changes made by the playwright with the same, clear purpose in mind: that of enhancing the dramatic effect of the performance in accordance with both the tastes and the cultural inheritance of his Dublin audience.

The first set of changes worthy of note have to do with stage propriety and the conventions of genre. The death of Belleforest's Fro (Frollo), for instance, is brought about by the Norwegian women who pursue and kill him in an act of collective revenge for his rapes (849). Burnell transforms this *Bacchae*-like spectacle into a heroic scene of single combat, in which Landgartha slays the usurper and avenges his assault on her honour. Fro/Frollo's death is one of several instances of an event shared by both narrative and theatrical versions, but significantly different in each. Burnell's disrupted and dislocated combat between Harrold and Reyner, for example (5. 329–56), is primarily used to comment on the Landgartha/Reyner relationship; in Belleforest it is a straightforward 'single combat' between the two men in which Landgerthe makes just a very short comment (872–3). In other instances, entirely new scenes are added to the play. Belleforest's account, as we might expect of a prose romance, exploits the narrative suspense of the courtship ritual. His Landgerthe resists Regner's courtship, and leaves for home; Regner pursues her, and having caught up with her, eventually persuades both Landgerthe and her parents that they should marry (858–64). *Landgartha*, the play, situates all of this action in the one place – Reyner's palace – and deals with the courtship rather more succinctly. Yet whereas Belleforest is uninterested in the marriage celebrations themselves, they take up the whole of Burnell's Act 3, where they serve to dilate celebration, offer the opportunity for performance in a range of theatrical modes, and defer the breakdown of the marriage to the opening of Act 4.

All this is proper to theatrical adaptation, and in similar vein Burnell either invents or fleshes out a range of minor characters, exploiting the dramatic potential of the subplot, the comic interlude and the supernatural visitation as they interweave with and comment on the main plot of the play. The subplot of Harrold and Eric's rebellion, for example, including the prophecy made to them in a dream by the Angel (5. 393–422), is a supplement to Belleforest (871). Burnell permits himself still further liberties with Belleforest's narrative, in respect of the main characters, for whom he invents new scenes. The climactic conclusion to Act 5 in which Landgartha, Vraca and Reyner all appear together (none-too-happily) on-stage is Burnell's intervention; in Belleforest, Landgerthe and Regner's (unnamed) second wife never meet. The differences in detail are also instructive. For the French account affords its heroine a moralized and dignified exit as – refusing to let Regner betray his second wife and their children – she retires 'le Coeur haut' ['her heart held high'] to Norway, there to reign with Regner's blessing as queen consort for their son (874). Burnell, by contrast, has Landgartha effectively summon her rival 'wife' Vraca on to the stage in order to dispose of her; and rather than waiting on Reyner's blessing, Landgartha herself dictates the terms of their decidedly ambiguous accommodation:

> Be just and vertuous, and you neede not
> Feare poyson, poynards, or conspiracie.
> To end: *Norway* shall be preserv'd for your young sonne;
> And as for me (though yours:) I'll end my life,
> An honest widdow, or forsaken wife.
> *Exit with Elsinora, Fatyma, & Marfisa* (5. 606–10)

Other events and references in Belleforest are not so much altered as expunged by the play. In relation to any attempt to locate Burnell's production in its Irish context, this is perhaps the most intriguing category of intervention. So, for instance, in Belleforest's version, Regner's second marriage is more formally delineated: when Regner returns to Denmark he sends an ambassador to Sweden to request a royal match; he petitions Landgerthe for a divorce which almost makes her 'mourir de tristesse' ['die of grief']; she refuses to consent (864). This dramatic moment allows Belleforest's narrator to intervene, praising her constancy and contrasting her behaviour with many other historical cases, or examples, where divorce has bred civil war: Medea and Jason; Anthony and Cleopatra; and, finally, 'Eleanore de Poitou' (867). This last example, moving the narrative history closer to home for early modern readers, is taken not from classical times, but from the rather more recent and turbulent history of Anglo-French (and indeed Anglo-Irish) relations. But the invocation of the infamous Eleanor of Aquitaine, wife to Henry II when he led the Anglo-Norman invasion of Ireland in 1171, and orchestrator shortly afterwards of a French revolt against her husband, is perhaps altogether too close to home for Burnell and his Old English kin: in any event, it is silenced in the play.[62]

This occlusion of all talk of invasion and rebellion is later compounded in Burnell's most telling omission, which occurs after Reyner's second marriage and before Harrold's campaign in Denmark. In Belleforest, the rebellion is made

---

62 Eleanor of Aquitaine (*c.*1122–1204) divorced Louis VII in 1152 and almost immediately married Henry Anjou, crowned Henry II in 1154, thus effectively creating the Angevin Anglo-Norman kingdom.

possible because Regner is – culpably – absent, taken up as he is with imperial adventures abroad. For Belleforest's narrator, Regner is a negative example: an expansionist, a prince 'fort adonné aux armes' ['addicted to arms'], who abandons his new wife, and leaves his kingdom to launch attacks on 'les isles de Hirlande, & la grande Bretaigne et Escosse' ['the islands of Ireland, Great Britain and Scotland'] (869). None of this back-story finds its way into Burnell's play. Rather than underline the relevance of this 'Ancient tale' for his Dublin audience, Burnell leaves some matters unspoken, and the territory closest to home apparently unexplored.

Saxo Grammaticus and the Ragnar Lodbrok Sagas: 'In an old/Worme-eaten Booke, in the Lady Elsinora's/Library'(3. 169–171)

Burnell stops short of extending *Landgartha*'s archipelagic map of Scandinavia to Ireland as Belleforest had done. Yet when we attempt to trace the origins of his heroine's story back further, beyond, that is, Burnell's possible French source and into the hinterland of Danish history and the sagas, it becomes impossible to ignore the shared histories of Ireland and Denmark. The story of Lathgertha is – as noted at the outset of this introduction – found in the *Gesta Danorum* or *History of the Danes,* a sixteen-book celebration of Danish achievements compiled from a mixture of oral and written sources by the twelfth-century writer Saxo Grammaticus.[63] Her tale is a minor episode in the early life of Ragnar (Reyner); so minor that of all the poets and chroniclers of his later legendary life as the Danish hero Ragnar Lodbrok ('Ragnar of the Hairy Breeches'), only Saxo Grammaticus thinks it worth the telling. And yet it is from this 'minor' episode in the Scandinavian hero's life that Burnell fashions his play.

The original story, as told in Book Nine of the *History of the Danes,* records how Regner, king of Denmark, fell in love with the Norwegian shieldmaiden Lathgertha when she helped him defeat the usurper King Frø of Sweden; Lathgertha attempts to protect herself from Regner's advances, returning home and setting a bear and a dog to guard her chastity; but Regner slays them, marries her, and they duly produce three children – two daughters and a son, Friedlef. Before long Regner's 'love turned away from his marriage' and he divorces Lathgertha, so as to pursue a royal bride: Thora, daughter of Herrod, king of the Swedes. He wins Thora by rising to the seemingly impossible challenge set by her father: Regner rids Sweden of the monstrous serpents Thora keeps as pets. According to legend, the invincible armour which his nurse gives him for this task earns him the heroic sobriquet 'Lodbrok'. Some time later, in spite of her one-time husband's rejection of her, Lathgertha, now herself remar-

---

63 K. Friess-Jensen (ed.), *Saxo Grammaticus: a Medieval Author between Norse and Latin Culture* (Copenhagen: Museum Tusculanum Press, 1981).

ried, comes to Regner's aid against the usurper Harald, and so plays a crucial role in the suppression of rebellion in Denmark. Saxo Grammaticus brings her story to an abrupt and scandalous end when she returns home after this victory and the same night murders her second husband rather than continue to share his throne.[64] Regner, for his part, goes from strength to strength: he forms a cele-brated standing army to attack Britain, then travels to Ireland where 'Dublin, crammed with barbaric treasures, was besieged, stormed and taken'. The sack of Dublin is, Saxo Grammaticus suggests, avenged by 'the Almighty' in the form of King Ælla of Northumbria, who imprisons Regner in a snake pit somewhere in England; here, isolated and far from home, Regner eventually dies.[65]

From one perspective, the Irish connection to Regner's story might seem an obvious point of interest to Burnell and his Dublin contemporaries; from another, it is clear why *Landgartha* occludes the notion that the king whom we are encouraged to read as a figure for Charles I might contemplate an invasion of Ireland. We cannot know why Burnell excised, or avoided, this part of the story but nor can we assume – as the dismissive critics mentioned above might have once done – that he did so out of ignorance. It is virtually impossible to trace the oral knowledge of such tales in early modern Ireland, and the possible references to and appearances of Ragnar Lodbrok in the known Irish annals remain tantalizingly opaque. It has, however, been suggested that Saxo Grammaticus drew his version of Ragnar's tale from a Latin manuscript of Irish origin, circulating in the twelfth century but now lost.[66]

Even if Burnell did not have access to such lore, it is clear that, for an Old English Palesman, Scandinavian history, far from being 'foreign material', was layered in the landscape. There is little space and time between the departure of Ragnar's progeny and the arrival of Burnell's ancestors; indeed Castleknock, the site of the Burnell family home was traditionally known as the former site of a royal palace of the Danes.[67] This archaeological presence of Ireland's Danish past

---

64 Saxo Grammaticus, *The History of the Danes: Books I–IX*, ed. Hilda Ellis Davidson and translated by Peter Fisher, 2 vols (Woodbridge: D.S. Brewer, 1996), I, pp 280–3. On the supernatural echoes of Lathgertha with the goddess Thorgerd and the Valkyrie see ibid., II, pp 151, 154.

65 Ibid., I, pp 290–1. See Rory McTurk, *Studies in Ragnars Saga Lodbrókar and its Major Scandinavian Analogues* (Oxford: Society for the Studies of Mediaeval Language and Literature, 1991), which makes the persuasive argument for a British–Scandinavian axis for oral transmission of the tales, pp 149–248. McTurk disagrees with the Saxo Grammaticus tradition that Ragnar died in Britain, preferring the alternative saga tradition which has him die in Paris in AD 845, pp 83–100.

66 See Rory McTurk, 'Ragnarr Lodbrok in the Irish annals', *Proceedings of the Seventh Viking Congress, Dublin, 15–21 August 1973* (Dundalk: Royal Irish Academy, 1976), pp 93–124; A.P. Smyth, *Scandinavian Kings in the British Isles, 850–880* (Oxford: Oxford University Press, 1977), p. 96.

67 A similar sense of the immediacy of Ireland's Viking past, this time drawn from Geoffrey Keating, *Foras Feasa ar Éirinn* (c.1634), is found in Sarah Butler, *Irish Tales* [1716] ed. Ian

makes Burnell's rather vague claim to staging an 'Ancient Story' all the more intriguing. As has already been suggested, the characters in this play show an obsession with kinship and lineage: the care taken to point out Reyner's hereditary right to invade and rule Sweden, Landgartha's awareness of and anxiety about her humble birth, the strident claims of kinship, 'cossenship' and brotherhood voiced between clowns, Amazons and nobility alike, all speak of the need both to delineate and confirm the relationships and alliances produced by annexation and conquest. The play itself, while it never quite names its own sources, is constantly preoccupied with the quest for, and the mythology of, origins. Nowhere is the urge to make dramatic capital of the question of sources more urgent than in Act 3, Burnell's wholly invented scene of wedding celebrations incorporating Valdemar's carefully researched and documented masque. From the 'Worme-eaten Bookes' found in a Danish castle, and an educated knowledge of classical Greek mythology, Valdemar weaves a celebration of Irish-Scandinavian connections which (as we shall explore further below) celebrates Stuart links with Catholic Ireland and precludes the more recent claims and interventions of the New English.

Given the fact that the play itself is so concerned with questions of the adaptation and interpretation of dramatic sources, and taking into account the echoes of Danish sources, written and oral, outlined above, it is worth considering one last change which Burnell makes to his possible sources. In Belleforest, Regner's second wife goes unnamed; she is characterized merely as the daughter of a similarly unnamed Swedish king; for his part Saxo Grammaticus names both king (Herrod) and daughter (Thora). Burnell makes two interventions here. First, he makes Reyner woo the daughter of a different Swedish king: Frollo himself. This is a canny dramatic move, for it identifies the rival 'wife' with the child of Landgartha's former conqueror and enemy, and in so doing heightens the slight done to her honour by her adulterous husband. Second, Burnell gives Landgartha's rival another name: not Thora but Vraca, a name found neither in Belleforest, nor in his source Saxo Grammaticus. This gives rise to the intriguing possibility that, alongside Belleforest, Burnell had some knowledge of other saga-based versions of the Ragnar story, distinct from those compiled and retold by Saxo Grammaticus. For in these sagas – which, as noted above, omit the figure of Landgartha altogether – Thora is Ragnar's first wife, and only after her much lamented death does he meet and eventually marry a second wife, Kraka. The echo of this second wife Kraka with Burnell's Vraca seems unmistakable.[68]

Campbell Ross, Aileen Douglas and Anne Markey (Dublin: Four Courts Press, 2010), see pp 9–30, 114–15.

68 Kraka (the crow), also known as Queen Aslaug or Randolin, appears most famously in 'Krákumál or the Lay of Kraka'. Ragnar woos her when she is disguised as a peasant; when he

It is, then, possible that Burnell knew of Kraka's story, and grafted it onto Saxo Grammaticus and Belleforest to make the most of his own Landgartha. This resonant echo of a name is richly suggestive; for it not only gestures towards a world of oral circulation and lost manuscripts, it also returns us to the possibility of other print sources and influences. For Kraka is also (very briefly) invoked in perhaps the best known textual legacy of the Lodbrok legends – 'The Death Song of Ragnar Lodbrok', published in a Latin translation by the Danish scholar Ole Worm (Olaus Wormius) just four years before Burnell's Landgartha appeared on the Dublin stage.[69] Whether or not Burnell knew of Worm and his work, the near contemporary publications resonate with each other. For the 'Death Song' returns Ragnar firmly to the Saxo Grammaticus tradition of his fate: a death that is inflected by his Irish ventures. Punished for his pride and foolhardiness in waging foreign campaigns, Ragnar spends his final hours in King Ælla's snake pit, remembering – but not regretting – his extraordinary life, and calling on the sons of Kraka for revenge.

Burnell does not mention Ragnar's 'Death Song' any more than he mentions other possible sources. He makes no direct reference to Reyner/Regnar's historical Irish connections; and he also omits any mention of the task which won Regner his second wife, namely that he drove out the monstrous serpents which were plaguing her father's lands. The question arises as to the significance of such apparent omissions. Why does Burnell not do as Shirley had done the previous year with his on-stage expulsion of the serpents by St Patrick?[70] Why does he throw away the possibility of the spectacular Irish scene? It is highly possible that changes to his source would have been recognized as such by at least some of Burnell's contemporaries. If so, in *not* drawing explicit attention to particular dimensions of his tale, might Burnell be encouraging that peculiar form of alle-

---

decides to leave her for a noble wife, Kraka reveals that she is the daughter of Sigurðr and Brynhilde. McTurk draws attention to similarities in Ragnar's treatment of Kraka and Lathgertha, *Studies in Ragnars Saga Lodbrókar*, pp 124–5. He elsewhere links the seduction of Kraka to Irish folklore, 'An Irish Analogue to the Kráka-episode of Ragnars Saga Lodbrókar', *Éigse: A Journal of Irish Studies*, 17 (1978), 277–96.

69 Ole Worm, *[Runer] seu Danica literatura antiquissima* (Hafniæ [Copenhagen]: Typis Melchioris Martzan, 1636, rev. 1651). Seaton suggests that Worm stayed with Sir Richard Preston, later earl of Desmond, while in London in 1612, *Literary Relations of England and Scandinavia*, pp 154–8. Preston was the first Scotsman to hold the Desmond title: until 1582, it had been held by the Old English/Irish Fitzgerald family but fell forfeit to the crown when the fifteenth earl led the Desmond Rebellion. Irish ownership of the title continued to be contested well into the 1630s. In another intriguing Irish connection, the 'Deathsong' was first translated from Worm's Latin into English by Thomas Percy, later bishop of Dromore, in *Five Pieces of Runic Poetry Translated from the Islandic Language* (London, 1763). See Robert Rix, 'The Afterlife of a Death Song: Reception of Ragnar Lodbrok's poem in Britain until the end of the eighteenth century', *Studia Neophilologica*, 81 (2009), 53–68.

70 Shirley, *St Patrick*, 5.3.

gorical interpretation that operates by way of an invocation of the right to silence? We are left with a strong sense that there is a silent kinship operating within the audience; that there are other Old English watching and reading who share Burnell's cultural idiom and make of this 'Ancient story' anything but 'foreign material'. Picking up not only on the references but also on the words not spoken, they appreciate that the play is a sharp riposte to those who would ignore prior claims – cultural and military – on Ireland.

Staging myths of origin: Goths, Cimbrians and 'Troy's Brutaines' (3. 303)
Contemporary debates on ethnic origins and the history of conquest in Ireland had found their way onto the Werburgh Street stage before Burnell's *Landgartha*. Just the previous year, Shirley had waded into the long-standing argument about the identity of Ireland's patron saint, with his *St Patrick for Ireland* offering a Laudian vision of the civilizing English High Church figure. In doing so, he followed in the wake of James Ussher, a man of Old English descent, now Protestant and Church of Ireland archbishop of Armagh. Ussher's tireless scholarly efforts to relocate St Patrick within a firmly British and proto-Protestant saintly tradition had produced a ferocious response from the Old Irish historian Philip O'Sullivan-Beare, a veteran of the Elizabethan wars now living in Spanish exile. His thoroughly Catholic account of St Patrick, *Patriciana Decas* (Madrid, 1629), was accompanied by a fierce personal attack on Ussher, and the promise of more to come.[71] If the primary interest of Shirley's play lies in its stridently English and confessional contribution to this debate (the contours of which we explore in more detail below), then Burnell's *Landgartha* deserves our attention for a different reason. For, rather than tell its own tale of cultural and ethnic domination, the play repeatedly concerns itself with the possibilities of negotiation and reconciliation: it explores the ways in which diverse ethnic and confessional groups might be united, even subsumed in a shared notion of the public good.

Landgartha both recalls and reconfigures tribal genealogies which had been elaborated in Ireland and among Irish communities in exile, by historians and poets, over the previous two or three decades.[72] Irish historiography of the 1620s and 30s – in so far as it was concerned to determine and demonstrate the right of a particular people to own land, make laws and govern – fell broadly into three camps: in the first, the native Irish, dispossessed in the aftermath of the Elizabethan Wars, wrote from continental exile not only to assert their prior claim on Ireland and challenge England's right to rule there, but also to encourage continental European powers to back their campaign. Here again Philip O'Sullivan-Beare, the

71 See Clare Carroll, *Circe's Cup: Cultural Transformations in Early Modern Ireland* (Cork: Cork University Press, 2001), pp 104–23.
72 Colin Kidd, *British Identities before Nationalism: Ethnicity and Nationhood in the Atlantic World, 1600–1800* (Cambridge: Cambridge University Press, 1999), esp. pp 146–81.

apologist for the Catholic St Patrick, blazed a trail with his highly-charged *Historiae Catholicae Iberniae Compendium* (Lisbon, 1621). A decade later, Peter Lombard's posthumously published *De Regnio Hiberniae, Sanctorum Insula, Commentarius* (Louvain, 1632) articulated the same claims with even more strident urgency. Dedicated and dispatched to the Pope, it sought to rally European counter-reformation support for Ireland's struggle against English rule; an intervention which caused Charles I himself to denounce it as 'a dangerous Book'.[73] Also in Louvain, but working at a quieter pace, Mícheál Ó Cléirigh and his colleagues – the 'Four Masters' – drew on the archival knowledge of the last generation of professional bardic poets to compile the *Leabhar gabhála* [Book of Invasions] (1631) and the *Annála ríoghachta Éireann* [Annals of the Four Masters] (*c*.1636), both of which confirmed in scrupulous detail the Gaelic origins of the native Irish. In doing so, they brought into written circulation the potent bardic myths of Irish origin which Edmund Spenser had worked so hard to discredit some forty years earlier in his 'View of the Present State of Ireland'.

Thus when a second camp of Irish historiography emerged – that which sought to defend England's right to rule in Ireland – it included Spenser's vitriolic but hitherto manuscript tract in its arsenal. Carefully edited to tone down its animosity towards the degenerate Old English, Spenser's 'View' is presented alongside the accounts of Meredith Hanmer and Edmund Campion in a collection entitled simply, *The Historie of Ireland* (Dublin, 1633). Although from different confessional backgrounds, the three authors in this anthology had two important things in common: they were English and they believed that English influence in Ireland had been a broadly civilizing force. Compiled by Sir James Ware, who was, like James Ussher, a scholar of Old English descent now turned Protestant, the collection sought to present a very different vision to that promoted by the dispossessed native Irish: an Ireland in which '*jam cuncti gens una sumus*' ['we are now united as one people'].[74] Ware's vision of an Ireland 'improved' by English governance also lies at the heart of his own narrative history of Irish letters, *De Scriptoribus Hiberniae*, published the year before *Landgartha* was performed. In Ware's Latin account, it is the arrival of Henry II and the Old English which rescues Ireland from a long, illiterate dark age:

> Constabit etiam per bella intestina, & Danorum Norwegorumq: tempestates, literas ibi, quasi intermortuas, diù jacuisse, ac insulâ tandem felicitèr in regis nostri Henrici secundi potestatem concessâ, Musarum fortes iterùm apertos.[75]

---

73 Windebank to Wentworth, 20 November 1633, in W. Knowler (ed.), *The Earl of Strafforde's Letters and Dispatches*, 2 vols (London, 1739), I, p. 161.

74 Ware (ed.), *Historie of Ireland*, Spenser, f. 3v.

75 Sir James Ware, *De Scriptoribus Hiberniae*, 2 vols (Dublin, 1639), I, f. A4v.

[It is also evident that, through the storms both of civil wars and wars with the Danes and Norwegians, literature there lay for a long time in ruins, as if utterly perished and only when at last the island happily submitted to the power of our good king Henry II, were the powers of the Muses again uncovered.]

Ware's invocation of the uncivil influence of the 'Danorum Norwegorumq[ue]' makes Burnell's staging of a narrative which predates their invasions of Ireland all the more intriguing. For the choice of both geographical and temporal location allies the author of *Landgartha* most closely with the third and final camp of Irish historiography – one which sought to graft Anglo-Norman inheritance onto Gaelic-Milesian origins, in order to construct a distinctly Old English legitimacy.

Geoffrey Keating's *Foras Feasa ar Éirinn*, yet another account of Ireland's history, this time from the Creation to the Norman invasion, was completed in 1634 and entered extensive manuscript circulation thereafter.[76] If the Four Masters set out to document and archive a distinctively Gaelic past, then Keating's project, as Bernadette Cunningham has persuasively demonstrated, was to use Irish language sources to forge a myth common to all Irish peoples. In Keating's account, Henry II does not invade or conquer Ireland, rather he annexes it with the blessing of the pope and at the invitation of the inhabitants. By this *translatio imperii*, the historical legitimacy of the Old English is secured by way of a grand narrative about Irish Catholicism. In 1633 James Ware had conjured up an Ireland at peace in which 'we are all united as one people'; a decade later, Keating's counter-reformation history of Catholic-Irish origins common to all, a myth which appears similarly intended to overcome ethnic divisions, served in fact as an inspiration to war against the New English. The point is made plain by those who drafted the Oath of the Catholic Confederation, to which Burnell, as we have seen, was to attach himself: 'pro Deo pro rege pro patria Hibernia unanimis' — united for God, king and our homeland, Ireland.

Returning to *Landgartha,* it is clear that the questions of ethnicity which animate contemporary Irish historiographers also haunt Burnell's play. Two moments in particular place these mythologies of origin at the heart of stage action: on the one hand they are invoked for war, by way of the battle speeches of Act 1; on the other, they sue for peace, in the masque which celebrates the marriage of Reyner and Landgartha in Act 3. Contemporary political tensions

---

76 B. Cunningham, *The World of Geoffrey Keating: History, Myth and Religion in Seventeenth-century Ireland* (Dublin: Four Courts Press, 2000) and 'Seventeenth-Century Interpretations of the Past: The Case of Geoffrey Keating', *Irish Historical Studies*, 25 (1986), 116–28; B. Bradshaw, 'Geoffrey Keating: apologist of Irish Ireland' in B. Bradshaw, A. Hadfield and W. Maley (eds), *Representing Ireland: Literature and the Origins of Conflict, 1534–1660* (Cambridge: Cambridge University Press, 1993), pp 166–90.

animate these twinned scenes, for Burnell is weaving an allegorical narrative history of the Three Kingdoms which places Irish-English unity firmly centre-stage and banishes New English (and, as we shall see, Scottish) interests to the wings. But there is also a powerful poetics in play, for these are also moments in which Burnell turns attention to his own literary roots, where he brings the particular forensic rhetoric of the poet to bear on the matter of imitation, inspiration and poetic inheritance. As he writes his battle-speeches, and as he invents his masque, Burnell both confronts and responds to the potent 'Irish' legacy of Spenser and Jonson.

In Act I of *Landgartha*, as the battle to determine the future of Norway/Ireland looms, each of the three warrior generals invokes the example of illustrious military forbears to encourage their troops: Landgartha rallies her Amazons with the achievements of their classical predecessors, the goddesses and queens of Greece, and the Amazon warriors who resisted the Roman Empire (I. 121–59); Reyner for his part encourages his Danish forces to act like 'Those valiant *Cymbrians* that almost gave/An end to Rome, the Mistris of the world' (1.192–3); while Frollo exhorts the Swedes to prove themselves to be worthy descendants of the Goths and Vandals, once masters of both Europe and Africa (1.227–70). Burnell is engaged in much more than scene setting here: rather from the opening scenes of the play, he is pitching the action precisely as a contribution to the historiographical debates on ethnicity and origins which were occupying not just the Irish historians outlined above, but also historians across early modern Europe.

Frollo's invocation of the 'Goths and Vandals' gives seventeenth-century voice to a sixteenth-century resurgence of interest in Scandinavian history.[77] The title 'King of the Goths and Vandals' was proudly adopted by Gustav Vasa, who liberated Sweden from Danish rule in the 1520s, then led it across the century into Lutheran Reformation. The royal title was largely authorized by the work of Johannes Magnus, the last papally-appointed bishop in Sweden, who died in 1544, in exile, in Rome. His *Historia de omnibus gothorum sveonumque regibus* [History of all Kings of Goths and Swedes] (Rome, 1554) – a work which draws heavily on Saxo Grammaticus – was published posthumously, by his brother, Olaus Magnus, also in Roman exile. The following year, Olaus published his own influential and hugely popular *Historia de Gentibus Septentrionalibus* [History of the Northern Peoples] (Rome, 1555). For those interested in the provenance

---

77 Kurt Johannesson, *The Renaissance of the Goths in Sixteenth-century Sweden: Johannes and Olaus Magnus as Politicians and Historians* (Oxford and Berkeley: University of California Press, 1991) and 'The Goths as Vision and Propaganda in Swedish History' in Carlo Santini (ed.), *I fratelli Giovanni e Olao Magno. Opera e cultura tra due mondi* (Rome: il Calamo, 1999), pp 157–66; Kristoffer Neville, 'Gothicism and Early Modern Historical Ethnography', *Journal of the History of Ideas,* 70 (2009), 213–34.

and resonance of early modern drama in English, these two works of Northern history offer – as Julie Maxwell has eloquently argued – compelling new perspectives on the Hamlet/Amleth story.[78] They also urge us to consider again the possible roots of Burnell's *Landgartha*, for 'Latgertha bellatrix' makes two brief appearances in Olaus Magnus' *Historia*: the first relating her links to 'Regerus'; the second placing her in a list of Amazon warriors which finds later echo in Belleforest and thence in Landgartha's Act I battle speech.[79]

As Maxwell demonstrates, the confessional politics which motivated and inflected the Magnus brothers' work found resonance with Belleforest as he assembled his *Histoires Tragiques* against a background of civil war in France. We might further extend this resonance to the late 1630s and the moment of *Landgartha*'s composition. For in continental Europe, the grandson of Gustav Vasa, Gustavus Adolphus, had very recently extended the claim of 'King of the Goths and Vandals' to the heart of the former Holy Roman Empire. It was a feat which sparked much admiration in England.[80] More particularly, however, it drew attention to the intricate and vital involvement of Scotland in Sweden's success.[81] Back in Dublin, in 1633, the year after Gustavus Adolphus' unexpected death, Ware's publication of Spenser's 'View' was a timely reminder that the Magnus brothers had already been recruited to the literary battle for Irish origins for, back in the 1590s, Spenser's Irenius had already invoked the authority of Olaus Magnus first to ratify the Scythian origins of the native Irish, and thence to justify their eradication.[82] As Burnell seeks out a historical example which might reaffirm the claims of the Old English – the tribe so particularly vilified by Spenser – he

78 See Julie Maxwell, 'Counter-Reformation Versions of Saxo: A New Source for *Hamlet*?', *Renaissance Quarterly*, 57 (Summer, 2004), 518–60.

79 Olaus Magnus, *Historia de Gentibus Septentrionalibus* (Rome, 1555) V, xvi and xxxii, pp 182, 199. In Germany, Lathgertha also finds earlier mention in Albert Krantz, *Chronica regnorum aquilonarium Daniae, Svetiae, et Norvagiae* (Strasburg, 1546) and thence finds her way into Cyriacus Spangenberg's collection of exemplary models of noble behaviour: *Adels Spiegel, historischer ausfürlicher Bericht*, 2 vols (Schmalkalden, 1591–4), I, pp 453–4.

80 The work of the Swedish cartographer Anders Bure, for example, was very swiftly translated and printed in English: *A short survey or history of the kingdome of Sveden* (London, 1632); *The History of Gustavus Adolphus* (London, 1633). See also Simon McKeown, 'Reading and writing the Swedish Renaissance', and 'The reception of Gustavus Adolphus in English literary culture: the case of George Tooke' in *Renaissance Studies: Special Issue: Reading and Writing the Swedish Renaissance* 23:2 (2009), 141–50; 200–20.

81 Alexia Grosjean, *An Unofficial Alliance, Scotland and Sweden, 1569–1654* (Leiden: Brill, 2003).

82 Spenser, 'View' in Ware (ed.), *Historie of Ireland*, pp 35, 40–2. See also Patricia Coughlan, '"Some secret scourge which shall by her come unto England": Ireland and Incivility in Spenser' in Patricia Coughlan (ed.), *Spenser and Ireland: An Interdisciplinary Perspective* (Cork: Cork University Press), pp 46–74; Matthew Woodcock, 'Spenser and Olaus Magnus: A Reassessment', *Spenser Studies*, 21 (2006), 181–204; Andrew Hadfield, 'The Idea of the North', *Journal of the Northern Renaissance*, 1:1 (Spring 2009), 1–18.

resurrects 'Latgertha bellatrix'. If Spenser twisted the words of Magnus to render the Scythians barbarous, then Burnell redresses the balance. His Landgartha gives eloquent classical voice to an alternative Scythian genealogy: Olaus Magnus' list of extraordinary Amazons who fight for justice in the face of tyranny. Whether or not Burnell came to this by way of the Magnus brothers, it seems appropriate that his inspiration can be traced to the works of these counter-reformation historians, working in exile in order to affirm a claim – at once ethnic and religious – to a homeland transformed by war and Reformation.[83]

If Landgartha's speech challenges Spenser's reading of historical sources, then Valdemar's masque – the centrepiece of Act 3 and indeed of the play as a whole – tackles the legacy of Jonson, in particular his *Irish Masque*. Burnell's Valdemar (like Jonson) produces his masque to celebrate a wedding; but it is also a celebration of a new community constituted in the wake of invasion and conquest: an emblem of peaceful coexistence. If Jonson's *Irish Masque* is a narrative disrupted by unforeseen events – storms at sea, mislaid clothes and masters, unwelcome Old English delegations to the king – then Valdemar's wedding masque celebrates stability. In 1640, as civil disruption threatens all sense of cohesion between the Three Kingdoms, Burnell's striking vision of political and dynastic cohesion bears scrutiny. For the marriage of Danes and Norwegian Amazons (English and Irish) is imbued with historical legitimacy: the authority of that 'old/Worme-eaten Booke, in the Lady *Elsinora's*/Library' (3. 169–71) affirms the royal couple's dynastic connections with the ancient classical world. And it does so by way of a still potent (though long discredited) myth of the Royal Stuart family's origins: the Brutus myth.

Even as, within the masque, Valdemar has his King Priam grieve the death of his son, Hector, he allows his Apollo to offer the king consolation in a prophecy of the future greatness of the Trojans. Burnell's spectacle here resurrects and re-enacts the Brutus myth found in the *Historia regum Britanniae* [History of the kings of Britain] (*c.*1139), written by a contemporary of Saxo Grammaticus: the twelfth-century legend-maker and historian Geoffrey of Monmouth. Like

---

83 The first English translation of Olaus Magnus appears almost ten years after *Landgartha*, printed by John Streater, republican critic of Cromwell, and dedicated to Bulstrode Whitelocke, the Commonwealth's ambassador to Sweden. *A compendious History of the Goths, Swedes & Vandals and other Northern Nations written by Olaus Magnus* (London, 1658). A very brief anonymous account of what appears to be Regner's reconquest of Norway aided by 'a company of noble and gentlewomen, excellently well-armed' – attributed in a shoulder-note to 'Johannes Magnus' – appears as part of an account of Scythians and Amazons in Sir Richard Barckley, *A discourse of the felicitie of man: or his summum bonum* (London, 1598), pp 259–60. The Norwegian pirate queen Avilda is also mentioned by name (260). This is repeated in Thomas Heywood's re-edition (London, 1631), pp 268–9; indeed the relevant section, which culminates with Elizabeth I, is a likely model for Heywood, *The exemplary lives and memorable acts of nine the most worthy women in the world* (London, 1640), see below pp 58–9.

Burnell after him, Monmouth claimed in the prefatory material to *his* history that he had access to and was translating from an ancient history; Monmouth defines his source, and his story as 'British'; Brutus, the exiled son of Aeneas, founded, he suggests, 'Brutaine'. During his long reign, Brutus is said to have protected his borders from the Danes (Cimbri) and founded a new Troy on the Thames. In authenticating Reyner as a descendant of Brutus by way of Valdemar's masque, Burnell thus not only identifies the Norwegian king as an ancestor of the Stuarts, but also, delving further back into the prehistory of his king, confirms that the Stuart dynasty could trace its lineage back to Troy.[84]

The Brutus myth was a popular one. By the late-sixteenth century Monmouth's historical claims had been largely discredited by archival historians such as Polydore Virgil, and yet the story was still acknowledged by many as a powerful foundation narrative, and a useful tool for building 'British' consensus.[85] The seductive qualities of the *Historia regum Britanniae* often led to selective quotation and use; writing in the 1590s, for example, Spenser has Irenius scornfully dismiss the entire Brutus saga in his 'View'; and yet the same author very happily capitalizes on Monmouth's subsequent heroic legends of Arthur in *The Faerie Queene*.[86] His championing of Arthur further reminds us that Monmouth's *Historia* was of particular value to the English in Ireland. For – in a move which parallels Keating's quest for a restorative account of Henry II's twelfth-century conquest – Monmouth's account of Arthur's early conquest legitimized the presence of the English in Ireland *before* the arrival of the Old English. Burnell, for his part, resurrects this compelling mythical genealogy and attempts to use it to reconfigure the map of Britishness at a time when the Bishops' Wars were putting particular pressure on the notional unity of the Three Kingdoms. In a move which chimes well with Wentworth's contemporary political ambitions, Valdemar's masque figures the vital and sacrosanct alliance between peoples as that between England and Ireland: Scotland is nowhere to be seen.

This matters, because if Scotland is eclipsed in Burnell's Trojan-inspired determination of the English-Irish alliance, it is also forcibly excluded from the Scandinavian claims to legitimacy which underwrite the action of this play. As Ó Buachalla has convincingly argued, the Stuart dynasty – from the accession of James, son of Mary, Queen of Scots, in 1603 – enjoyed the loyal support of the

---

84 Geoffrey of Monmouth, *The History of the Kings of Britain and Edition and Translation of De gestis Britonum (Historia regum Britanniae)* ed. M.D. Reeve and N. Wright (Woodbridge: D.S. Brewer, 2007).

85 Polydore Virgil, *Anglica Historia* (Basel, 1534). See David Armitage, *The Ideological Origins of the British Empire* (Cambridge: Cambridge University Press, 2000), pp 24–60.

86 See A. Hadfield, 'Briton and Scythian: Tudor Representations of Irish Origins', *Irish Historical Studies*, 28 (1993) 390–408; W. Maley, '"This ripping of the Auncestors": the ethnographic present in Spenser's *A View of the Present State of Ireland*' in P. Berry and M. Tudeau-Clayton (eds), *Textures of Renaissance Knowledge* (Manchester: Manchester University Press, 2003), pp 117–36.

Catholic Irish across the seventeenth century.[87] But that loyalty had been threat-
ened on a number of occasions by Ireland's rivalry with and distrust of Scotland.
In 1640, as Charles struggles to deal with the Scottish Bishops, Burnell's masque,
with its assertion of matrilineal inheritance, and its celebration of the links of
Anne of Denmark and Elsinore to England and Ireland is timely.[88] For even as
the masque celebrates more recent Stuart dynastic links, by way of Charles I's
mother, to Denmark; even as it identifies Landgartha and Reyner with Anne of
Denmark and James I and so calls to mind a long tradition of British royal links
to Scandinavia, it does so expressly to bypass the claims of Scotland as England's
favoured partner, or match.[89]

Landgartha thoroughly subverts the twinned legacy represented by Spenser's
'View' and Jonson's *Irish Masque*. Burnell's celebration of English-Irish legitimacy
on the Dublin stage offers a long-awaited response both to Spenser's demonizing
of the Old English/Scythian Irish and to Jonson's ventriloquizing of the Irish
ambassadors in his *Masque*. Perhaps the clearest indication of Burnell's cultural
confidence in so doing lies at the heart of the play, in a scene of his own invention:
the masque in which he redresses an old insult, one compounded by the fact that
in 1613, the *Irish Masque* had been played by 'five English and five Scots'.[90]

---

87 Breandan Ó Buachalla, 'James our True King: the ideology of Irish royalism' in D.G. Boyce,
   R. Eccleshall, V. Geoghegan (eds), *Political Thought in Ireland since the Seventeenth Century*
   (London: Routledge, 1993), pp 7–35.

88 The 1633 Edinburgh coronation of Charles I, for example, raised concerns that Irish interests
   were under threat, see Lisa Hopkins, 'We were the Trojans: British national identities in 1633',
   Renaissance Studies, 16:1 (2002), 36–51, and more generally, S. Murdoch, *Britain, Denmark-
   Norway and the House of Stewart, 1603–1660* (East Linton: Tuckwell, 2003).

89 James spent some five months in Sweden, including substantial time at Elsinore, at the time of
   his marriage (Nov. 1589– April 1590), see David Ward, 'The King and *Hamlet*', *Shakespeare
   Quarterly*, 43 (1992), 280–302. There had previously been the possibility of a Scandinavian
   match for Elizabeth I: Eric XIV of Sweden was one of her most pressing suitors and Adolphus,
   duke of Holstein, his Danish rival, see Susan Doran, *Monarchy and Matrimony: The Courtships of
   Elizabeth I* (London: Routledge, 1996), pp 13–39. Some forty years after *Landgartha*, Joshua
   Barnes wrote 'Landgartha, or the Amazon Queen of Denmark and Norway', a masque to cel-
   ebrate the marriage of Anne, daughter of the future James II, and Prince George, son of
   Christian V, King of Denmark and Norway, in July 1683. Designed for a Cambridge marriage
   celebration which never came to fruition, the masque was neither performed nor published;
   but it was revised and entered manuscript circulation in anticipation of Anne's accession to the
   English throne in 1702, Emmanuel College, Cambridge, Special Collections: Barnes' MSS
   James, 170, ff.1–53; 172, ff.150–79, 183–8. It appears that Barnes learned of Burnell's *Landgartha*
   after writing his first version but before his later revision – Langbaine's 1691 account of the play
   is bound into Joshua Barnes' MS James 72 – however, Barnes' version does not suggest that he
   had read Burnell. See Alan Swanson, *An Annotated Edition of Joshua Barnes' The Academie, Or,
   The Cambridge Dunns: With an Introductory Essay on the Place of Joshua Barnes in Seventeenth-century English Theatre* (Lewiston, NY: Edwin Mellen Press, 2011), pp 34–40, 125–40.

90 N.E. McClure (ed.), *The Letters of John Chamberlain*, 2 vols (Philadelphia: American

BURNELL'S AMAZONS

Voicing Landgartha

Landgartha and her troops were not the only Amazons in the limelight in early 1640. On 21 January, at the climax of *Salmacida Spolia* – a masque by Sir William Davenant, the playwright who had in the end succeeded Ben Jonson as poet laureate – a heavily pregnant Queen Henrietta Maria was lowered to the stage from fantastically coloured clouds:

> The Queenes Majesty and her Ladies were in Amazonian habits of carnation, embroidered with silver, with plumed Helmes, Bandricks with Antique swords hanging by their sides, all as rich as might be, but the strangeness of the habits was most admired.[91]

Sent from Pallas Athene to Philogenes (Lover of the people), himself played by the king, the 'Queenes Majesty' is 'a Reward of his Prudence, for reducing the threatning storme into the following calme' (Av). The spectacle was certainly impressive. But if the image was intended to promote the idea of a conciliatory King Charles, accompanied by his Amazonian queen, acting together to unite their discordant kingdoms in peace and harmony, then it did not quite ring true. For this was the last masque to be staged at court before the outbreak of war across the Three Kingdoms.

It is tempting to speculate that news of this court production prompted Burnell to take up his pen and hurriedly write *Landgartha*, the last production to be staged in the Dublin theatre before the outbreak of war. It makes neat sense of the apology in the epilogue that 'This Tragie-Comedy with the expence/Of lesse then two Months time he pen'd.' (Epilogue, 11–12) Whether or not Burnell was inspired by these particular examples, he would certainly have been aware of the long-standing interest of the Stuart queen consorts – both Anne of Denmark and Henrietta Maria – in the staging and playing of Amazons. For their interests had been fostered respectively by his theatrical hero, Ben Jonson, and his local theatrical rival, James Shirley.

The English tradition of festive masques in which aristocratic women silently portrayed Amazons and goddesses was of long standing; it also, again, raises

Philosophical Society, 1939), I, p. 498. On Jonson's strong connections to Scotland see Ian Donaldson, *Ben Jonson, A Life* (Oxford: Oxford University Press, 2011), pp 22–51.

91 Sir William Davenant, *Salmacida spolia. A masque* (London, 1640), f. D2r. On the political contexts see Martin Butler, 'Politics and the Masque: *Salmacida Spolia*' in T. Healey and J. Sawday (eds), *Literature and the English Civil War* (Cambridge: Cambridge University Press, 1990), pp 59–74 and Karen Britland, *Drama at the Courts of Queen Henrietta Maria* (Cambridge: Cambridge University Press, 2006), pp 176–94.

intriguing links with Scandinavia. James I's Danish wife Queen Anne made her first appearance as Pallas Athene in Samuel Daniel's *The Vision of the Twelve Goddesses* (London, 1604). With the able assistance of Ben Jonson and Inigo Jones she eventually took her own place in the pantheon of Amazons: in Jonson's *The Masque of Queens* (London, 1609), eleven of the twelve queens are famous Amazons from history; the twelfth is 'Bel-anna' herself.[92] When Henrietta Maria descended from the clouds in her Amazon costume – also designed, some forty years later, by Inigo Jones – she was invoking the theatrical legacy of the late Danish queen mother. But by 1640, Henrietta Maria also had an established, and increasingly fraught, theatrical reputation of her own; one which was thoroughly enmeshed with her compromised – albeit contractually codified – position as a Catholic queen in a Protestant country.[93] From France, she had imported the court entertainment and throughout the 1630s she and the king performed masques for each other on Twelfth Night and Shrovetide. As noted above, the fact that the queen herself performed on stage had enraged puritan critics, most notoriously William Prynne. In addition, the fact that her favoured collaborator-playwrights – Walter Montagu, James Shirley, and William Davenant – were all rumoured to be Catholics only served to reinforce the Puritans' opinion that this theatrical exhibitionism was part and parcel of the Marian cult of Catholicism which Henrietta Maria and growing numbers of her female attendants practised at court.[94] The 1640 performance of *Salmacida Spolia*

92 Ben Jonson, *The Masque of Queens* (London, 1609), f. D3r. See Stephen Orgel, 'Jonson and the Amazons' in Elizabeth Harvey and Katherine Eisaman Maus (eds), *Soliciting Interpretation: Literary Theory and Seventeenth-Century English Poetry* (Chicago: University of Chicago Press, 1990), pp 119–39; Clare McManus, *Women on the Renaissance Stage: Anna of Denmark and Female Masquing in the Stuart Court, 1590–1619* (Manchester: Manchester University Press, 2002), pp 97–135 and, more generally, S. Shepherd, *Amazons and Warrior Women: Variations of Feminism in Seventeenth-century Drama* (Brighton: Harvester Press, 1981); Kathryn Schwarz, *Tough Love: Amazon Encounters in the English Renaissance* (London: Duke University Press, 2000), pp 109–33. Harbage lists a number of anonymous lost Amazon masques across the last half of the sixteenth century, e.g., in 1551, 1579, *Annals of English Drama*, pp 32, 51.

93 Anne of Denmark was Catholic and refused to take communion when she came to London in 1603, Albert J. Loomie, 'King James I's Catholic Consort', *Huntington Library Quarterly*, 34 (1971), 303–16. Henrietta Maria's Catholicism was a much more public and publicly negotiated matter; her right to practise was circumscribed in a series of international and papal prenuptial agreements, see Malcolm Smuts, 'Religion European Politics and Henrietta Maria's Circle, 1625–41' in E. Griffey (ed.), *Henrietta Maria: Piety, Politics and Patronage* (Aldershot: Ashgate, 2008), pp 13–38.

94 On Henrietta Maria's theatre see Butler, *Theatre and Crisis*, pp 25–54. Britland mentions the possibility of an abandoned Amazon entertainment as part of the Queen's 1628 progress, an Amazon costume for a Shrovetide masque in 1633, and the 'Amazonian Maides' of the antimasque in *Florimène* in 1635, *Drama at the Courts of Queen Henrietta Maria*, pp 64–5, 26, 165. For a persuasive analysis of the connections between court theatre and Catholicism see Rebecca Bailey, *Staging the Old Faith: Queen Henrietta Maria and the Theatre of Caroline England, 1625–1642*

seemed to confirm their worst fears, for it appeared to celebrate the queen's role as an Amazon defender not only of the monarchy but also of Catholicism.

Outside Whitehall, rumours grew concerning Henrietta Maria's involvement in 'popish plots' and the fact that she was actively lobbying abroad, including in Rome, for funds for a Catholic army – one which would include, some said, Irish recruits. Before long, the fears which bred rumour seemed actualized when the silent Amazon stepped out of the private court masque and onto the very public stage of civil war. For in 1643, Henrietta Maria struck a dramatic pose at the head of a very real army, the Earl of Newcastle's controversial Catholic regiment, which included James Shirley among its ranks.[95]

We explored something of the Irish pre-history of such a regiment above in relation to the first performance of Burnell's *Landgartha*. But, clearly, Wentworth's vice-regal politics, and Old English hopes for extension of the right to serve in the military are not the only determining context for the play. It is rather, to the London court that we must look for the motivation behind the extended play on the Jonsonian masque of Act 3. A spectacle which can productively be read within the matrix of recent courtly Amazon performance, Burnell's masque offers an appreciative Old English Catholic response to Henrietta Maria's Marian poetics of female fortitude and leadership. But there is also an important difference. For the court masque tradition, in making a spectacle of the Amazon, relied on the silence of the female performer.[96] Burnell not only transposes the Amazon to the public stage, he also – crucially – gives her voice. Landgartha speaks.

There is, of course, a price to pay for this new Amazon voice: the legal restrictions preventing women from appearing in the public theatre held sway in Ireland as in England until the Restoration and so, in 1640, Landgartha and her Amazons would have been played by men. But if gender ventriloquism is the price to pay, what is there to be gained? First, this new speaking Amazon has a very different physicality: Scania brandishes a battle-axe in her hand – not an 'Antique sword' by her side – as she delivers her 'armed Prologue' (Prologue, 6); Marfisa is always dressed for action, whether that be fighting, horse-riding, or

(Manchester: Manchester University Press, 2009) in particular the chapters on Shirley (though sadly it does not follow him to Ireland), pp 49–88 and on Davenant, pp 175–216. On Montagu, see also Sarah Poynting, 'The Rare and Excellent Partes of Mr. Walter Montague' in Griffey (ed.), *Henrietta Maria*, pp 73–88.

95 See Bailey, *Staging the Old Faith,* p.195 and Michelle White, *Henrietta Maria and the English Civil Wars* (Aldershot: Ashgate, 2006). In letters to the exiled Charles, the queen calls herself 'her she-majesty generalissima', M. Green (ed.), *Letters of Queen Henrietta Maria* (London, 1857), p. 222.

96 On women's voices in the masque see McManus, *Women on the Renaissance Stage*, pp 179–201 and Melinda Gough, '"Not as Myself": The Queen's Voice in *Tempe Restored*', *Modern Philology*, 101:1 (2003), 48–67.

dancing; and even the Amazon Queen, Landgartha, is not given to holding spectacular, architectural poses, such as those designed for the ladies of the court by Jonson, Davenant and Jones; indeed it is striking that she rarely ever sits still in the play, unless ordered to do so (2. 404).

Second, and perhaps most importantly, the new Amazon does not merely speak; rather her speeches demonstrate rhetorical eloquence, political clarity and moral conviction. That Burnell placed great importance on giving his Amazons – and in particular Landgartha – more than merely adequate voice is clear from a brief consideration of two instances where he adapts her speeches from Belleforest's tale. The first relates to the crucial test of the inspirational general: the speech given on the verge of battle. Belleforest gives his Landgerthe two battle-related speeches: in the first, she deploys the imagery of the natural world – of lions, tigers, little birds and the motherly instinct to protect – so as to persuade her women to join Reyner and overthrow Fro (844–5); in the second, she performs a 'traditional' general's exhortation (853–4). Burnell fuses the two into the one major exhortation of Act 1, where he deftly displaces all talk of natural womanly protective instincts, and has his Landgartha urge her troops into battle supported by a fluent and forceful command of classical Greek examples (some of them stolen from Belleforest's learned and moralizing narrator).

If Landgartha's martial rhetoric in Act 1 is properly attuned to the matter of war, then she further demonstrates her humanist strengths in Act 2 by speaking in a manner entirely appropriate to the politics – at once personal and public – of peacetime. When Regner proposes marriage in Belleforest, we read of Landgerthe's concern that her ruler might change his mind about her in due course because of her low birth; the tone she adopts is that of an obedient, but anxious subject (860–1). In Burnell's hands, Landgartha's private anxiety is voiced by way of an extended – and ever more public – conversation (2. 361–511). Her immediate response to Reyner's unexpected proposal is to consult with her Amazons (2. 361); conscious of the force Reyner might exercise on them as conquered women (though former allies), she emerges from this consultation to offer the king a hedging reply, which is both wary and interestingly plural: 'Your poore subjects (sir)/Must rather expect (in duty) your commands' (2. 387–8). Pushed further by the king to give voice to her own desires, she takes a seat, and speaks. What she delivers is a carefully fashioned and highly politicized discourse on the rights and responsibilities, not just of the good subject, but also of the good king (2. 406–37). She accepts Reyner's proposal, but the terms of her doing so are those of hesitant gratitude and careful duty, rather than passionate love:

> I cannot (nor will my heart permit it) but
> In way of gratefulness, reciprocally
> Requite with love againe, as dutie binds;
> Nay more then so. (2. 418–21)

This assent is, moreover, buried right in the middle of a long, thirty-line speech, in which she carefully reminds the king that she herself could have been queen before, and that in agreeing to marry him she is not acting from ambition. And even after she has 'requite'd' his request, she offers both parties to the agreement a get-out clause; she begs him to 'to decline a while/The vehemencie of your fleete desires;/And take full time to thinke on what you doe' (2. 424–6).

With the circumspect caution voiced in that second, monosyllabic line, Burnell's Landgartha breaks open the tradition of the masquing Amazon. Not only does she take on the part of the female warrior who speaks, she also assumes a role which none of the men of Reyner's court are prepared to play: that of the good political advisor who is mindful not of the desires, but of the honour of the king. This new-found power of speech lends her on the one hand an extraordinary freedom: it enables her to voice the wisdom of both soldier and politician. But this also produces profound frustrations. For the love-sick Reyner does not listen: unprepared for the extension of the role of the Amazon Queen beyond that of the quasi-Marian object of adoration, he hears none of Landgartha's fears or warnings; he hears only that she will marry him, and is miraculously cured. It is left to Landgartha to wonder at the wisdom of her own transformation, giving voice in the last lines of Act 2 to the fear that all her warnings will prove prophetic, and that her decision to change from self-governing Amazon to subject-wife may have dire consequences. And so, when Valdemar asks her for Scania's hand in marriage, Landgartha – even as she playfully puts him right about the nature of the power she holds over her fellow Amazons – already senses the loss of her own agency and self-determination:

> She is not my warde; and may take whom she fancies
> I may my selfe repent, to be perswaded (2. 492–3).

Marfisa Revisited

As suggested above, critical readings of *Landgartha* are often dominated by discussion of the appearance in Act 3 of Burnell's 'Irish' Amazon, Marfisa. Critics have focused in particular on her extraordinary and unexpected first entrance, and on the 'whip of Dunboyne' which she and her Danish admirer Hubba dance near the close of the Act; they comment on its spectacular qualities and its local colour; its superfluity and its crowd-pleasing entertainment. Her appearance in Act 3 might suggest that if Landgartha gives fierce voice to the Amazon, then Marfisa restores her to her habitual status as entertaining, seductive spectacle. Even the stage direction which introduces Marfisa seems designed to grab the audience's attention:

> *Enter Hubba and Marfisa in an Irish Gowne tuck'd up to*
> *midlegge, with a broad basket-hilt Sword on, hanging*

in a great Belt, Broags on her feet, her hayre
dishevell'd, and a payre of long neck'd
big-rowll'd Spurs on her heels. (3. 97)

It is at once over-specified in its Irish detail and tantalizingly vague. On the one
hand the 'Irish Gowne ... Broags ... Spurs' all invoke a long tradition of English
commentary on Irish dress in general and Irish women's dress in particular. Yet,
on the other hand, for all her signs of Irishness, Marfisa brings on stage an air of
mystery. Why the 'big-rowll'd Spurs', and from where has she ridden? Has she
come to celebrate the wedding, or to disrupt it? And why the outlandish name?
It seems at first that her arrival is precisely timed so as to dilate still further the
comic preamble to the 'official' masque. But Marfisa is no stage Irish clown;
rather she exudes a seductive self-confidence which instead makes a fool of her
Danish (English) suitor, Hubba. Marfisa's arrival not only delays the central
masque, it also threatens to eclipse it: for she enters, raises audience expectations
and then promptly disappears. Later in the scene, once she has returned to the
stage, the newly wed Landgartha gives voice not only to her own desires, but
also to those of the audience as she cedes her right to lead the dancing with the
words: 'Let's stand. I long to see Marfisa dance' (3. 340).

It is important to realize that if we judge Marfisa's place in the play on her
appearance in Act 3 alone, we risk casting her – and perhaps even the play as a
whole – as an exotic and rather quaint Irish exception in the canon of early
modern English drama. In truth, the role Marfisa plays in *Landgartha* extends far
beyond that of offering a dash of local, ethnically charged colour. From the
moment she enters – coincident with Landgartha's decision to stop being an
Amazon – Marfisa is a significant presence in the play. Moreover, she gives con-
sistent voice to the Amazon values which Landgartha seems to have abandoned.
While the fourth act (in the single occasion in which she appears not as part of
the Amazon group) develops her courtship with Hubba, it does so in order to
stress her continued sexual chastity. The courtship scene, rather than serving as
a comic romance, becomes, in effect, a commentary on Landgartha's ill-judged
decision to marry, as Marfisa voices her astonishment that the king can treat his
wife so badly (4. 178–232). Her importance grows as the play progresses. By Act
5, Landgartha is consulting Marfisa on strategy, and sends her with Fatyma to
recruit reinforcements; in so doing she quietly accepts the Amazon's criticism of
her all too ready acceptance of Reyner's infidelity (5. 146). When Landgartha
finally exits the play, having reasserted both her rights as consort and a new form
of Amazon independence, she does so in the company of Marfisa (5. 610).

At once alter-ego and stage ally to Landgartha, Marfisa serves to offer a run-
ning critical commentary on the play's central heroine. But she also enters the
drama with a significant historical and literary pedigree of her own. This deserves

brief exploration, because it suggests that in calling his 'Irish' Amazon by the apparently unlikely name of 'Marfisa', Burnell is engaging in a series of further conversations – at once political and literary – that extend beyond the immediate context of the Dublin stage. If the character of Landgartha was fashioned both to resonate with and respond to the Amazons of the court masque, then Marfisa demands to be read as a response to a second persistent tradition of Amazon writing. Rooted in poetry and prose – that is to say in romance, travel-writing and historiography, rather than on the Jacobean stage – this particular Amazon figure is consistently identified with Englishness (rather than 'Britishness'), and with the cult, not of Mary, nor of Catholic queen consorts, but of Elizabeth I. Indeed, even as Henrietta Maria was being lowered from the clouds on to the stage, Elizabeth was being celebrated, in Thomas Heywood's *The exemplary lives and memorable acts of nine the most worthy women in the world* (London 1640), as the last and most glorious of them all.[97]

As he comes to create the character of Marfisa, Burnell seems at once to invoke this Elizabethan tradition and to look beyond it for his inspiration. It is worth again recalling the fact that – apart from that teasing reference to 'an Ancient story' – he is altogether silent about his sources. But it is likely that in the first instance, he draws on the historical figure of the Amazon queen Marpesia/Marthesia, who ruled with her sister Lampedo in Asia Minor and thence expanded the Scythian Amazon empire into Europe.[98] Marpesia appears in the chapter on Amazons in the 1521 English translation of Christine de Pisan's *Cyte of Ladies*.[99] She also enters Elizabethan prose by way of translations of the travel narratives of Thevet and Muenster – as indeed of their source, Justinus, who, thanks to the indefatigable Arthur Golding, made it into English first.[100]

97 Modelled on the traditional male Nine Worthies, Heywood's list contains three Jews, three Gentiles and three Christians: Deborah, Judith, Esther, Boudica, Penthesileia, Artemisia, Elfleda, Queen Margaret (Henry VI's wife), Elizabeth I. See also Celeste Turner Wright, 'The Amazons in Elizabethan literature', *Studies in Philology*, 17 (1940), 433–56.

98 Marpesia and Lampedo appear in the earliest collection of exemplary female biographies, Giovanni Boccaccio, *De claris mulieribus* [written and revised 1361–75], Chapter 11; this chapter appears in Henry Parker, Lord Morley's manuscript English translation [c.1534–47] dedicated to Henry VIII, Herbert Wright (ed.), *Forty Six Lives from Boccaccio* (London: Early English Text Society, 1943), pp 39–42.

99 Christine de Pisan, *The boke of the cyte of Ladies* [c.1407] (London, 1521), I, xvi.

100 Sir Walter Ralegh, *The discouerie of the large, rich, and bewtiful empire of Guiana* (London, 1596), p. 24, reproduced in Richard Hakluyt, *The principal nauigations, voyages, traffiques and discoueries of the English nation* (London, 1599–1600), p. 638; Sebastian Munster, *A briefe collection and compendious extract of the strau[n]ge and memorable things, gathered oute of the cosmographye of Sebastian Munster* (London, 1572), f.56v; André Thevet, *The new found vvorlde, or Antarctike* (London, 1568), p. 102; Marcus Justinus, *Thabridgment of the histories of Trogus Pompeius... translated into English by Arthur Goldying* (London, 1564), ff.10v–11r.

Asia Minor's Marpesia survives into the Jacobean period by way of the compilation of earlier travel narratives that is Purchas, and the early women's history of Thomas Heywood.[101] For, as well as crowning Elizabeth in the ways noted above, Heywood also carries Marpesia to the threshold of *Landgartha*'s performance and publication: she is mentioned in his 1640 collection of exemplary women as an ancestor of the fifth Worthy, Penthesilea.[102]

Heywood's Marpesia offers one possible analogue to Burnell's Marfisa, not least since she begins to make sense of a number of features of Burnell's character which commentators have previously dismissed as absurd. The geography of Marpesia's Euro-Asian empire, for example, makes it entirely possible that there should be an Amazon named Fatyma accompanying the Scandinavian women, and that Fatyma should be Marfisa's 'Cossen-german' (3. 126). It is further conceivable that the two might ride together to Salzburg to raise Amazon reinforcements for a Northern war (5. 156). These Northern wars, as Harrold's alliance with Louis the Pious attests, have a pan-European dimension; Burnell's play once again calls to mind the contemporary European context.[103]

The point is reinforced when we consider a second, and in many respects more obvious, 'line' from which Burnell's figure derives: that of the woman warriors celebrated in Ludovico Ariosto's *Orlando Furioso*, the definitive version of which was first published in Ferrara in 1532, among whom we find the eastern Amazon who goes by the name of Marfisa. Burnell's Marfisa shares many of the exotic qualities of her namesake in Ariosto. Saracen and twin sister to prince Ruggiero, Marfisa also stands as counterpoint to the Christian woman warrior Bradamante who is in love with Ruggiero but will marry him only if he converts to Christianity. Bradamante gladly renounces her warrior status when she eventually marries Ruggiero and proceeds to found a dynasty of Christian rulers. Marfisa on the other hand has neither ambition nor desire to marry; she very happily remains an Amazon throughout. Eventually – after demonstrating considerable resourcefulness in battle across Ariosto's romance – she converts to Christianity and devotes her considerable energy to ruling rather than fighting. But she does so – crucially – with her Amazon status still intact.[104]

---

101 Samuel Purchas, *Purchas his pilgrimage* (London, 1613), p. 334; Thomas Heywood *Gynaikeion, or, Nine Bookes of Various History Concerning Women* (London, 1624), p. 221.

102 Heywood, *Nine the most Worthy Women*, p. 101.

103 The military successes of Gustavus Adolphus sketch a similar geography. Seaton's analysis of seventeenth-century English library catalogues confirms that contemporary interest in Gustavus Adolphus led to increased acquisitions from and about Scandinavia, *Literary Relations of England and Scandinavia*, pp 258–74.

104 Marfisa herself delineates her eastern origins when she meets the Holy Roman Emperor and converts to Christianity, Robert McNulty (ed.), *Ludovico Ariosto's Orlando Furioso translated into English Heroical Verse by Sir John Harington (1591)* (Oxford: Oxford University Press, 1972), Book 38, Stanzas 12–18, pp 437–8. Marfisa also appears in Matteo Maria Boiardo's *Orlando*

Burnell most likely knew of Marfisa from the popular English verse translation by Sir John Harington first published in 1591, and most recently reprinted as *Orlando furioso in English heroical verse* (London, 1634). Ever the loyal servant of Elizabeth I, Harington takes pains in his notes to underline the achievements of the heroines where possible. In the case of Marfisa, he saves his best praise for her success not in arms, but in statecraft: from Marfisa's example 'we may see that that sex is capable of rule and government and not to be excluded from the highest degree thereof'.[105] It is through Harington that we find the first tentative connection of Marfisa with Ireland for, while serving in Ireland during the Essex campaign of 1599, Ariosto's translator had visited the 'rebel' Hugh O'Neill, Earl of Tyrone, and presented his two sons with a copy of his book.[106]

This moment of cultural exchange points towards a further echo of Marfisa to be found in late sixteenth-century Ireland. For *Orlando Furioso* had already proved to be both an inspiration for and powerful influence on Spenser's *The Faerie Queene* (London, 1590, 1596), the poem which might be said to have inaugurated the tradition of the woman warrior in Renaissance English literature. The striking figure of Britomart, the chaste female warrior and one of the many possible avatars of Elizabeth I within Spenser's poem, shares many of the qualities of Ariosto's Bradamante. Marfisa does not appear in Spenser; but she has strong affinity with Britomart's nemesis, the tyrant Amazon Radigund. Indeed their climactic contest is, as many critics have demonstrated, closely modelled on the battle between Bradamante and Marfisa in Ariosto.[107] As we move to consider

Innamorata (1482). On Marfisa's Amazon qualities, see Margaret Tomalin, 'Bradamante and Marfisa: An Analysis of the "Guerriere" of the *Orlando Furioso*', *The Modern Language Review*, 71, 3 (1976), 540–52 and Thomas P. Roche, Jr, 'Ariosto's Marfisa: Or, Camilla Domesticated', *Modern Language Notes*, 103, 1 (1988) 113–33.

105 McNulty (ed.), *Orlando Furioso*, 'Morall' to Book 37, p. 433. Harington is commenting on Marfisa's parliament and insititution of the law for women following her defeat of the tyrant Marganor, ibid., pp 37, 97–103, 432–3. Jonson famously stated 'That John Harington's Ariosto under all translations was the worst', see 'Informations to William Drummond of Hawthornden', Bevington et al. (eds), *The Works of Ben Jonson*, 5, 351–98 (361). It has nonetheless received much recent critical attention, see Jason Scott Warren, *Sir John Harington and the Book as Gift* (Oxford: Oxford University Press, 2001); Miranda Johnson-Haddad, 'Englishing Ariosto: *Orlando Furioso* at the Court of Elizabeth I', *Comparative Literature Studies*, 31:4 (1994), 323–50 and on Marfisa in particular, Selene Scarsi, *Translating Women in Early Modern England: Gender in the Elizabethan Versions of Boiardo, Ariosto and Tasso* (Aldershot: Ashgate, 2010), pp 36–43. On the Irish inflections in Harrington's translation, see Carroll, *Circe's Cup*, pp 69–90.

106 N.E. McClure (ed.), *The Letters and Epigrams of Sir John Harington* (London: H. Milford, 1930), p. 78.

107 McNulty (ed.), *Orlando Furioso*, Book 36, Stanzas 18–67, pp 413–18; Edmund Spenser, *The Faerie Queene*, 5. 7. 26–34. On the Irish contexts for Radigund, see Carroll, *Circe's Cup*, pp 28–47. Spenser's Radigund is consistently referred to as an 'Amazon' but the term is deroga-

more closely why Burnell makes his Marfisa 'Irish', it is intriguing to note that Spenser's contest of Amazons takes place in the fifth book of *The Faerie Queene*, the book which is most firmly inflected and infected by the author's views on and experience of Ireland.[108] Ireland, it seems, may be a place where Amazons spring to the literary imagination, where, indeed, Amazons thrive.

There are strong indigenous reasons for this being so: the powerful Irish-celtic tradition of warrior queens might well compel an Irish playwright to conjure up an Irish companion for *Landgartha*. Andraste, the Celtic warrior goddess, Queen Medb of the Ulster cycle *Táin Bó Cúailnge* [The Cattle Raid of Cooley], Aífe, lover of Cú Chulainn: all offer possible inspiration for an Irish Amazon. From more recent history, the life of the Irish pirate Gráinne Ní Mháille was already legendary: her meeting with Elizabeth I in 1593 would, over centuries to come, be further rewritten as a dramatic encounter between equal queens of Ireland and England.[109] But if Burnell's Marfisa trades on Irish Amazon mythology, then she also responds more specifically to her local, contemporary Dublin context; for she offers, as suggested above, a critical riposte to James Shirley's recent depictions of both Irish and women on the Werburgh Street stage. In the first instance, she stands in dignified contrast to his excruciating stage Irish bard in *St Patrick for Ireland*. In the second, she offers a stern corrective to his vision of a villainous, feminized Scandinavia; the chastity, loyalty and bravery of Burnell's Marfisa all stand in stark opposition to the Machiavellian scheming and rampant infidelity of Shirley's Marpisa in *The Politician*.

Having considered some of the reasons *why* Burnell might make Marfisa Irish, it is worth pausing for a moment, both to consider exactly *how* we recognize Marfisa as Irish, and to ask – in a play which continually seeks to demonstrate the nuances of Irish identity – what kind of Irishness she might represent.

tory (e.g., 5. 5. 1). Her enslavement of Artegall might be said to parody Marfisa's law of women (above). Spenser's combat ends not with a recognition scene and the happy reunion of lover, brother and sister but with the death of Radigund and the (albeit short-lived) recovery of the emasculated Artegall. See also Robert Headlam Wells, *Spenser's Faerie Queene and the cult of Elizabeth* (London: Croom Helm, 1983); Mary R. Bowman, '"She there as Princess rained": Spenser's Figure of Elizabeth', *Renaissance Quarterly*, 43:3 (1990), 509–28.

108 Some of the most influential recent studies to reshape our understanding of the relationship of Spenser with Ireland by way of *The Faerie Queene* include Andrew Murphy, *But the Irish Sea Betwixt us: Ireland, Colonialism and Renaissance Literature* (Lexington: University Press of Kentucky, 1999); Patricia Palmer, *Language and Conquest in Early Modern Ireland: English Renaissance Literature and Elizabethan Imperial Expansion* (Cambridge: Cambridge University Press, 2001); Richard McCabe, *Spenser's Monstrous Regiment: Elizabethan Ireland and the Poetics of Difference* (Oxford: Oxford University Press, 2002) and Andrew Hadfield, *Edmund Spenser: A Life* (Oxford: Oxford University Press, 2012).

109 See Miranda Althouse-Green, *Celtic Goddesses: Warriors, Virgins and Mothers* (London: British Museum Press, 1997); Anne Chambers, *Granuaile: Ireland's Pirate Queen, c.1530–1603* (Dublin: Gill and Macmillan, 2009).

The matter turns out to be far from simple. Critics have tended to identify Burnell's Marfisa as native or Old Irish, distinguishing her from the Old English Landgartha. Wheatley and Donovan, for instance, describe her as the Old English's 'very Irish ally', while Kerrigan figures her more carefully as 'the Amazon who represents Gaelic and/or Gaelicized Ireland'. Kerrigan further – and properly – presses this distinction from Landgartha in his reading of the play, as he anticipates the moment in October 1641 'when Landgartha joined Marfisa in rebellion'.[110] There are, however, some suggestions in Burnell's text that Marfisa is, like Landgartha, of Old English descent, though of a different social background. That much-commented moment where Marfisa and Hubba 'Dance the whip of Dunboyne merrily' (3. 340) is one such instance.

If we recall that Spenser anchored Irish dancing to Scythian origins then we might read their dance as a sign of shared 'wildness', celebrating the shared Scythian background of the Old Irish and the Amazons. We might imagine it staged as an exuberant even 'wild' Irish contrast to the courtly 'grand dance in foure couple' (3. 342) which follows and closes the scene. Burnell, however, is quite specific in his choice of dance. 'The whip of Dunboyne' has a very particular cultural resonance: it is mentioned in Jonson's *The Irish Masque* in 1613 and in Fynes Morison's unpublished itinerary of Ireland a decade before that.[111] As Seán Donnelly has persuasively demonstrated in his historical exploration of the dance, it originated in Northern England or Scotland, and was exported to the Irish Pale with the waves of transmigration which followed the twelfth-century Anglo-Norman conquest. Even after it had long fallen out of fashion in England, 'the whip of Dunboyne' was still being danced in the early-seventeenth century in the Dublin Pale, more specifically in Fingal, Burnell's childhood home.[112]

All of this suggests that Marfisa's 'Irishness' has a degree of specificity to it, which may well be personal to Burnell himself. It also makes of her a closer cousin to Landgartha than we might at first have thought; like her Amazon leader, she too is of Old English descent. It is, perhaps, no surprise that her Danish/English dance partner knows the steps; they share a past. Marfisa and the wise, subversive Captain Hubba also share something else: a timely absence. In their zeal to focus on Marfisa's appearance, critics miss a simple but crucial piece

110 Wheatley and Donovan (eds), *Irish Drama*, I, p. xii; Kerrigan, *Archipelagic English*, pp 180–1.

111 Ware (ed.), *Historie of Ireland*, Spenser's 'View', p. 42; Jonson, 'Irish Masque', *The Works of Jonson*, 4, pp 239–50 (l.68); Graham Kew (ed.), *The Irish Sections of Fynes Moryson's unpublished Itinerary* (Dublin: Irish Manuscripts Commission, 1998), p. 112.

112 Seán Donnelly, 'The "Whip of Dunboyne" and other Irish dance tunes from Tudor and Stuart Leinster', *Ossory Laois and Leinster*, 3 (2008), 127–267, including a lute setting from the early 1660s (141). Cunningham notes Keating's link to the Butlers of Dunboyne, suggesting they were possible patrons of a 1668 transcript of his history and that family members were at the Irish College at Bordeaux at the same time, *The World of Geoffrey Keating*, pp 176–7, 184.

of plotting; neither Marfisa nor Hubba watch the masque. The formal celebration of the Brutus myth, the careful archaeology of Danish links, the prophetic delineation of English-Irish relations – all of the detail explored in part three above: they are oblivious to it all. They have, it is nudgingly suggested, much more interesting things to do: Marfisa and Hubba leave the stage, after a good deal of flirting and innuendo, to find 'some honest place, where I may/ Unspurre, untucke my Gowne, wash, and so forth' (3. 120–1). They re-enter 'untuck'd' and 'in pudding time' (3. 339) – after both the masque and the company's polite discussion of it has ended – to hijack the last dance.

Imagining *Landgartha* in performance, we might well decide to play their absence for smutty laughs; we could have Marfisa enter still more 'dishevell'd' than she had exited. But in doing so, we would need to reconcile such a decision with her subsequent appearances, and more specifically with Marfisa's insistence on – Landgartha's admiration of, and Hubba's doleful acquiescence in – her unfailing chastity. Following arguments explored earlier in this introduction, and reading marriage in this play as a figure for political accommodation, we might, more reasonably, understand both Marfisa's chastity and her absence from the masque as emblematic of a certain political defiance. For it is striking how the masque silences Landgartha, transforming her from the fighting talking Amazon of Acts 1 and 2 into a silent spectator. Burnell arranges his plot so as to ensure that Marfisa does not bear witness to this silencing. Might Marfisa's wilful absence also be read (like her chastity) as a refusal to be like Landgartha – a refusal to be either silenced or sidelined? If so, then we must pause to acknowledge that the performance she avoids having to be part of is central not only to Act 3 but also to the play as a whole: a celebration of the renewal of an English-Irish destiny.

If we return one last time, now with sharper critical caution, to the moment when Marfisa first bursts onto the Werburgh Street stage, we realize that from the very outset she is something of a mystery. We realize this because Burnell shows Hubba attempt to decipher the mystery of her origins, and fail. Marfisa has, as the stage direction with which she is introduced makes plain, the costumes and the props of 'Irishness'; but when Hubba subjects these to close scrutiny, when he attempts to identify her with her gown by way of the only mention of 'Ireland' in the entire play – 'I thinke you had/The patterne on't from us, as we from *Ireland*' (3. 131–32) – Marfisa simply dodges the implied question about her ethnic identity and resists his categorization.[113] She reminds both Hubba and the audience that gowns are, after all, only accessories:

113 Recent feminist scholarship on Ariosto's Marfisa has stressed her ability to combine unassailable Amazon integrity with a chameleon-like ability to perform appropriately in any given situation. See J. Chimène Bateman, 'Amazonian Knots: Gender, Genre and Ariosto's Women Warriors', *Modern Language Notes*, 122.1 (2007), 1–20; Ita Mac Carthy, 'Marfisa and Gender

> That I know not but am sure a handsome woman
> Lookes as well in't, as in any dresse, or habit
> Whatsover (3. 133–5).

The slippery evasiveness of this response might, by the English commentators mentioned above, be read as itself proof of 'Irishness'. But it is remarkable that here and throughout the play, Marfisa's speech has none of the verbal quirks and accent markers that distinguish the voices of her stage-Irish contemporaries.[114] Burnell's warning from this first appearance is clear: watch and read carefully, he reminds us, take nothing – not even that splash of local colour which critics have so often focused on – for granted. The world of this play is bigger than you imagine.

EPILOGUE: 'BETWIXT BOTH': DEFINING TRAGICOMEDY

In conclusion, we turn our attention to the last of the liminary materials added to the play-text: Burnell's defensive but uncompromising afterword:

> Some (but not of best judgements) were offended at the Conclusion of this Play, in regard *Landgartha* tooke not then, what she was perswaded to by so many, the Kings kind night-imbraces. To which kind of people (that know not what they say) I answer (omitting all other reasons:) that a Tragie-Comedy sho'd neither end Comically or Tragically, but betwixt both: which *Decorum* I did my best to observe, not to goe against Art, to please the over-amorous. To the rest of bablers, I despise any answer (158).

This tells us a number of things: that the play was not universally well received, that the playwright was angered by his critics, and that he makes of his anger the spur to engage in a reasoned theoretical defence of his artistic decisions. This last move is intriguing: for Burnell here articulates, as F.H. Ristine has pointed out, an English-language definition of the genre of tragicomedy unique for the period.[115] The closing remarks of the 1640 edition point, in other words, to yet another aspect of this play's exceptional status, or singularity.

Performance in the *Orlando Furioso'*, *Italian Studies*, 60:2 (2005), 178–95. I am grateful to both authors for illuminating discussions of Burnell's Marfisa.

114 J.O. Bartley, 'The development of a Stock Character I: The Stage Irishman to 1800', *Modern Language Review*, 37:4 (1942), 438–47.

115 F.H. Ristine, *English Tragicomedy, Its Origin and Development* (New York: Columbia University Press, 1910), p. 137. See also Rankin, '"Betwixt Both": Sketching the Borders of Seventeenth-Century Tragicomedy', pp 196–200.

But they also suggest – once again – that Burnell is aware of, indeed seeking to participate in, arguments and debates which extend far beyond the dually inflected contexts of Dublin and the metropolitan centre of London. In addressing the matter of genre directly in this way, Burnell is participating in one of the burning international literary debates of the day: the nature and 'Decorum' of tragicomedy. Just a few years earlier, in 1637, the decision by the French playwright, Pierre Corneille, at the close of *Le Cid,* to invoke – but defer beyond the end of the play – the marriage between Chimène and her father's murderer, Don Rodrigue, had become a *cause célèbre.*[116] *Le Cid* proved tremendously popular among the London courtly theatre set: shortly after the first Paris performance, Joseph Rutter's translation was staged at James Shirley's former London home, the Cockpit Theatre, and then published; at Charles I's request, Rutter then went on to translate Nicholas-Marc Desfontaines' *La Vraye Suitte du Cid,* also performed in Paris in 1637. This sequel 'solves' the problem by bringing Chimène's 'dead' father back; he licenses the marriage and thus brings to fruition the happy ending which Corneille had deliberately declined to stage.[117] Burnell's response to this literary 'quarrel' was distinctly different.

It is certain that news of the spectacular argument about Corneille's violation of the rules of generic 'Decorum' had spread to Dublin; it is very probable that the literary coterie which had coalesced around Shirley during his residency at the Werburgh Street Theatre discussed its implications. While it is impossible to ascertain if Burnell had read any of the various texts generated by the *Querelle du Cid,* we do know that James Butler, favourite of Wentworth and a leading young aristocratic figure of the day, owned many of them. They are listed, along with many otherwise unidentified volumes of French drama, in a library catalogue compiled after the Restoration; that is to say after Butler – by now ennobled as the Duke of Ormond – had both served as Charles I's Lord Lieutenant during the years of the Irish Confederation and survived the intervening Cromwellian legislation to serve again for his restored son Charles II.[118] It is tempting to imagine

---

116 For related documents and detailed critical commentary, see Jean-Marc Civardi, *La Querelle du Cid (1637–1638)* (Paris: Honoré Champion, 2004). For a succinct summary of the arguments focused on their relevance to English tragicomedy see David L. Hirst, *Tragicomedy* (London: Methuen, 1984), pp 48–61.

117 Joseph Rutter (trans.), *The Cid a tragicomedy, out of French made English: and acted before their Majesties at court, and on the Cock-pit stage in Drury-lane* (London, 1637) and *The second part of the Cid* (London, 1640). Rutter was acknowledged as a 'sonne' to Jonson in his dedicatory poem to Rutter's first and only original play, *The shepheards holy-day: a pastorall tragi-comaedie acted before both their majesties at White-hall, by the queenes servants* (London, 1635), ff. A3r-v. See also A. Lefevre, 'Au temps de la reine Henriette-Marie: Le Cid à Londres', *Revue de Littérature Comparée,* 45 (1971), 74–90.

118 Royal Commission on Historical Manuscripts, *Calendar of the Manuscripts of the Marquess of Ormonde, preserved at Kilkenny Castle,* 8 vols (London: HMSO, 1902–20), 7, p. 515. See also

Burnell, somewhere between 1637 and 1641, borrowing Ormond's books; to imagine, however improbable the scene, the two discussing the implications of the *Querelle* for drama in English, and in Dublin in particular. The two men certainly had much in common: both proudly traced their lineage to Henry II's twelfth-century conquest of Ireland; both were of Anglo-Norman origin, and both, it seems, read French. Ormond, however, had already made the important decision which would ensure his survival over the coming decades in a fast-changing Ireland: he had converted to Protestantism. Burnell's own persistence in defending both Old English rights and Catholic culture could not ensure a happy ending either for his play or for himself. As Morash has suggested, if Landgartha embodies the Old English sense of betrayal by Reyner and the (New) English, then 'cohabitation might be possible, but not full [or more precisely continued] consummation.'[119] It is important to remember that Burnell's Landgartha has already had a child by Reyner; they are not newly-weds. But the point about closure deferred still stands since it is clear that neither at the moment of *Landgartha*'s performance, nor at its publication, were relations between England and Burnell's Ireland defined in terms which admitted of either the much-hoped for reconciliation of comedy, or the final devastation of tragedy.

The liminary materials to the published version of *Landgartha* tell their own story. Combining 'Tragie-Comedy' with 'Ancient History', political history and allegory is clearly a tricky business; you may hope for 'good applause' (title-page), but you must also be ready for the disruptive 'bablers' (afterword). Perhaps the best that Burnell could still hope for in 1640–1 was to fall 'betwixt both'; to be, at least, still part of the civil – which is to say at once literary and political – conversation. When the Werburgh Street Theatre re-opened after the Restoration, once again under the management of John Ogilby, once again Master of the Irish Revels, Ormond was one of the enthusiastic backers of the staging of another play in the tragicomic mode: Katherine Philips' translation of Corneille's *Pompey* (Dublin, 1663).[120] For in the wake of Charles II's return from Parisian exile and fuelled by the enthusiasm of dramatists such as the New Englishman Roger Boyle, Lord Orrery, tragicomedy was flourishing in both London and Dublin. The intervening years, however, had extinguished the possibility of renewed conversation with the genre's first, Old English, theorist, practitioner, and defender: Burnell had disappeared from the scene.

David Edwards, *The Ormond Lordship in County Kilkenny, 1515–1642* (Dublin: Four Courts Press, 2004).

119 Morash, *History of Irish Theatre*, p. 9.

120 See my '"If *Egypt* now enslav'd or free, A Kingdom or a Province be": Translating Corneille in Restoration Dublin' in Sarah Alyn Stacey and Véronique Desnain (eds), *Culture and Conflict in Seventeenth-century France and Ireland* (Dublin: Four Courts Press, 2004), pp 194–209.

A note on the text

The *English Short Title Catalogue* lists seven extant copies of *Landgartha*: three in the British Library (General Reference Collection: 162.c.27; G.11220; 644.b.5); one in the Bodleian Library (Malone. 203 (2)); one in Boston Public Library (G.3967.21); one in Harvard University Library (Houghton, 14424.2.19*) and one in the Henry E. Huntington Library (Rare Books, 151860). This edition takes Bod. Malone, 203 (2) as its copy-text.

This present edition follows the copy-text as closely as possible. Inconsistencies in spelling have been retained with the following concessions: the early modern character 'i' has been modernized to 'j'; the spelling of the characters' names in speech prefixes has been silently expanded and regularized throughout to the form listed in 'The persons of the Play'; elsewhere expanded character names are indicated by square brackets. Where the early modern spelling might cause confusion, the word has been glossed at first appearance. All other emendations to the text are listed on p. 159.

The play is set in verse: a loose hypermetrical pentameter line which at times does not scan consistently and tends towards prose. This present edition avoids re-lineation of the original and retains the original presentation of the text at a left-hand margin: the em-dashes, of varying lengths, have also been reproduced. The stage directions have been reproduced in their entirety. Those indicating an 'aside' or emotion of delivery have been moved from the right hand margin and placed in square brackets in the main text.

LANDGARTHA

Landgartha.

A Tragie-Comedy, as it was presented
in the new Theater in *Dublin*,
with good applause, being
an Ancient story,

Written by H.B.[1]

HORAT.
Hunc socci cepere pedem, grandesq; cothurni.[2]

Printed at *Dublin* Anno 1641.

---

1 H[enry] B[urnell]. His full name is revealed in the Epistle Dedicatorie. On the author and his influential Old English Catholic family see Introduction, pp 17–21.

2 HORAT. … cothurni = 'HORACE: This foot the socks took up and buskins grave.' The line from Horace's *Ars Poetica*, l. 80, offers an image for the iambic 'foot' invented by the poet Archilochus for comic invective; a fusion of the ancient Roman and Greek stage footwear for comedy (socks or light shoes) and tragedy (buskins or high boots). Burnell here reclaims the image for his tragicomedy. This translation is taken from Jonson's near-contemporary posthumously published 'Horace, his Arts of Poetry, Made English by Ben Jonson' [London, 1640], *The Works of Ben Jonson*, 7, pp 1–68, (21).

The persons of the Play.[3]

Frollo	King of *Sweland*,[4] and conqueror of *Norway*.
Hasmond and *Gotar*	two courtiers to *Frollo*.
Landgartha	a *Norwegian* Lady.
Scania	sister to *Landgartha*.
Elsinora	Aunt to both.
Fatyma	cousin to *Land[gartha]* & *Scan[ia]*.
Marfisa	an humorous gentlewoman, cousin to *Fatyma*.
Fredericke and *Wermond*	two noble men of *Norway*.
Reyner	King of *Denmarke*.
Valdemar	neer cousin to *Reyner*.
Inguar	a *Danish* noble man.
Hubba	an humorous merry *Danish* Captaine.
Cowsell and *Radgee*	two foolish Coxcombes.[5]
Rolfo	a Drawer.[6]
Harrold	a competitor for *Denmarke*.
Eric	his brother.
Lothaire	a *German* noble man.
Vraca	daughter to *Frollo*.

Two posts, a Scout, & two Gentl[emen],

Phoebus, Pallas, Pyram, Hector, Achylles, and *Satyres*, in a maske: which may be Acted by the forenam'd persons.

---

3 For the characters, see Appendix. For further consideration of the historical and literary sources, see Introduction, pp 36–51.

4 Sweland = Sweden.

5 Coxcombe = a jester's hat, hence fool.

6 Drawer = beer-drawer, tapster.

THE EPISTLE
Dedicatorie.

To all faire, indifferent faire, vertuous, that are
not faire and magnanimous Ladies.

I Have here plac'd a patterne, yea, more then⁷ one (Ladies) for you to imitate. Chastity and other vertues joyn'd to beauty, vertue single and manly fortitude in the female Sexe, doe here present themselves unto you. What you cannot reach one way take another: & know that the form & faculties of the minde, doe farre excell in worth those of the body. Yet, both joyn'd (as in *Landgartha)* is of all the most excellent: in regard that that externall beauty allures (nay commands) the minde of man (that affects visible objects) to the love of vertue, which it selfe do's possesse, and suffers (as most coveted) greater combats in the resisting of vice. Bodily force too in a woman (were it but to defend it's owne Fort) is a perfection; though it cannot be expected but from a few of you, it will be sufficient that you never fall willingly, but in the way of honour. If I have not draw'n this faire visage, as a chiefe Arts man:⁸ I hope yet (you will say) that I have made it indifferent handsome, and that my good will to effect it after the best fashion for your sakes: will notwithstanding my weaknesse, purchase an excuse at least for my boldnesse both in undertaking the worke and in offering of it (in part a poore braine borne Infant of mine, that covets to looke at the light)⁹ to be cherish'd by such hands as yours, to kneele at the feete of your pietie. Whatsoever it be, or whosoever got it: let it be yours, as is

The affectionate honourer

of your perfections,

Henry Burnell.

---

7 then = than.

8 chiefe Arts man = a highly skilled artisan and/or an artist.

9 poore braine borne Infant... to looke at the light = a book which wants to be published. The image of the book as child recurs in early modern dedicatory prefaces, cf. Sir Philip Sidney who refers to the 1590 *Arcadia* as 'this child which I am loath to father'. On the journey of *Landgartha* from performance to publication see Introduction, pp 25–36.

Patri suo Charissimo operis Encomium.

Multiplici ratione, sator,[10] mea carmina (quamvis
    Non limata) tuis jungo; nempe ipse petisti,
    Cui teneor parere libens; formosa virago
Huc me vestra movet, virtutis dotibus exors,
In fracte[11] potius carnis quæ compede solvi
Certa fuit, fœdata foret quam crimine; cujus
Iactatis Pyrrhæ decus immortale resurgit
Nobilibus gestis; ad quod præcordia magna
Lætitia diffusa mihi, quando auribus hausi
Arrectis (genitor) te (per quem essentia, & à quo
Impetrata mihi, fruor & quibus, omnia) culte,
Consulto, graviter, cum suavitate, venuste,
Prægnantem causam peragisse.[12] Sed indere amoris
Non probo delicias: quod te fecisse sequutum
Historia[13] normam; belle, sciteque jocantem
Lætificando alios, non te, mens certa revolvit.

Aliud.

Melpomene tua tela (parens) contexta Thalia et,
    judicio quamvis non trutinanda meo est:
Me tua sed certam solers facundia, verax
    expertorum hominum & fama diurna facit,
Te nullis potuisse tuis errare, decorum
    omnimodo Scœnis, sed tenuisse triplex;
Nempe modum retinendo (docent ut scripta sagacis
    Flacci) personæ, temporis, atque loci.
Ad te à Invernis flexit victoria vatem,
    partibus his cedunt Brutiginæque tibi,
Fama quidem tendet, quacunque auratus Apollo
    se tua: tu vives dum vehet amnis aquas.

---

10 sator = 'sower' or 'planter' hence father or sire. 'Planter' has interesting resonance, here applied to an Old English writer.

11 fracte emended to *fractu*: by the breaking of.

12 peragisse emended to *peregisse*: s/he has completed.

13 Historia emended to *Historiae* (gen.): the rules of history.

Tu pater Aonio deducens vertice musas,
  gloria (non fallor) posteritatis eris.
Terra tuas certum est exhauriet extera laudes;
  clarescet scriptis insula nostra tuis.

Eleonora Burnell[14]

14 Eleonora Burnell, daughter of Henry. This is a unique example of Latin verse written by an
Old English woman in Ireland. The translations of the Latin poems, presented in square brackets (pp 76–7 and 81) do not appear in the original. I am deeply indebted to Will Poole for his
work on the translations of – and discussions of the difficulty of – the Latin verse. I am also very
grateful to Colin Burrow for his translation of the first poem. The second poem is discussed in
Jane Stevenson, *Women Latin Poets: Language, Gender, and Authority from Antiquity to the
Eighteenth Century* (Oxford: Oxford University Press, 2005), pp 385–6.

[An Encomium on his work to her dearest father.

For many reasons, my father, do I join my verses, unpolished though they are, to yours. Surely you yourself asked me to do so, to whom I am bound freely to obey. Your beautiful virago of a heroine also moves me to do this, who is outstanding in the gifts of virtue—who was certain to be set free from those bonds by breaking of flesh rather than by criminally breaking her vow,[15] and by whose noble deeds worthy of Pyrrha[16] she rises to immortality. Towards which deeds great joy flooded my whole body when I drank in through pricked ears (father) that you (through whom I enjoy my essence and from whom my all accomplishments derive), in a cultured, considered, grave, sweet and elegant manner, have narrated the pregnant cause. But I do not seek to introduce the pleasures of love, or to say that what you have done followed the rules of history.[17] Know that your fixed mind has considered beautifully jocular matters that might have been deadly to others, but not to you.

Another.

Your warp woven, father, by Melpomene and Thalia,[18] although it is not to be weighed in the balance of my judgment, yet your skilful eloquence, the truthful opinion of tried and tested men, the diurnal report, makes me assured that you were unable to err in your verse, but have in every way held to the triple decorum for dramatic writings: namely the manner of maintaining – as the writings of wise Horace teach – the standards of person, time, and place.[19] Victory bends to you, as Bard, from the Iverni; the Brutus-born women cede these regions to

---

15 i.e. Landgartha whose virtue means she will die in battle before breaking a vow. In the play, Landgartha has not made an Amazon vow of chastity and therefore cannot break it by marrying Reyner; she then remains faithful to her marriage vow, see Act 2. 394–6.

16 In Ovid's *Metamorphoses*, Jupiter permits Pyrrha and Deucalion to survive the universal flood. They then repopulate the world by throwing stones over their shoulders: Pyrrha's produce women, Deucalion's men (I. 319–95). Pyrrha is described as 'red-haired' – from *pyrrhus*, flame-coloured – here suggesting an Irish resonance.

17 The 'rules of history', i.e., following historical truth, are mentioned here; the dramatic unities in the second poem.

18 Melpomene is the muse of tragedy and Thalia of comedy; Burnell has woven both together in his 'Tragie-Comedy'. There may be a punning (if a-grammatical) play on 'tua tela' (n. pl. 'weapons') suggesting the difficulties his hybrid play encountered.

19 Eleonora Burnell refers to Horace – not Aristotle – to defend her father's observation of three unities of dramatic composition, echoing his defence of tragicomedy cited on the play's title-page. Given the episodic sweep of *Landgartha* in terms of both geography and time – not to mention the reversals in Reyner's character – the claim is tenuous.

you.[20] Assuredly Fame and golden Apollo himself will stretch forth to whatever you do: you shall live while the river bears water. You, father, leading down the muses from the Aonian mount, you will be (I am not deceived) the glory of posterity. Sure it is that a foreign land will drink up your praises;[21] our island will become illustrious through your writings.]

20 'Bard' is used to invoke the twinned resonance of 'vatem' as poet and prophet; Ptolemy refers to the *Iverni*, a Celtic tribe occupying the south-west of Ireland, hence, by extension the ancient Irish, see K. Müller (ed.), *Claudii Ptolemæi Geographia,* (Paris, 1883–1901), II, ii; *Brutaginaeque* = those (women) of the race of Brutus, i.e., the English. Thus the poet claims that her (Old English) father's poetry has conquered both the native Irish and the English. On the discussion of origins, in particular the use of the Brutus myth within the play, see Introduction, pp 44–51.

21 Eleonora Burnell assumes that the printed text will win – and thus suggests that it was intended to win – literary favour abroad. 'Terra … extera' may include, but is not exclusive to, England.

To his worthy to be much honoured Cousin Henry Burnell *Esq, on this his Tragie-Comedy, & c.*

Though my prayse cannot adde ought here: Yet give
Me leave (Cousin) to rayse my selfe, and live
Past time with thee; for, what thou writ'st is fine,
Pleasant, profound, chaste, morall, and divine;
Beyond the childish flashes of this age,
Affected non-sence, and *Canarian* rage;[22]
Or *Gargantuan* foppery.[23] Not one word
That's immateriall do'st thou affoord,
Vaine, or superfluous. Thy phrase is good;
Nay, strong, and elegant, though understood
Not by light-headed ignorance that do's admire
Strange language only. Wave, vote, flames, and fire,
Tempests and whirlewinds, *Scorpions,* and *Hags,*
Are stuff that take such, though indeed but rags,
Base rags that they patch on, and thou do'st scorne;[24]
Or any dialect that is much worne,
Though by the best; thy words thou mak'st to fit
(Not contrary) th' Conceptions of thy wit.
And, though thou *England* never saw'st: Yet, this
(Let others boast of their own faculties,
Or being Sonne to *Iohnson*)[25] I dare say,
That thou art farre more like to *Ben*: then they
That lay clayme as heirs to him, wrongfully:

22 Canarian rage = drunkenness induced by the popular sweet wine from the Canaries.
23 Gargantuan foppery = monstrous or excessive foolishness, from François Rabelais' series of novels about the giant Gargantua, first published 1532–52. Anne Lake Prescott notes that for Ben Jonson, Rabelais was associated with the comedy of excessive wordiness and social climbing: *Imagining Rabelais in Renaissance England* (London and New Haven: Yale University Press, 1998), pp 57, 116–23.
24 This general attack on overly spectacular theatre could be more specifically directed towards the effects used in James Shirley's recent Dublin play *St Patrick for Ireland* (1640).
25 i.e. Ben Jonson, poet laureate *c.*1617 until his death in 1637. The 'sons of Ben' was the name adopted by followers of Jonson in the seventeenth century, see Joe Lee Davis, *The Sons of Ben: Jonsonian Comedy in Caroline England* (Detroit: Wayne State University Press, 1967) and Ted-Larry Pebworth and Claude Summers, *Classic and Cavalier: Essays on Jonson and the Sons of Ben* (Pittsburgh: University of Pittsburgh Press, 1982). On Shirley, Burnell and the contest for the laureateship see Introduction, pp 32–4.

For he survives now only, but in thee
And his own lines; the rest degenerate.[26]
Nay, I can more affirme (and truly) that
In some things thou do'st passe him: being more sweet,
More modest, mylde, lesse tedious; Thy owne feet
Go thou on stoutly then: if thou proceed,
Him (though't be much) in all points thou'lt exceed.

Io. Bermingham.[27]

26 The degeneration of the Old English, especially those who intermarry and foster their children, is a persistent trope in early modern English writing about Ireland, see, for example, Edmund Spenser, 'A View of the State of Ireland' in Sir James Ware (ed.), *The Historie of Ireland, collected by three learned authors viz. Meredith Hanmer Doctor of Divinitie: Edmund Campion sometime fellow of St John's Colledge in Oxford: and Edmund Spenser Esq.* (Dublin, 1633), pp 45–8. Bermingham here reverses the trope: the English language survives intact only in Ireland, in the 'true' Englishman, Burnell.
27 Io.[hannes] (i.e., John) Bermingham, a relation of Burnell's and member of another influential Old English family of the Dublin Pale. See Introduction, pp 33–6.

Ad nobilissimum ingeniosissimum, dissertissimumque suum amicum Dominum *Henricum Burnellum* operis Elogium.

Vellera laturus signorum principis, anceps
    Ausonides lecto milite cepit iter:
Mox longos tentare sinus, votoque potiri,
    Aeolios cives, Ioniumque domans.
Mascula, casta, decens, suavisque (Henrice) *virago*
    Sola tibi invicta pubis ad instar adest.
Ergo procellosæ Niseidis, atque Charibdis
    Securus turbae, carbasa pande Notis.
Pande palam cedro tua digna volumina, Meci,[28]
    Multorumque prius pensa bilance virûm.
Pande nihil mancum: nil non laudabile: nil, quod
    Sympathicum non est, symmetriæque tenor.
Currum Phoebus equis sic, sic robusta Bootes
    Septem concordi plaustra Trione regit.
Magnes gnarorum: in rabiem Marpesia cautes,
    Quorum Cerberea toxica fauce fluunt.
Carmine sublimi morum icon, stilus honesti,
    Calcar virtuti es, criminibusque jugum.
Per g[29] *Minervali tutus munimine: fiet*
    Nobilior studijs gens tua clara tuis.
Munera, vive, tibi fulvo mage grata metallo,
    Æquora dum biberint proxima signa polo.

                              Philippus Patricius.[30]

---

28 Meci = possibly Mece (abl.) so 'palam … Mece' = in the presence of Mecus.

29 *Sic*: this 'g' may be a typographical error or a reference to a foot- or side-note that was then omitted, though there are no other such notes within the text. The line scans lawfully without it, but as entirely spondaic bar the penultimate dactyl.

30 Philippus Patricius = Philip Patrick. I have been unable to identify this author, though the quality of his Latin verse and the range of his references suggests that he was probably a graduate. Patricius plays on a number of meanings: of Patrick's stock or loyal to St Patrick; from a patrician family; possibly on 'patrico', an uneducated vagabond priest.

[To the most noble, intelligent, and eloquent Master Henry Burnell, his friend, an Elegy on his work.

He, in two minds, about to take up the fleeces, the prince's tokens, made the journey from his martial bed to the Ausonides: soon to assail far-off shores, and conquer, by the loyal oath of the Aeolian citizens, subduing Ionia.[31] That she-manly, chaste, seemly and sweet virago, Henry, is at hand for you, in the image of a young warrior, alone invincible. Therefore, untroubled by the stormy daughter of Nisus and Charybdis, untroubled by the tumult, show forth your sails to the south winds.[32] Show forth openly, Mecus,[33] your volumes worthy of the cedar-oil,[34] weighed first in the balance of many men. Show nothing defective, nothing unpraiseworthy, nothing which is not pleasing, holding fast to symmetry. Thus Phoebus rules his chariot with his horses, thus Bootes his seven wains with the twin Bears.[35] Lodestone of skilled men: Rock of Marpesia,[36] from which in a torrent flow toxins from the Cerberian pass. In sublime poetry the icon of decorum, of honourable style, you are the spur of virtue, a bridle for slanders. Safe through Minervalian[37] defence, may your distinguished people be nobler through your studies. Live, with rewards more pleasing to you than the golden metal, while the constellations closest to the pole drink in their seas.]

---

31 The 'He' refers to Aeneas. According to Virgil's *Aeneid*, Aeneas leaves his native Troy when it falls to the Greeks and travels – by way of the Greek Aeonian Islands and the Ionian sea – to Ausonia (Southern Italy) where he founds Rome.

32 In Greek myth Scylla (daughter of King Nisus) and Charybdis were treacherous women transformed into sea-monsters and placed on either side of the Strait of Messina, between Italy and Sicily. Odysseus travels through the Strait twice, first sailing close to the whirlpool Charybdis; next to the dangerous rocks, Scylla, (Homer, *The Odyssey*, Book 12).

33 Unidentified.

34 cedro is a metonymy: the backs of books were usually anointed with cedar-oil to preserve them from moths and decay, see C. Lewis & C. Short, *A Latin Dictionary* (Oxford: Clarendon Press, [1879] 1998).

35 Bootes ... the twin Bears: *Boötes* (the herdsman or the hunter) is one of the earliest noted constellations of seven stars, first referred to in Homer's *Odyssey* and described in Ptolomy's *Geography*. Appearing in the Northern sky, it is associated with the twin constellations of *Ursa Major* and *Ursa Minor*, see Landgartha's battle speech, I, 121–8.

36 Marpesia, the legendary queen of the Amazons, was said to have founded a city in the Caucus Mountains known as the Rock of Marpesia or the Marpesian Cliff. The phrase 'Marpesia cautes' is famously used by Virgil to describe Dido's stony silence when Aeneas attempts to address her in the Underworld (Virgil, *The Aeneid*, VI, 470–1). On Marpesia as one of the possible sources for Burnell's Amazon Marfisa, see Introduction, pp 58–9.

37 Minervalian = of the goddess Minerva.

Prologue delivered by an Amazon *with* a Battle-Axe in her hand.[38]

The best of English Poets for the Stage[39]
(Such was the envie, nicenesse and the rage
Of pettish weakelings, and detracting fooles,
That could prayse no man; and, i' th' muddie pooles
Of their owne vices, were o'rwhelm'd) was faine   5
An armed Prologue to produce, on paine
Of being tongue-strucke.[40] Therefore, marvell not
The present author (having not forgot
How in's first Play, he met with too much spite)[41]
Sho'd sent an armed *Amazon,* t'invite   10
(If it be possible) all minds to affect
What of himselfe, he could not well expect
From his detractors: Or, to let those know,
He cares not each of them prove still a foe.
Yet, this his second (as the first) he made   15
To please you, not for Money; to invade
Your wills for your owne profit. For, if his minde
He had sought by it to content you'd finde
Another method in't; and not a word
Of any mirth or love, wo'd he afford   20
To make you laugh or languish. All, rich stuffe
(Though not so pleasing) he'd expose, to cuffe[42]
(And generally too) the monster vice;
Which he performes but gently, in this piece.
Yet its beleev'd 't will please the most and best,   25
In all the passages; and for the rest,
Let 'em (if they will needs) in pudles swim:
For, he sleights them more, then they can wrong him.

---

38 Later identified in the Epilogue as Scania. Gerald of Wales (Giraldus Cambrensis) identified the
   battle-axe as a dangerous and distinctively Irish weapon 'borrowed from the Norwegians and
   Ostmen', 'The Topography of Ireland' in T. Wright (ed.), *The Historical Works of Giraldus
   Cambrensis* (New York: AMS Press [1863], 1968), pp 1–164 (123, 135–6).

39 Lines 1–7 refer to Ben Jonson and his 'armed prologue' to *The Poetaster* (1601). This derisive
   response to John Marston's 'armed epilogue' to *Antonio and Mellida* (*c.*1599) was a controversial episode in the London 'War of the Theatres' (*c.*1600–2). Burnell replays this conflict as a
   challenge to Shirley over the legacy of Jonson, see Introduction, pp 34–6.

40 tongue-strucke = harshly criticized.

41 The author refers to an earlier play, now lost. See Introduction, p. 15.

42 cuffe = strike, beat or box.

Landgartha.

The first Act.

Enter Fredericke and Wermond.

FREDERICKE

Ｉt's a noble, noble act!
   WERMOND And cannot
  But vex the bloudy usurper, let him put
  Ever so good a face on't, though they were
  But women only, that conspire against him.[43]   5
FREDERICKE It stirs him not: for since his conquest made
  On us, and murdring of our lawfull Prince,
  Things have succeeded so to all his wishes,
  That he's grow'n carelesse: nay blindly besotted
  By security, and selfe-perswasion,   10
  Lock'd by the tempest of his lust; so as
  He feares no force of man; much lesse weake women,
  As he is pleasd to tearme 'em; he minds nothing
  But whom to kill, or foulely ravish: and
  The conversation of his Bawds, and Spintries.[44]   15
WERMOND Is't possible, he sho'd be so secure,
  And passe away in such a dying slumber?
FREDERICKE He thinkes the gods doe slumber too, or winke
  At what he do's, or rather snore supinely;
  Or that there are no gods, and what's spoke of 'em   20
  Is but a meere foolish fable; He'll beleeve
  No mans intelligence, not his own spyes
  That this fleet of Denmarke, now launch'd forth, sho'd move
  Against him hither.

---

43 Lines 1–28: according to Saxo Grammaticus, Frø [Frollo, king of Sweden, killed Siward, king of the Norwegians and grandfather to Regnar [Reyner], usurped the throne and put Siward's wives to work in a brothel. When Regnar arrives to claim the throne and avenge his grandfather, the women join his army (*History of the Danes*, I, p. 280). Belleforest's version echoes, indeed stresses, the Amazons' desire for revenge; see, for example, Landgerthe's battle speech, *Histoires Tragiques*, pp 853–4. On Burnell's sources, see Introduction, pp 36–51.

44 Bawds, and Spintries = pimps and male prostitutes.

WERMOND It's not all the power,   25
   He for the present can command that will
   Resist it, if he doe; joyn'd to the valiant
   Landgartha, with her faire lock'd troope of Ladies: *Musicke of*
   But, let's be silent; here the wretch himselfe comes.   *Recorders.*

Enter Frollo leading a weeping Lady,[45]
Hasmond and Gotar.

FROLLO Come my pretty sweet-heart, dry up those pleasing   30
   Eyes; this liquor's too precious to be spilt
   In such a cause, for a lost Maydenhead,
   And to a King that will become thy slave for't,
   And for more of that sport: who to please thee
   In that, and whatsoever else thou canst conceive,   35
   To rayse content to thee, and varri'd to thought,
   Will ransacke Kingdomes.
LADY Leave me yet blacke Devill,   *Breakes from him.*
   Thy words sound farre worse than the voyce of Hell.
FROLLO Some kicke the Spyder out at the Court gates;   40
   An angry scratching cat. We wo'd not be   *Exeunt Fred[ericke]*
   So vex'd another night with such a foole.   *and Werm[ond]*
GOTAR She'll soone repent Sir, and turne backe, to offer   *with the Lady.*
   Her dainty body to your mylder usage
HASMOND I rather thinke, she'll to the mad *Langartha*;   45
   And there make one amongst her furious troope
   Of Furies, that will yet endure no horsing,[46]
   Though they manage bravely.
FROLLO There's a Wench indeed,
   What luck had I, never to lay my hands   50
   On her? They say she's very faire and handsome.
HASMOND The clappers of mens tongues proclayme that; and
   Speak strange things of her.
FROLLO We shall finde 'em (the best
   Is of it) altogether, to make a royall   55
   Choyce. We meane to single forty at least,
   Of the most buxome (of which she shall be

45 The 'weeping Lady' is not listed in the Dramatis Personae. In all other respects this first scene
   is a model of exposition, introducing the principal characters and beginning in the midst of the
   action.
46 horsing = riding, covering a mare.

Chiefe generall, as now she is) for our
Owne private pallat.

HASMOND I may hope (Sir) you'll grant   60
Me halfe the number, with her wise and modest
Aunt *Elsinora,* to precede: Or her fine
Valorous sister *Scania,* for I must
Imitate your manly vertue, Sir, as neere
As I can.   65

FROLLO Marke well what I say now: for thy
Good service as my honest smocke Atturney[47]
(Though sometime, yet thou did'st begin to us, thou'lt say
For fear they'd beene diseas'd:) thou shalt not have
One woman (wert thou e'er so willing) more   70
Or lesse than thirty.

HASMOND [*Jeeringly*] O Prodigious!
I doe beseech you, Sir, to hear me speake,
Like so many Basilisks[48] (with angry shots
From their sharpe venom'd eyes) they'd strike me dead: 75
Or (as the Porcupyne) send fether'd arrowes
At me,[49] for my slacknesse.

FROLLO You must have thirty,
Or none.

HASMOND Nay, if I must, I shall: and that's   80
As bad.

GOTAR [*Solemnely*] You will not (Sir) be altogether
Unmindefull of my good endeavours.

FROLLO By no meanes, good Sir, thou shalt possess for thy
Share, twenty five; with the pretty smugge[50] *Fatyma,*   85
To leade'em.

GOTAR I humbly thanke your grace, though I
Sho'd not covet so many desperate femals:
Yet, with the assistance of my kindest friends,
I shall be strongly back'd.   *Enter Wermond.* 90

---

47 smocke Atturney = (variation on smock agent) pimp, procurer of women.

48 Basilisk = or cockatrice, a fabulous reptile whose look was believed to kill. See P. Holland, trans., Pliny the Elder, *The historie of the world: commonly called, The naturall historie of C. Plinius Secundus* (London, 1601) II, 356. On the image in early modern poetry see Sergei Lobanov-Rotovsky, 'Taming the Basilisk' in D. Hillman and Carla Mazzio (eds), *The Body in Parts: Fantasies of Corporeality in Early Modern Europe* (London: Routledge, 1997), pp 195–217.

49 Lines 76–7: Refers to the myth that porcupines can shoot their quills in defence, Holland, trans., Pliny, *The historie of the world,* I, 215.

50 smugge = neat, trim. Fatyma's small stature is referred to every time she appears.

WERMOND May it please you, Sir,
    Here are arriv'd two posts at once, all full
    Of sweat and durt; and bring bad newes, it's fear'd.
FROLLO Curse on thy feares, Goe, send 'em hither to us;   *Exit.*
    It's but these women that affright fooles thus.   *Enter first post.* 95
    What newes? be briefe.
GOTAR He's full of durt, indeed!
FIRST POST *Landgartha* with a mighty troope of women,
    Gathered to her from all the parts of *Norway,*
    Make havocke of your souldiers, sir; and killing   100
    All the Sweds[51] they light upon, they likewise threaten,
    They will grant you (ere long) no better quarter.[52]
FROLLO My Sweds and I will make some, here in *Norway,*
    Pay dearely for that vant.[53] Come, doe thou croake too. *Enter 2. post.*
    The worst tale thou canst.   105
SECOND POST You had neede, Sir, make quicke
    Resistance, or shift for your selfe: for, the King
    Of *Denmarke,* with a mighty fleete, has now
    Put in at *Mastrand;*[54] and begins to land
    His forces, to joyne with *Landgartha's:* who   110
    With maine speede, marches to meete him thither.
FROLLO Which he shall soone repent, and so shall that
    Male-harted Traytresse, withall the curll'd knot
    Of rebels that attend her;[55] We are not
    So unprovided, as they doe suppose yet,   115
    Fly therefore *Hasmond,* gather thou our troopes
    Within and neere the Citie. *Gotar,* thou
    Haste to the quarters further off; and with
    All possible speed draw unto us. Away
    When need compels, men must use no delay.   *Exeunt omnes.* 120

A march, then enter Landgartha, Scania, Elsinora, Fatyma,
and one or two Ladies more, all attyr'd like Amazons,
with Battl-axes in their hands, and Swords on.

51 Sweds = those from Sweland, i.e., Swedes.
52 grant ... quarter = spare the life of a defeated, captured or surrendered enemy.
53 vant = vaunt, boast.
54 Mastrand = Marstrand, a port on the southwest coast of Sweden, thus granting easy access to the southeast coast of Norway.
55 the curll'd knot/Of rebels = the serpent hair on the head of the Medusa multiplied when cut off. This was a common figure for rebellion, here given extra force as the rebels in question are female.

LANDGARTHA We now (sweet Ladies and deare sisters) march not
    Against th'intemperate *Frollo:* but ascend
    The milkie way, that leads to immortall fame,
    Not to be rank'd among the starre-made harlots:
    But stated in the high'st Empyreall heaven,   125
    To side the gods, where *Pallas* and chast *Phoebe*
    (Arm'd chiefely with the weapons of their vertues)
    Keepe all the Masculin deities in awe.[56]
    This our designe may well exalt us thither,
    As their good deeds did them: that in defence   130
    Of that all sho'd hold dearest, our honours, Ladies,
    Doe now expose our selves to death, and what
    A cruell, vicious, revengefull Tyrant
    May inflict on us, if vanquish'd. Yet, this act
    Of ours we must not vainely boast of: for,   135
    The little birds will (with their beaks and wings)
    Offend the ravishers of their young issue.
    What then should we performe thinke you, that farre
    Passe these? yeild up your bodies basely to
    Foule rape and lust, and so to infamie   140
    For ever? No, no: farre be this from us
    Honour'd virgins, that have such armes to wield
    These cutting weapons, being (too) to fight authoriz'd,
    By the examples of the noblest women,
    Semiramis, Zenobia, faire *Cinana*   145
    Sister unto great *Macedon,* stout *Alvilda,*
    Camilla, and the Amazonian Queenes,
    Great *Mithridates* Queene, and severall others,
    Are patterns now for us to imitate;[57]

---

56 Lines 121–8: Landgartha invokes the myth of Callisto, chaste servant of the goddess of hunting
    (known as Artemis, Phoebe or Diana), who was pursued and raped by Zeus, then later turned
    into the *Ursa Major* constellation (also known as the Great Bear or The Plough). See also
    Philippus Patricius' poem above. For Landgartha, this 'starre-made harlot' is contrasted with the
    true goddesses, Pallas Athene, goddess of war and the aforementioned Phoebe, both of whom
    embody Amazon values of fearlessness and chastity. Landgartha's battle speech draws on Greek
    mythology; this is not the case in Belleforest's account and in Saxo Grammaticus she has no
    speech.
57 Lines 144–9: Landgartha invokes a multi-ethnic pantheon of Amazons: Semiramis = Greek
    name for a legendary Assyrian queen, born of a goddess, and based on the historical queen
    Shammuramat (*c.*800 BC), ruler of Babylon; Zenobia = Empress of Palmyra (267–72) led a
    rebellion against Rome, seizing control of Egypt and became known as the new Cleopatra;
    Cinana = Cynane, the warrior princess, half sister of Alexander the Great; Alvilda = Alfhild,

O most brave patterns! Yet this we may say,   150
That our chast glories shall passe theirs, as farre
As th' worth of our intentions doth exceed
The cause they undertooke: nor ought you doubt it.
Let then the King of *Denmarke* fight where he list:
We will pursue no other than our worst   155
And strongest adversary in's owne squadron;
Where I, as first, will loose my life, or give
A suddaine end to his blacke purposes,
That sought a conquest on our chastities.
ELSINORA Thy vertues and example, Neece: that are not   160
To be reach'd by any imitation
(At least of our endeavours) doe farre more
Excite our courages, then *Hermes*[58] could,
Were he now here, to play the Orator:
Lead on then; you shall find us no bad seconds.   165
SCANIA I have more than a womans longing to begin.
LANDGARTHA I know *Fatyma*, though she be not great[59]
Has not the least desire to fight among us.
FATYMA Stay till you see me knocke some great ones downe;
Untill when, I shall well remit your prayses.   170
LANDGARTHA Then follow me; and as you see me wooe
The *Swedish* King, to his doe you so too.[60]   *Exeunt. A march.*

Enter Reyner, Valdemar, Inguar, Hubba, and
one or two more Souldiers with Axes.

runaway princess and legendary pirate leader who was eventually captured by her former suitor,
married him and became queen of Denmark; Camilla = Queen of the Volsci, Roman Amazon
and servant of the goddess Diana. Virgil recounts in *The Aeneid*, Book 11, how she fought fire-
cely for Turnus against Aeneas; Mithradates Queene = Hipsicratea, wife of Mithradates VI,
who rode to war with her husband against Rome. In Belleforest, the narrator compares
Landgerthe to four Amazons: 'Semyramis ... Zenobie ... Cinane ... Valasche' (*Histoires
Tragiques*, pp 841–2) and Landgerthe invokes 'Avilde' in her first battle speech (ibid., p. 845).
Burnell replaces the Bohemian Valasche with the classical Camilla, perhaps because the former
was involved in internal civil wars rather than a foreign campaign, more specifically a campaign
against Rome. Landgartha's Amazon examples would be well known to Burnell's audience:
Camilla, Hipsicratea, Zenobia and Valache appear in Jonson's *The Masque of Queens* (1609); all
except Avilda appear in Heywood's *Nine the Most Worthy Women* (1640), see Introduction, pp
52–3, 58.
58 Hermes = messenger of the Greek gods and patron of orators and poets; the Roman Mercury.
59 great = large, tall.
60 Lines 171–2: i.e., what I do to Frollo, you do to his men.

REYNER It's my chiefe comfort noble *Cymbrians*,[61]
    Subjects and friends, to be your guide to day,
    Against a valiant wicked adversary; 175
    And for our right, th'inheritance of this kingdome,
    To shewe that vertue and the cause, doe more
    Prevayle than any humane fortitude,
    Or setl'd Councels, when they're joyn'd to vice;
    And by injustice seeke to advance their states: 180
    Which wisely our forefathers mask'd beneath
    The fables of the *Titans* 'gainst the gods.[62]
    But it sho'd seeme the vertue of our foes
    (Wisedome and valour) has forsooke 'em, by
    Their palliardise,[63] by ease, and hourely ryot; 185
    This kingdom being more fatall unto them,
    Then *Capua* was to *Hannibal*:[64] and therefore,
    Not worth your meanest feares: I must not then
    Inlarge my selfe in words too farre, because
    You need 'em not; nor need you be beholding, 190
    Unto the fames of your brave Ancestors,
    Those valiant *Cymbrians*, that almost gave
    An end to *Rome*, the Mistris of the world,[65]
    And not in her declyning dayes, when her
    Owne vices had confounded her; as when 195

61 Cymbrians = Cimbri, ancient tribe of Jutland (Denmark), commonly believed to be descended from Japeth, son of Noah. Usually described as Germanic, they were also identified as Celtic and thus linked to the Cymri of Wales and Britain. Just like Landgartha, Reyner identifies his forces (the Danes) with some of Rome's most dangerous enemies (see below). See also Introduction, pp 47–9.
62 Titans = a race of deities from the classical Golden Age. The first generation, the children of Uranus and Gaea, rebelled against their father. Their descendants were eventually overthrown by the Olympian gods. Burnell also invites, by way of his own allusion, an allegorical 'mask'd' reading of the triumph of justice over tyranny implied in his own fable.
63 palliardise = (from French) fornication, lechery. The word is lifted directly from Belleforest's description of Fro [Frollo], *Histoires Tragiques*, p. 843
64 Lines 186–7: The Italian city Capua defected to Hannibal in 216 BC during the Second Punic Wars (218–201 BC) and became his Italian capital. His army took winter quarters there (216–215 BC) and, according to historians, emerged much weaker. In Renaissance military hand-books, reference to Hannibal in Capua became shorthand for the dangers of permitting military discipline to relax in settlement. For its relevance in early modern Ireland, see Rankin, *Between Spenser and Swift*, pp 149–56.
65 The Cimbrian Wars (113–101 BC) occurred when, together with the Teutons, the Cimbrians migrated south into Roman territory, causing the first serious threat to the Roman Empire since the Second Punic Wars (see above).

The *Gothes* and *Vandals*[66] (now our enemies)
Did trample on her, being downe before.
She liv'd full man, when great King *Beleus*[67]
Did (on the borders of rich *Italy*)
Vanquish three of her bravest Generals,   200
Sylanus, Cæpio, and *Manilius.*[68]
This (if you please) you may consider; and
That our foes are more famous for their whoredomes,
Than conquering of *Norway*. Reflect also
How for this cause, we are assisted by   205
An Angel troope, of chast and noble Ladies:
Whom neyther losse of life, or other evils
Can fright, from seeking to revenge the wrongs
Done to their Sex, their parents, and their friends.
Then, let's not shame our selves now in their presence,   210
Or to posteritie: by being out-gone
By women in a battle. Lastly, consider
The everlasting honour due to vertue;
Of which we now shall make a glorious purchase.
HUBBA I am affraid you will consider (sir,)   215
So long of these women; untill you forget
What you applaud so feelingly, your vertue.
REYNER Thou'rt always merry, *Hubba,* honest withall;
And from my heart I wish, that each man here
Performe a Souldiers parts, no worse than thou;   220
We shall not then be beaten.
VALDEMAR Let's march on, sir:
And you shall quickly find the meanest of 'em,

---

66 Gothes and Vandals = normally identified as East Germanic/Slavic tribes who played a large
part in the downfall of Rome in late Antiquity. Reyner here invokes their Swedish origins in
order to identify them with Frollo's enemy forces. The Goths inhabited Gotland, the southern
part of the Swedish peninsula; the Vandals were associated with Vendel, a province in Uppland.
See Introduction, pp 47–9.

67 King Beleus = probably Boiorix, king of the Cimbrians.

68 Lines 199–201: Sylanus = Consul Marcus Junius Silanus who refused to negotiate with the
Cimbrians on the possibility of peaceful settlement and was defeated in Southern Gaul in 109
BC; Coepio = Pro-consul Quintus Servilius Caepio; Manilius = Consul Gnaeus Mallius
Maximus. The combined Roman forces of Caepio and Mallius were defeated by the Cimbrians
at the Battle of Arausio (105 BC) largely because the two commanders utterly refused to coop-
erate with each other. The huge Roman losses caused the two generals to be called to trial and
in the longer term famously produced a full scale re-organization of the Roman military. This
invokes the 1640 controversies around Wentworth's 'Irish' army; see Introduction, pp 21–5.

Valiant and strong to purchase what's your birth-right.[69]

REYNER Then let us move; and prosper too, as we   225
    Affect[70] injustice, or impietie.   *Exeunt. A march.*

Enter Frollo, Hasmond, Gotar, and two or three
more with Axes.

FROLLO We must not loose our confidence, brave Warriors,
    Though we be taken somewhat tardy, by
    A sort of raw fresh-water souldiers,[71] weake
    Unmartiall women fitter for night encounters,   230
    And some poor fugitive *Norwegian* rebels,
    Conquer'd and beaten oft by us before.
    What then although our numbers be the lesse?
    Yet not by much: the glory of the adventure,
    Would not be worth the paines we under tooke else.   235
    Besides, if we consider what our Ancestors[72]
    Have (by their never-equall'd vallors) oft
    Perform'd against the noblest nations of
    The world, this our designe is nothing: nothing
    To what they did: What we have done our selves,   240
    And mean to doe hereafter. Notwithstanding,
    Let me commend unto your memories,
    After a generall fashion (for now
    The time exacts deeds more than words) what some
    Of their large conquests were, not onely in   245
    Europe, Which was all theirs a'most: but in
    Affricke,[73] a third and richest part of th' world;
    Which from the *Ocean* unto *Nyle* they won;
    And from the *Mid-land* Sea,[74] to the torrid *Zone*.
    Great *Rome* herself (that wisedom boasted most,   250

69 birth-right = a reminder that Reyner has a rightful blood claim on Norway by way of his
    grandfather Siward and is not, like Frollo, a usurper.
70 Affect = aim at, aspire to.
71 A sort of raw fresh-water souldiers = a sortie (sally or attack) by unskilled untrained recruits.
72 Ancestors = i.e., the Goths and Vandals above. For Burnell's audience, Frollo also invokes the
    more recent successes of the Swedish King Gustavus Adolphus (1594–1632) in the Thirty Years
    War (1618–48), see Introduction, pp 36–7, 48.
73 While the Goths extended their empire along the Northern shores of the Mediterranean and
    into Asia, the Vandals moved into North Africa in 429 BC and over the next ten years built up
    a sizeable empire there.
74 Mid-land Sea = Mediterranean.

And next her vallor) was by our fathers taken,
Pillag'd, and burnt foure times at least;[75] and her
Large Empyre brought to nothing. She master'd all:
We master'd her;
And will not now degenerate[76] first of ours.   255
What though men say, we are not religious?[77]
Religion is but a toy, and first invented
By politicke States, to keepe fooles in awe;
And of all men observed least by themselves,
If she but thwart the least of their intendments.   260
They glorifie her much for their owne ends;
And that's even almost all: and so may we.
Yet, honour by warre, riches, and our pleasure,
Shall be the Altars, and the gods we'll bow to
In our free mindes; and what we gain we'l keepe.   265
King *Reyner* therefore was not wise, in seeking
To dispossesse the bravest Nation breathing,
Of what they have atchiev'd by the right of conquest;
And shall (I hope) in snatching at our Crowne,
By your more pow'rfull armes, soone misse his own.   *Ex[eunt]* 270
                                                                               Allarums.

> *A good while after the allarums are begun,*
> *Enter Frollo and a gentleman.*

FROLLO Furies and plagues: these wild, wild, bloudy whores,
        Fight like so many Tygers: without the least
        Apprehension of feare, or any kind

75 foure times = the four sackings of Rome referred to were by the Gauls after the Battle of the Allia
    (AD 387); by the Visigoths (AD 410); by the Vandals (AD 455) and by the Ostrogoths (AD 546).
76 See note 26 above.
77 Lines 256–70: Frollo's speech here draws on English stage-Machiavellianism, more particularly,
    on Machevil's 'Prologue' to Christopher Marlowe, 'The Jew of Malta', ed. Roma Gill in E.
    Esche, D. Fuller et al. (eds), *The Complete Works of Christopher Marlowe*, 5 vols (Oxford:
    Clarendon Press, 1987–95), 4, pp 3–4. In particular, Frollo plays on the idea of atheism or lack
    of respect for the gods: 'I count Religion but a childish Toy,/And hold there is no
    sin but Ignorance.' (Ibid., ll. 14–15); and the notion of right of rule by conquest rather than (as
    in Reyner's case) blood birthright: 'What right had Caesar to the Empery?/Might first made
    Kings, and Lawes were then most sure/When like the *Dracos* they were writ in blood.' (Ibid.,
    ll. 19–21). On Marlowe's (mis-)representations of the political thought of Niccolò Machiavelli
    in this prologue see Irving Ribner, 'Marlowe and Macchiavelli', *Comparative Literature*, 6:4
    (1954), 348–56 (351).

Of mercy: the pursie[78] *Danes* come nothing neere 'em:
Having cut off our vauntgard,[79] and right wing,   275
They presse on our maine battle too; and force
It to give ground. Goe, fly thou: and charge *Hasmond*
To fetch the reare with speed up; that we may   *Exit gentl[eman].*
(There being no other hope for safety left us)
Upon one desperat onslaught hazard all.   *Enter Scania.* 280
SCANIA I am glad I've met you, sir.
FROLLO [*aside*] A pretty fine peece.
    I wo'd faine save this. I sho'd preferre
    Thy beautie, unto ought that's ours; prove kind
    And gentle unto thee, sweetheart: if thou'lt   285
    But yeeld ———
SCANIA To thy imbraces, that must 'a' had
    My sister, me and forty more. We now
    Shall see what you can doe 'gainst one. Come quickly
    Then, unto your guard sir: or I shall soone send forth   290
    Your too hot bloud, to coole your lustfull heart.
FROLLO Plague on you for a company of spiteful,
    Venomous tong'd bitches. Ye had rather lye
    With the worst Hynde of your owne,[80] than the best of us.
SCANIA Villaine, I'll answer thee another way.   *Offers to fight on which* 295
LANDGARTHA Hold sister. This must only be my mate: *Land[gartha] enters.*
    Goe, seeke you out another somewhere else?[81]   *Exit Scania.*
FROLLO Art thou *Landgartha*? Or some supernall[82] goddesse,
    Descended in her fairer shape, to make
    A conquest now on *Frollo*, that must yeeld   300
    Himselfe thy captive?
LANDGARTHA Thou once call'dst me subject;
    And I am come to tender my alleagence,
    To your ungracious wickedness, thus ———   *stricks[83] at him.*

---

78 pursie = (pursy) fat, also short of breath, cf. 'In the fatnesse of these pursie times/Vertue it selfe
    of vice must pardon beg', Shakespeare, *Hamlet*, 3. 4. 144–5.
79 vauntgard = vanguard.
80 Hynde of your owne = Frollo here plays on three meanings of the word hind, none of them
    complimentary: a female deer, associated with Phoebe/Diana and her virgin huntresses; a low-
    ranking household servant; backside. He thus, against the Norwegian women, interweaves
    accusations of lesbianism and inappropriate behaviour with the lower classes with a xenopho-
    bic rejection of their Swedish conquerors.
81 Burnell invents the single combat scene between Frollo and Landgartha; in Belleforest, Frollo is
    pursued and cut to pieces by all the women, *Histoires Tragiques*, p. 855, see Introduction, p. 38.
82 supernall = heavenly, celestial.   83 stricks = strikes.

FROLLO Hold, for heavens sake hold, and patiently   305
    But take my faithfull vow. Doe thou withdraw
    Thy troopes from our defeat: and by the *Olympian*[84]
    Gods, I shall no sooner
    Have strucke King *Reyner* with his punie *Danes*,
    But I'll make thee my Queene.   310
LANDGARTHA Thy Concubyne.
FROLLO All miseries light on me then for ever;
    Or if I ever mixe with woman but
    Thy selfe: for thou art worthy of a *Mars*,
    A *Hercules*, or *Iupiter*.[85]   315
LANDGARTHA And have
    Fully resolv'd never to kisse any man,
    But him that shall first master me in fight:
    You are best therefore looke well to your selfe, sir;
    Or I shall quickly marry your hearts bloud   320
    To this weapon.   *They fight & he's hurt.*
FROLLO I bleed you see: let which
    Serve as an offering, to appease thy wrath
    Conceiv'd against a wretch, that now repents *Here Rey[ner] Vald[emar]*
    (Unfainedly) his former evill life.   *Inguar & Hubb[a] are discovered.* 325
    May the gods chiefe attribute then (mercy)
    Find roome for me (a Convertite) in thy
    Noble and vertuous soule: and I shall still
    Become thy pious imitator: be
    Govern'd by thee in all things, and thy husband,   330
    By heaven and all, I will.
LANDGARTHA But I hope you shall not: *They fight, and she*
    For I must try your manhood once againe.   *strikes him downe.*
REYNER O brave mayde!
FROLLO Faire *Furie*, thou hast kill'd me,   335
    Hell take thee for 't: my love is now cool'd indeed.
    But I will be reveng'd. I cannot, cannot rise:

---

84 Olympian = dwelling on Mount Olympus.

85 Lines 314–15: In contrast to Landgartha's references to Greek mythology, Frollo's references
    are firmly Roman. Mars = Roman god of war, son of Jupiter and Juno, and father to Romulus
    and Remus, founders of Rome; Hercules = half mortal son of Jupiter and Alcmene, hated by
    Juno who causes him to kill his family in rage. He is allowed to atone for this act by complet-
    ing the Twelve Labours of Hercules. At one point during the labours, commanded by the
    Delphic oracle, he becomes slave to an Amazon, the Lydian queen Omphale; Jupiter = (Greek:
    Zeus), chief of the Olympian gods.

The losse of bloud, and paine, strike faint my pow'rs:
That I were now on high transform'd *Atlas*:[86]
This being no fable, but a truth: that I   340
Might cut the axle-tree of heaven in two:
And tumble downe the gods, and breake their necks,
Proud gods, if such there be. Then, like *Enceladus*
(Loaden with flaming *Etna*)[87] I sho'd turne,
And shake out all the starres: The sunne, and with   345
That fire, burne all to cinders. Thus I'd turne:
O divels, I cannot: but doe feele a pitchy
Cloud (darker than night) hang o'r my drowsie temples:
And must (there is no remedy) descend, to stalke
Along th'infernall waves, or wafted over,   350
Grapple with the damned *Furies*, receive my soule
You beastly Hags, then: that shall torment you more,
Than you can any.[88]   *Dyes.*

LANDGARTHA The gods are now reveng'd
On thee, by me, libidinous Woolfe, foule Tyrant.   355

REYNER And rid me (worthy Lady,) of a dangerous
Adversary.

LANDGARTHA I doe beseech, sir: *Kneels on one knee.*
As my duty onely to receive that,
Unto them and your grace, though a woman.   360

REYNER This to me (Madame) is too great an honour.
Pray stand up. I should rather kneele to you,
Whose beauty and incomparable vertues,
Exact no slender adoration,
From all those that love goodness; or the image   365
Of heaven in your face. We must acknowledge,

---

86 Lines 339–41: The Titan Atlas led the revolt against Zeus and the Olympians (note 62 above)
and as punishment was transformed into a mountain and forced to hold up the 'axle-tree' or
celestial axis on which the world and the heavens turn. The Atlas mountain range in North-
west Africa bears his name, cf. Virgil, *The Aeneid*, VI, ll. 796–7 where Anchises foretells the
extent of Augustus' empire, reaching: 'where ancient Atlas turns on his shoulders the starred
burning axle-tree of heaven.' Frollo continues his echoing of Christopher Marlowe, who asso-
ciates the word axle-tree with his over-reaching heroes: *Doctor Faustus* 2. 3. 40, *1 Tamburlaine*
4. 2. 50 and *2 Tamburlaine*, 1.1.90.

87 Enceladus = one of the hundred-armed giants who revolted against the gods. Killed by Zeus,
he was buried under the volcano, Mount Etna in Sicily.

88 Lines 349–53: There are echoes here, in the '*Furies*' and '*Hags*', of Bermingham's dedicatory
poem (above, ll. 12–15). It is the Marlowian Frollo who comes closest to the excessive theatre
invoked there. Burnell here kills off one of his best and certainly most dramatic characters.

Notwithstanding our right to the crowne of *Norway*,
What pow'r so'er we have in't, gain'd and confirm'd
Chiefly by you, that are our strongest friend.
LANDGARTHA Your poore and humble vassall,[89] that desires 370
No other recompence for her small service,
Than your Kingly licence, to remaine
(When your foes are wholly vanqish'd) from all
Imployment sever'd: to lead a solitary
Quiet life, being compell'd (in the defence 375
Of what I ever most esteemed) to march
Thus among men; which I did not covet, but
The contrary.
REYNER You will not wrong the world
(The race of man, sweet Lady,) so to robb it 380
Of such lustre: nay of all light, by
Dedicating of what is onely good in't,
Your selfe, to solitude.
LANDGARTHA I must not be
Compell'd to any state of life, sir. 385
REYNER You cannot
Madame, I see that; and (by your force my foes
Now put to flight) I shall continue alwayes,
Not onely a meere servant, but for ever
Your bondman; not to offend you i' th' least thought. *Enter Scania,* 390
VALDEMAR Here be other noble friends (sir) to whom you *Elsinora &*
Stand bound in no small summes. *Fat[yma].*
ELSINORA Of Princely favour
Onely.
REYNER Rise faire Ladies, you shall command 395
Us, being your creature.
HUBBA They're delicate fine wenches, pretty youths.
LANDGARTHA You are now, sir
To consider, how to use your victory.
SCANIA For us, we shall hereafter (we doubt not) 400
Partake the fruits of your most Royall bounty,
Which we shall begge more, for the generall
Good, than our particular interests, sir.

89 Lines 370–85: After the straightforward task of war, this marks Landgartha's first articulation of
the conflict of interests facing the Amazon in peacetime. On the one hand she desires Amazon
separatism and freedom from servitude; on the other, she recognizes the duty of a subject, see
Introduction, pp 55–6.

REYNER You shall be the Law-makers, to your selves:
    For those, by whom we raigne, shall be our guides: 405
    In the meane time, thou *Valdemar* and *Inguar,*
    Pursue the flying foe, but most with mercie,
    Not[90] of circumspection; yet, least th' Van
    Turne by some accident, by us not thought on;
    Save all that yeeld, whom we doe meane to send   410
    Home ransomelesse; to see if that benefit
    May worke a peace betwixt us.[91] If it doe not,
    We shall the next time be the more excus'd,
    In our extending of severitie.
    Come Ladies, we'll to counsell to conclude   415
    Concerning what we have (by you) subdu'd.[92]

---

90 In the following copies, the word 'void' has been inserted here in early manuscript to read: 'Not *void* of circumspection.': Boston Public Library; British Library (162.c.27 and G.11220); Houghton Library; Bod. Malone (203). This frequency might suggest a printer's or authorial addition.

91 Reyner intends to follow seventeenth-century laws of war as regards the holding and negotiated release of hostages as opposed to secret ransoming or the killing of captives, cf. the publication which appears just before *Landgartha*, James Butler, duke of Ormond, *Lawes and orders of warre. 1641. Established for the good conduct of the service of Ireland* (Dublin, 1641), Br. See Introduction, p. 30–1.

92 Lines 415–16: Reyner's consultation with the Amazons on the terms of post-war settlement invokes the influence of Queen Henrietta Maria on Charles I's policy-making in the pre-Civil War years. Perceived as fair and benevolent by the Old English, she was considered by Protestants in both England and Ireland to be aggressively pro-Catholic, see Introduction, pp 52–4.

The second Act.

Enter Valdemar, and Inguar.

VALDEMAR It's a strange humour that has seaz'd upon him;
    Whatsoever the cause be.
INGUAR When you are
    Ignorant of it, all others must be so.
VALDEMAR He discovers nothing to me save onely   5
    That he is full (and that he often sayes)
    Of griefe and heaviness; and sometimes sicke.
INGUAR His sicknesse may (in time) prove dangerous,
    If some fit remedy be not apply'd.
VALDEMAR He'll heare of none; I urg'd his Physitians,   10
    At which he storm'd, and bad me leave him to
    Himselfe; and since I dare not come in sight.
INGUAR It's a deadly malady, that will admit
    Of no cure. We are best put Captaine *Hubba*,
    Or the wise *Cowsell* on him: for the wit   15
    Of the one and th'others folly may remove
    More of that grief he speaks on, than good counsell.   *Enter Rey[ner].*
VALDEMAR Here comes the man himselfe, in his usuall
    Meditation and therefore let's away.   *Exeunt ambo.*
REYNER She is divinely faire, and in her mind[93]   20
    The noblest vertues keepe their residence,
    As in their lovli'st habitation,
    Being all in love with her, I thinke, as I am,
    From my sad heart warme teares (teares of affliction)
    The fire of my affection doth send up   25
    Into my eyes, that thence distill in streames,
    Which yet to me, are torrents of sweet joyes,
    Joyes, that this is for her, my griefe proceeds
    From a profound feare I shall never gaine her,
    Injoy that unpeer'd modell of perfection.   30
    There is no way but one to pull the fruit

---

93 Lines 20–44: Reyner's soliloquy, the first of the play, marks a shift from the public world of battle to the private world of romance. On his symptoms, see Lesel Dawson, *Lovesickness and Gender in Early Modern English Literature* (Oxford: Oxford University Press, 2008).

Jove would turne Goose, to taste:[94] she's so reserv'd
To the least vicious acts; Wretch, that hope
Is not (yet) left thee: For, being nobly borne[95]
(Though she no fit match be for us, in lieu   35
Of worldly substance, being in her selfe
An ample dowry for a richer Prince)
We sho'd (and gladly) sue to be her husband.
But a report goes, she will joyne with no man,
In such an obligation, which (that she   40
Will not at all have me) is that which striks
A blacke despaire into my soule, and will
(Unless I meete some comfort) quickly kill me;
Being sicke in body, as in mind already.   *Enter Hub[ba] & Cowsell.*

HUBBA See, where he stalks. Doe you but put him out   45
Of his sad humor; and thou sha't have ————

COWSELL O Captaine,
I am affraid, for he looks sowre upon't.

HUBBA No matter: feare you nothing, but proceed;
And care not what you say, so you say something;   50
It's your fooles fashion, and you now must seeme one.

COWSELL But hearke, you, Captaine. How sho'd I begin?

HUBBA Say that you come from the Ladies: so I leave you.   *Exit Hub[ba]*

REYNER Sirra. what make you here?   *& peeps.[96]*

COWSELL Come from the Ladies.   55

REYNER Well sayd, speake that againe.

COWSELL Come from the Ladies.

REYNER Very good, and what of them?

COWSELL Come from the Ladies.

REYNER What, againe. Pray tell me, what did occasion   60
Your so kind friendly visit to the Ladies?

COWSELL I went thither (being some two myle of)
To be joviall with a new acquaintance
Of mine, my brother *Radger*.[97]

94 Jove would turne Goose, to taste = Reyner contemplates the possibility of rape by way of the
   myth of Leda and the swan in which Jove/Jupiter transformed himself to rape Leda, queen of
   Sparta. The 'Goose' implies stupidity, cf. Falstaff, 'You were also, Jupiter, a swan for the love
   of Leda. O omnipotent Love! how near the god drew to the complexion of a goose!'
   Shakespeare, *The Merry Wives of Windsor*, 5.5. 5–8.
95 Lines 35–38: The niggling question of Landgartha's humble birth is introduced at this point.
96 peeps = Hubba observes the following scene in secret to find out what ails Reyner.
97 Radgee is twice named as 'Radger' in the text; here and in the stage direction following 4.111
   below.

REYNER Some such wise man,   65
    As thou art.

COWSELL He's a very honest man.

REYNER And takes his cup soundly,[98] I warrant.

COWSELL So
    Doe many honest men beside him; and   70
    Keepe wenches too, that's more.

REYNER And yet are honest.

COWSELL 's honest and fairecondition'd gentlemen,
    As live, I know severall of 'em, my selfe.

REYNER The Ladies are well. How did they use thee? tell.   75

COWSELL They're all exceeding well: and us'd me kindly
    For your sake; they gave me a banquet, strawberries
    And creame; we drunke helter-skelter[99] too; the Ladies
    Tooke your health themselves, and ask'd me how you did;
    Landgartha sayd, you were a good man, and that   80
    She lov'd you with all her heart.

REYNER Let me imbrace   *Imbraces him.*
    Thee from my heart, for that good newes.

HUBBA [*Aside*] Sweet King,
    Have I found your malady?   85

COWSELL O kind Prince!

REYNER What sayest? are they not delicate fine creatures?[100]

COWSELL Indifferent handsome, passable, and so forth ——

HUBBA You'll with a knocke be sent forth, I see that.

REYNER I was not from thy want of wit, to expect   90
    Any true censure. But yet, tell me truely:
    Which of 'em all dost thou thinke is the fairest?

COWSELL The Lady *Elsinora* in my opinion,
    Is th' rich Pearle among 'em; *Landgartha* to her
    Is but a meere milkemayde.   95

REYNER He makes me sicke,
    A dunce to wrong the worlds chiefe ornament.   *Kicks, & beats him.*

COWSELL Oh, oh my bum! my bum!   *Exit, and enter Hubb[a].*

HUBBA I perceive I must
    Venture a beating too.   100

---

98 takes his cup soundly = drinks heavily.

99 helter-skelter = in disorderly haste and confusion.

100 Lines 87–97: The vocabulary of this discussion echoes that of Burnell's address to the 'Ladies'
    in the 'Epistle Dedicatorie'.

REYNER Thou mett'st a foole
    Going out that way.
HUBBA And he complaines of something
    Under favour.
REYNER We gave some cause for't, but   105
    Doe now repent it. Prethee *Hubba* call him;
    He sayd some 'at of the Ladies.
HUBBA I can tell
    You more of 'em than he: for, I was lately too
    Where they (like a companie of fine ducklings)   110
    Wag together.
REYNER Thy words are base.
HUBBA What wo'd
    You have me say? They are all very valiant;
    And made King *Frollo* pay for seeking (and   115
    But in's goodwill) to domineere a little
    Over'em; he lost his life and kingdomes by't.
REYNER We therefore ought the better to love them.
HUBBA As your subjects onely, sir, but not to cast
    Under you on a bed, couch, or cleane mat;   120
    You know what fine *Furies* they are, if you vex 'em.
REYNER We are not so unwise, as to consult
    Of their dishonour.
HUBBA Nor so farre (I hope)
    Mistaken to marry any of 'em.   125
REYNER Why *Hubba*? Are they not faire and vertuous,
    Think'st thou?
HUBBA I doe admire, sir, you sho'd talke
    So much of vertue: a thing th'arrantest Asse
    Will scorne, if Money be not joyn'd to it;   130
    And then (although he hate it, and the possessor
    Of it) he will prayse't.
REYNER Thou'rt now in thy old humors.
HUBBA Besides, you thinke *Landgartha* faire: but I say,
    Th'Emperors daughter's worth a thousand of her.[101]   135
REYNER I'de loathly beat thee *Hubba:* yet, I tell thee;

---

101 Th'Emperors daughter = The Emperor, Louis the Pious (778–840), also known as Louis the
    Debonaire, had four daughters. This probably refers to Gisela (b. 821) whose dowry was
    famously rich. Louis the Debonaire is invoked again in Act 4 as a supporter of the rebel
    Harrold when Harrold and Eric flee to him in defeat.

Were *Charlemaine* (the Emperors father)[102] now
Alive, and in his Pryme of youth and glory,
Landgartha (being his Paralell in vallor;
By vertue much more) were a wife enough good   140
For him; were she not neere so faire as she is.
But all, all being joyn'd *Hubba*; I suppose
He wo'd esteeme her his chiefe earthly blessing.
I, I, and more, a Paradise on earth.

HUBBA Were she ten times better: you cannot have her.   145

REYNER Thou shoot'st a suddaine feare (colder then death)
Into me; You were best give no bad reason,
For what you say.

HUBBA She has vow'd Chastity,
Unto the gods:[103] which bond though you sho'd be   150
Content to forfeyt, it is sure she will not.

REYNER The strongest poyson could not sincke me deader,
Then thy sad tongue has.   *Exit.*

HUBBA Flunge away in a rage:
Well; I was to blame to tell him, what I was not   155
Sure on: For now I truely doe conceive
There is no plaster but one, that can cure him;
And that the faire *Landgartha* must apply too;
No garden hearbs will doe it, any one
That has as much braine as a Wood-cocke, may now   160
Finde that, that knowes what his disease is. He's worse
Then horne-mad[104] already; I'll therefore after him,
And what betwixt lyes and true tales, I shall goe very neere
To fetch him to himselfe, and hope againe.   *Exit.*

Enter Inguar in the middle.[105]

INGUAR The King stretch'd on his Couch, strangely distemper'd,   165
And most unlike himselfe (his courage lost)

---

102 Charlemaine = Charlemagne (742–814), king of the Franks, Holy Roman Emperor and
    father to Louis the Pious.
103 Lines 149–51: Refers to the classical Greek idea that Amazons took a vow of chastity to
    Artemis/Diana. The vow is again referred to at the end of the act, ll. 394–6.
104 horne-mad = raging like a beast in heat; linked to rutting or, more specifically, the horns of
    a cuckold.
105 in the middle = this could mean in the middle either of the stage or of his musing soliloquy.
    See the beginning of Act 1 above which also begins in the midst of the action.

He pules[106] and whynes most pitifully: Good heaven,
What strange disease sho'd render so devicted[107]
Such a man? So valiant? So each way noble?
We see no outward cause, that sho'd distract him;   170
Sho'd it be love?   *Enter Vald[emar] to Inguar.*
VALDEMAR Lord *Inguar,* I have newes
    For you.
INGUAR I long to hear 'em: For your count'nance
    (Showing alacrity) speaks comfort to the King.   175
VALDEMAR Did you never heare of a little blind
    Boy,[108] that wounded many a proper man?
INGUAR Has *Cupid* shot his Highnesse?
VALDEMAR No mortall man,
    Nor god so deepe, 't will be proclaym'd in open   180
    Market shortly.
INGUAR Who should the object be?
VALDEMAR Who but *Volsca de gente Camilla?*[109]
    Th' fairest and best of women, brave, *Landgartha*
    Hubba is sent (on paine of his best joynt)   185
    To fetch her hither: from whence ere she part,
    Her duty and th' Kings gracious affection
    Consider'd, she may be glad to yeeld to his
    Commands; as I hope her sister will, to my
    Intreaties to serve her.   190
INGUAR I beleeve, you 'ill finde
    Your selfe mistaken in those vertuous Ladies.

        Enter the foure Ladies in womans apparell
            with Swords on, and Hubba.

LANDGARTHA The gods defend so good, and merciful
    A Prince; I know it's but a cold that troubles
    His grace.   195

106 pules = whimpers, the mewling cry of a young animal or bird.
107 devicted = overcome, subdued.
108 little blind Boy = Cupid, who was often depicted as blind-fold or unseeing in Renaissance
     art, see Jane Kingsley-Smith, *Cupid in Early Modern Literature and Culture* (Cambridge:
     Cambridge University Press, 2010).
109 *Volsca de gente Camilla* = 'Camilla of the Volscan tribe', Virgil, *Aeneid,* 7, l. 803, see 1, 148
     above. Virgil's catalogue of the enemies of Aeneas and Rome, headed (unusually) by a
     woman, still remains a favourite for translation exercises, see Barbara Weiden Boyd, 'Virgil's
     Camilla and the Traditions of Catalogue and Ecphrasis (*Aeneid* 7.803–17)', *American Journal of
     Philology,* 113:2 (1992), 213–34.

HUBBA Not so (Madame) I can assure you;
    His disease proceeds rather of heate.[110] He burnes
    Extreamely; and its thought by some, that his
    Physitians cannot cure him.

LANDGARTHA I hope   200
    They are deceiv'd that thinke so.

VALDEMAR Welcome to Court,
    Faire Ladies; Which, till now (that you lighten it
    With the divine splendor of your beauties)
    Was darker than a dungeon: and but a Hell   205
    Compar'd unto the Paradise of the Campe,
    Where in the fruition of your pleasing'st
    Conversations, being rapt beyond our selves
    With hope of future favours, we in you
    Plac'd the whole summe of our felicities.   210

LANDGARTHA You are merrily dispos'd it seemes, sir,
    Which (to be plaine) becomes you but most foulely,
    The King being sicke, when all (and chiefly you)
    Sho'd (and not for ceremony onely) put
    A darke face of sorrow on; and contayne   215
    Their slippery tongues, from talking over-idley;
    Some may conceive your mirth proceeds, from being
    Next heire to him in bloud.[111]

VALDEMAR It rather springs
    (Sweet Lady) from your comming now to cure him.   220

LANDGARTHA Which, with a joyfull heart, I sho'd performe
    If I knew how: Pray you therefore, kind sir,
    Be somewhat cleerer in what you conceive.

VALDEMAR [Jeeringly] 'ts quickly learnt; nature will teach you Madame,
    His grace will shew you too; you will not prove   225
    Perverse.

LANDGARTHA Are you so blinde a Goate, to forget *Gives him a box, on which*
    Frollo so soon?[112] to open your eyes take that. *all draw, and Scania steps in.*

110 heate = according to the physiological theory of the four Humours, lust was caused by excess
    of heat.

111 Next heire to him in bloud = Burnell invents the character Valdemar and, in making him
    Reyner's heir, introduces the possibility of dramatic rivalry. Valdemar has many of the attributes
    of the well-educated literary gentleman, he invokes Virgil and Homer and, in the next act, devises
    the wedding masque. In acts 4 and 5, he also proves to be a good advisor to Reyner and a strong
    fighter. It is tempting to read this embodiment of humanist values as a figure for Burnell himself.

112 Lines 227–8: Goats, like Frollo, are associated with lechery, cf. 'Were they as prime as goats,
    as hot as monkeys', Shakespeare, *Othello*, 3.3.406.

SCANIA Pray sister hold. What doe you meane to quarell
    On a surmise? I know the Lord *Valdemars*   230
    Intents are noble and much more the Kings.
ELSINORA Y'are to blame, Neece, to be so suddaine in such
    A fond conceit.
LANDGARTHA Doe we come to be abus'd?
    I'll backe agen. For your part sir, you shall   *Exit, and the other* 235
    Not fayle to meete me, when and where you list.   *three follow her.*
HUBBA His grace will now run mad indeed.
VALDEMAR Lord *Inguar,*
    As you love me, follow that severe Lady;
    And reduce her (if ever you did ought for   240
    A friend) to mildnesse, and this way backe; or I
    Am lost for ever to the King and people: *Exit Inguar.*
    Captaine, goe thou too once more, for my sake.
HUBBA And as you meane to doe, forsweare my selfe
    That you meant no hurt. I have already told her   245
    A hundred lyes at least; and am now o' th' faith,
    That double the number will scarce serve to quiet her;
    It's such another untoward piece of flesh   *Exit Hub[ba].*
VALDEMAR *[Jeeringly]* She is an excellent Mistris, and has taught
    Me such a Lesson, I have cause to thanke her: 250
    For she has given me patience, and wisedome;
    Honesty too I thinke. The flat truth is
    She has wrought strangely with me, very strangely,
    The ravishing notes of a *Cycilian Cyren,*[113]
    Could not so have taken my Eare (and from thence   255
    My heart) with a most alluring kinde of
    Delight, as the smart-touch of her white hand has:
    It strucke into me such a love,
    To her Sister I meane,[114] that came so kindly
    Betwixt us, as I doe now account my selfe,   260
    A gainer by the blow; in hope to gaine
    What I now love so much, and nobly too.

113 Cycilian Cyren = Sicilian Siren. These bird-women lured sailors to their deaths on the rocks
    near Sicily with their enchanting singing. Odysseus famously resists them by following the
    advice of Circe: he blocks the ears of his men and has himself tied to the mast of his ship,
    Homer, *Odyssey*, Book 12.
114 To her Sister = Valdemar's swift clarification that he has fallen in love with Scania, not
    Landgartha, both evokes and quickly forecloses the possibility of the 'rival lovers' plot
    common in tragicomedy.

Well, they will come backe this way againe, I know;
And I must sing a very dolefull ditty,
A Palinode;[115] or pray, where they may see me,   265
Being a thing I've only done but twice
These seven yeares: once, that I went to sea:
Secondly and lastly, before the last battle.   *Exit.*

Reyner is discover'd on a Couch, and a gentleman
with him.

REYNER Are th' Ladies come yet to Court?
GENTLEMAN They are sir,   270
And will soone be here.   *Enter Inguar & Hubba.*
REYNER Whose that?
GENTLEMAN My Lord *Inguar.*
REYNER Where have you left the Ladies?
INGUAR Comming after (Sir,)   275
    Sad and much troubl'd for your want of health.   *Enter the 4. Ladies.*
SCANIA You'll be extreamely hated, if you use.
    So much exception, on so little cause.
LANDGARTHA If he accost me any more, with his
    Base jeering countenance and whorish language;   280
    My sword shall (for such kindnesse) kisse his midriffe.
FATYMA Pray pacifie your minde, you need not stand
    At so much distance.
REYNER Are not they come yet?
HUBBA They now are here, by much adoe.   285
REYNER Good *Inguar,*
    Intreat 'em to approach.
INGUAR Madame, the King
    Desires you wo'd be pleas'd to draw neerer.
REYNER You honour me, sweet Ladies, in this visit: 290
    Which, beyond expression adds comfort
    Unto a wretched sickely man. Chayres there,
    Pray you sit downe; y'are all exceeding welcome.
LANDGARTHA Our duty charg'd us (sir,) to obey your summons:
    Yet, our affection to your grace's welfare,   295
    And to that depends of it (the generall good

115 Palinode = an ode or song in which the author retracts the views or sentiment of an earlier
    song.

Of the republicke) were the chiefe motives
To our journey.[116]

SCANIA And being able (sir,) to stead you
    In loving wishes onely, we must expect   300
    (With griefe to see his weakness, whose good health
    We most desire) your highnesse royall pleasure.

REYNER Thankes worthy Ladies. We must also pay
    You in good wishes; being otherwise
    Too indigent[117] to cancell what we are   305
    Ingag'd to you for many wayes.
    We have beene still opprest since your departure
    From us (whose vertuous presence, was all
    The comfort we had) with a heavy sadnesse,
    Nourish'd by griefe; nor doe we ever hope   310
    To see the Sunne againe. but at a window.

LANDGARTHA The gods defend you (sir,) from giving way
    To such despayre.   *Enter Vald[emar].*

VALDEMAR I follow after (like
    A Theefe) aloofe, to see what good successe   315
    The King has in his love suite; and to venter[118]
    For my particular, as he makes his voyage.

SCANIA Your Majestie must never entertayne
    Darke melancholy thoughts, but quite cashire[119] 'em.

VALDEMAR Her voyce sounds sweeter, then the celestiall spheres,   320
    In their harmonious motion. I am more
    Then ravish'd when I heare it; and thinke I shall
    Fall sicke too, or runne franticke, ere 't belong.

FATYMA I heard no meane Physitian often say, Sir,
    That Musicke and mirth were good for sickely men.   325

REYNER Bid the Boy sing the Song we made of Love.

     Song.
   Love's farre more pow'rfull than a King,
   And wiser then most Statesmen are:
   For it commands him, and doth spring
   In them strange thoug'ts; in both much care   330

---

116 Lines 294–8: Landgartha makes it clear that she attends the king as a dutiful subject not as a
    personal favour. See Introduction, pp 55–6.
117 indigent = deficient, falling short.   118 venter = venture.
119 cashire = cashier, dismiss, disband, esp. of troops. Scania's vocabulary of war persists as she
    deals with peacetime emotions.

(Besides th'affaires o' th' Common-wealth)
To crouch and to obey. Nay more:
It makes 'em loose all joy and health
And not be the men they were before;
Untill wise love, all pow'rfull love,   335
The gracious Physitian prove.[120]

LANDGARTHA This is a very loving song,
　　Your grace made: but the contents of it, not
　　To be apply'd to you sir, that may command
　　(If pow'r and person can compell) the best   340
　　And fairest Lady i' th' world to be yours,
　　In a noble way; and otherwise your vertue forbids it.
REYNER It does indeed forbid us what is vicious.
　　And seeing we doe not hope for life, we must
　　Crave your kinde pardon now, to heare us tell   345
　　Th'occasion of our sicknesse, briefly thus:
　　You are the onely cause on't.
LANDGARTHA How? I my liege?
　　My knowledge sayes not so.
REYNER Your beautie, vallor,   350
　　And all the perfections (parted to others,
　　But) in you conjoyn'd, protest it: and I
　　For one can sweare it. But, being repell'd
　　By a severely-awing rigor from your brow
　　(Yet sweet withall, though killing) and being told   355
　　Of a sad purpose y'have, never to marry;
　　We now are fall'n thus low, beneath the Center
　　Of deepe despaire and sorrow: and desire,
　　You will say something, eyther to hasten our death,
　　Or to recall it by a loving sentence.   360
LANDGARTHA I must take some time thence to deliberate
　　Aside.   *She goes aside &*
REYNER Being yours, in that you may command us.   *the Ladies with her.*

120　Lines 327–36: Music, dance and song is an important feature of Werburgh Street theatre pro-
　　ductions, as of the contemporary London theatres. While no external account of the music
　　and dance for *Landgartha* survives, Katherine Philips' letters to Poliarchus (Charles Cottrell)
　　offer a detailed account of how John Ogilby, Master of Revels and himself a dance-master,
　　pulled together Dublin's resources for the later staging of her *Pompey: A Tragoedy* in 1663, G.
　　Greer, R. Little and P. Thomas (eds), *The Collected Works of Katherine Philips: The Matchless
　　Orinda*, 3 vols (Stump Cross: Stump Cross Books, 1991–93), 3, pp 3–4, 90–1. On the music
　　in Act 3, see also Introduction, pp 62–3.

LANDGARTHA We expected no such entertayment.
ELSINORA My minde foretold me still of some disaster.   365
SCANIA Notwithstanding your resolution,
    Not to marry: you have not vow'd against
    Obedience to a man, in that friendly
    Yoake of Wedlocke.[121]The Kings sound affection
    Is not then to be rejected, if you ever   370
    Take any.
LANDGARTHA If I doe, he shall be the man.
FATYMA You must not study now long for some answer.
ELSINORA He's desperatly ill: and if you sho'd
    Give him a flat deniall, we might be   375
    All seazed on heere at Court, and some villanie
    Committed on us; being to defend our selves,
    Too few by many.
SCANIA They shall take our lives,
    Ere we'll endure to be defil'd.   380
FATYMA And with
    The loss of some of theirs.
REYNER Have you consider'd
    Yet, of the doome y'are to pronounce?
ELSINORA All stand   385
    Warily on their guard.
LANDGARTHA Your poore subjects (sir)
    Must rather expect (in duty) your commands.
REYNER Nay sweet Lady. Doe not increase my torment,
    By adding affliction to misery,   390
    With a complement: but something say, that
    May appertaine to th'matter, to rid me
    Quickely of my paine.
LANDGARTHA It's sure; I have not
    (Although I ever meant it) bound my selfe,   395
    Unto a single life.
REYNER Then dearest Lady,
    Consider who I am; and what I now am,

---

121 Lines 366–9: Scania makes the distinction (also recognized in law) between a 'resolution',
    made with oneself, and a 'vow', a binding promise to God. Scania's distinction invokes the
    forthcoming Irish parliamentary debates around bigamy and the state-sanctioned marriage
    vow, see Introduction, pp 27–9. It also resonates more broadly with post-Reformation ten-
    sions around Catholic compliance with State oaths of allegiance, see Edward Vallance,
    *Revolutionary England and the National Covenant: State Oaths, Protestantism and the Political
    Nation, 1553–1682* (Woodbridge: Boydell Press, 2005).

Lodg'd thus: for though I clayme you not as by desert,[122]
Or dutie: Yet being your Prince, you owe me   400
Some regard; and all, I e'r must glory in,
Shall be to make you Queene of what is ours.
LANDGARTHA May it please you, Sir.
REYNER Pray you sit and speake;
Or I must rise, if weaknesse will permit.   *She sits, and the rest stand.* 405
LANDGARTHA Had I beene ambitious, when you were not
Crown'd King of *Norway*: I could then perchance
Have written Queene, unto your prejudice.
But, for that *Frollo* once intended foulely,
I (that could not affect vice) did refuse   410
What he with earnestnesse, and many Oathes
Sought to confirme; and was his bane[123] at last,
Though I beleev'd that what he said, he meant.
    Now therefore (Sir,) your affection (grounded
In way of honour, without taint of basenesse;   415
With such exterior signes too, of deepe love
To me, unworthy of so great a Prince:)
I cannot (nor will my heart permit it) but
In way of gratefulnesse, reciprocally
Requite with love againe, as dutie binds;   420
Nay, more then so. But yet, gracious Sir,
I (that am meane and poore to be your Consort;
And that things of this kinde are oft repented)
Doe now beseech you, to decline a while
The vehemencie of your fleete desires;   425
And take full time to thinke on what you doe:
Were't but to take a neerer view of me,
And that in all points. For know sir, the honour
You now affoord me, compar'd to th'infamie
That would redound[124] to both of us, and to others   430
(By whom you are to be advis'd) if ought
Sho'd chance amisse, when things were consumate,
Is nothing: would but heighten your disgrace.
    Your wise demurre[125] too, I shall take as full payment

---

122 desert = deserved prize, i.e., because Reyner rescued Landgartha and Norway from Frollo.
123 bane = agent of ruin, slayer.   124 redound = reflect on, come back on.
125 demurre = hesitation or objection. Given the formality of Landgartha's speech, this may
    invoke the Anglo-norman legal term 'demurrer': this occurs when one party temporarily
    admits the facts as stated in the opponent's plea, denies that they are entitled to relief and thus

For all my services; and rest devoted   435
  More deepely yours: and evermore continue
  Your loyall subject onely, sir.
REYNER I was sure
  (Noblest and best of Ladies:) That your words
  (Being such as now they are) could not but worke   440
  A cure upon me. See, I can stand up:
  Nay goe; I'll throw my Cap[126] off too. Some of you
  Give me a Hat; I will walke with you forth
  Into the Gallery, and tell you there,
  I have consider'd so much what you are,   445
  Though not to your full value this being
  Impossible: that if you thinke me not
  Unworthy (as indeed I am for you)
  We shall soone be Man and Wife. To morrow
  I'll wayte on you further, into the Garden.   450
HUBBA [Aside] And there (in one of the little bawdy houses)
  Seale the Covenant,[127] if it be receiv'd
  Though he were sure to die in an houre after.
ELSINORA [Aside] I see she does affect him in good earnest.
  But wisedome bids be silent; This poore kingdome   455
  Being already torne too much, by tyrannie and troubles.
  Things past our helpe, with patience must be borne,
  Untill a fit time.
REYNER Lady Elsinora,
  Me thinkes you do not signe our loving motion,   460
  With a friendly countenance.
ELSINORA I hope, great Sir,
  You will be pleas'd to entertayne farre better thoughts
  Of your humblest hand-mayd.
REYNER I hope we shall.   465
LANDGARTHA In licensing our departure, for some small time
  (Days five or sixe, and for a private Cause:)
  You will for ever bind us (sir) to your commands;[128]

  stops the action until the court determines the outcome (OED).
126 Cap = nightcap, here a sign of his swiftly cured illness.
127 Seale the Covenant = consummate the marriage. The 'bawdy houses' in the garden were pre-
     sumably for Frollo's use. Hubba also acknowledges that Landgartha, if raped, would have no
     hesitation in killing Reyner in revenge.
128 Lines 466–8: In Belleforest, Landgerthe leaves the court to allow Regner's passion to cool off
     but he follows her and marries her with her parents' blessing, Histoires Tragiques, p. 862; in

And to returne with all convenient speed,
To obey your Highnesse pleasure in all points.   470
REYNER That ask'd agen, would throw me on my Couch;
    Never to rise.
VALDEMAR Madame, I sho'd make bold
    To stop your journey, though the King were pleas'd
    To grant his licence: for you (I must say   475
    Somewhat roughly) saluted my left eare
    With your right hand, as these can witnesse for me.
LANDGARTHA For which, you are resolv'd to challenge me:
    But not to be your wife; I gave you no
    Such promise.   480
VALDEMAR I must have satisfaction.[129]
LANDGARTHA You may declare what that is, when you list.
VALDEMAR Nay, you shall know it now; and thus it sounds:
    That you perswade this Lady, to become   *Takes Scan[ia] by*
    My second.[130] For, love has strucke me too, so sore   *the hand.* 485
    A cuffe (caus'd by her beautie, and what else
    Is good in her, in my opinion
    Superlatively:) that I shall ne'r be rid
    O' th' paine on't; unlesse you that are like to be
    My Cossen,[131] advance me higher, to the honour   490
    To be your brother. We shall then be kind friends.[132]
LANDGARTHA She is not my warde;[133] and may take whom she fancies;
    I may my selfe repent, to be perswaded.

Saxo Grammaticus, Regner pursues Lathgertha to her home and slays the beasts she has set to
guard her chastity, *History of the Danes,* p. 283.

129 satisfaction = the opportunity of restoring one's honour by way of a duel, repayment,
    atonement. Valdemar's use of the language of challenge refers to the fact that Landgartha
    struck him (l. 228 above); it is also a galant replaying of the language of duelling as that of
    courtship.

130 second = (in duelling) appointed assistant. In asking for Scania's hand in marriage, Valdemar
    refers to the fact that one of the duties of the second was to seek reconciliation of the quarrel
    and thus avoid combat.

131 Cossen = kinsman, distant relation.

132 kind friends = this phrase suggests a double relationship: that of kin or kind, i.e., related by
    birth and blood, and of friends, related by choice and /or marriage. Valdemar's optimism here
    contrasts with English suspicion of intermarriage between the native Irish and Old English,
    see Introduction, pp 27–9.

133 warde = ward of court. Landgartha is not the legal guardian of Scania, who can make her
    own choice. Landgartha's comment amplifies contemporary Old English antipathy towards
    the Court of Wards. They regarded it as an English tool for disrupting Catholic inheritance
    and for proselytizing, see Hugh Kearney, 'The Court of Wards and Liveries in Ireland, 1622–

REYNER Speak Ladie, doe you like the man? He is
    As good a Gentleman as We are: Say,   495
    Will you have him?
SCANIA You make me blush (sir,) to aske
    Me such a question.
VALDEMAR Nay then, it's granted.
SCANIA I will not grant at first; nor shall you say   500
    Hereafter I deceiv'd you.
FATYMA You deceive
    Your selfe. [To Elsin[ora]] Well Madame, I perceive we two
    Must matelesse home to prove the Vestals.[134]
INGUAR Not, sweet Lady, if you'll daigne to grace me, with   505
    The title husband.
FATYMA For your goodwill, sir,
    I thank you: but will heare of no more coupling.
INGUAR I yet must love you still.
REYNER Then let's from hence,   510
    To entertayne heavens happy influence.[135]   *Exeunt.*

41', *Proceedings of the Royal Irish Academy,* 57 (1955–56), 29–68 and Victor Treadwell, 'The
    Irish Court of Wards under James I', *Irish Historical Studies,* 12, 45 (1960), 1–27.
134 Vestals = the virgin priestesses in charge of the sacred fires at the temple to Vesta in Rome.
135 influence = an etherial substance which flows from the stars and shapes human destiny.

The third Act.

*Enter Fredericke and a Servant
at the dore.*

FREDERICKE Let 'em not presse so fast in, to behold
    A semi-maske:[136] for now't can be no more,
    For want of fitting Actors here at Court;
    The Warre and want of Money, is the cause on't.[137]
SERVANT Stand further off, my masters, or I shall —— ——   5
FREDERICKE Let fly amongst 'em.
VALDEMAR Pray you my Lord, have a care   *Enter Vald[emar] and Lady.*
    (For my sake) of this Lady; a kins-woman
    Of my wives.
FREDERICKE (I know you are Uxorious.)[138]   10
LANDGARTHA He shall not need: for I will have a care
    Of my selfe.
FREDERICKE I sho'd gladly serve your Highnesse:
    But can hardly yet from hence.
VALDEMAR Come Cousin,   15
    I will be your Gentleman usher my selfe.   *Exeunt ambo.*
COWSELL [*within*] Make roome I say there, for me and my brother.
FREDERICKE What kind of Cossens are those?
SERVANT A payre of Coxcombes,
    So individuall by the littleness   20
    Of their understandings, they cannot be parted.   *Enter Cow[sell]*
COWSELL Come away brother *Radgar*, we'd need make haste,   *& Rad[gee].*
    To take our places.
RADGEE I shall be proud brother,
    To be seated after you.   25

136 semi-maske = semi-masque, a short entertainment involving music, dance and elaborate set presented as a complement to a longer play. Usually performed at court, they involved courtiers as players. Absent from both Belleforest and Saxo Grammaticus, the wedding celebrations of Act 3 are Burnell's invention. This act constantly invokes the court masques of both Ben Jonson and the contemporary Caroline court, see Introduction, pp 34–6, 49.

137 Warre and want of Money = this invokes the forthcoming debate in the Irish parliament on the funding of Wentworth's controversial 'Irish' Army, to be recruited as support for Charles I's Scottish campaigns, see Introduction, pp 21–5.

138 Uxorious = dotingly fond of one's wife.

COWSELL And I fortunate
    To sit next before you.
RADGEE It shall be my ambition brother, to
    Be still (as now) your most humble servant.
COWSELL It must be all my study then, brother; To   30
    Command things onely pleasing: for marke you
    Deere brother. I must strive chiefly to precede,
    But ————— in my affection.
FREDERICKE A pretty Antimasque:[139]
    I will sit downe, and heare what it concludes.   35
RADGEE But hearke you now, brother. Shall we have any
    Drinke, Banquets, or so ————— —————
COWSELL Not a drop betwixt meales, brother,
    That's but a simple Countrey fashion.
FREDERICKE Are they already fall'n from complement?[140]   40
RADGEE Yet, me thinks brother, 't were n't amisse to lay
    The pots hard by;[141] and let him drinke that wo'd.
COWSELL I sho'd a part keepe with you, in that Catch[142]
    Brother, but now (with griefe enough) I say't
    (Wo'd I co'd not say 't:) I cannot now (being puff'd   45
    Up here for want of ayre) drink nere as much,
    As when I liv'd abroad i' th' Countrie; nor eate
    The quarter quantitie.
RADGEE That must be beleev'd
    Generally, as a Maxime infallible: 50
    For to day brother, the stinke of your perfum'd
    And stuffing meates,[143] took my stomacke quite away
    From me. Yet, we drunke pretty well you know.
COWSELL It's certaine (brother,) those that cannot eate,
    Must drinke, and I can drinke indifferent well still   55
    But, time there was I could 'a' payde it soundly.
RADGEE As, how much? Pray sweet brother.
COWSELL It is scarce
    Credible, I now shall tell you: at one short
    Sitting, I'd a drunke you of Wine sixe Flaggons,   60

139 Antimasque = a comic or grotesque prelude to a masque, usually involving lower characters.
    This comic disorder is replaced by courtly order when the masque begins.
140 complement = mutual completion and harmony.
141 lay the pots hard by = set out some tankards near to hand.
142 a part keepe with you, in that Catch = I would agree with you that it was a problem.
143 perfum'd and stuffing meates = highly seasoned forced meat used to stuff a joint.

And two dozen of Beere at least, all at eight draughts;
And never 'a' seene the colour of my face,
In a Chamber pot; or sought ease, by visiting
My kind friend *Aiax*.[144]

RADGEE That's more by a little,   65
Then I ever could vent the right way. But yet,
I dare speak it brother, we are very neere
As good drinkers, as you be here i' th' Citie:
For you see, when we come to Towne, we doe
Nothing but runne from Taverne, to Taverne;   70
Oft to blind[145] Alehouses, to visit the fine
Wenches, of purpose there plac'd, to draw custome;
Now and then to see a Play, when we want
Other exercise; and once a weeke (upon
A holy day, when all doores are shut up)   75
To a godly exhortation,[146] and sleepe out
(At least) three parts on't.

COWSELL Especially if you
Take your liquor before hand.

RADGEE Right brother, but   80
Tomorrow we will, both from hence, to th' Countrey.

COWSELL Wo'd this night were over once.

RADGEE We've excellent Mayds with us,
And while my Ladies dance and feast it here,
Both night and day: We both will keep Court there;   85
Throw out the house at th' windowes,[147] and fetch in
All our Towne-fidlers, with all the young fellowes
In fifteen villages about us; is't not good?

COWSELL O rare!

FREDERICKE I' th' meane time Sir, let me perswade you   90
To conduct your brother to a place: For I
Am weary of your company.

COWSELL 'thanke your Lordship.   *Exeunt ambo.*

---

144 Aiax = the Ajax, or flush toilet was invented by Sir John Harington and featured in his con-
     troversial political allegory *A New Discourse of a Stale Subject, called the Metamorphosis of Ajax*
     (London, 1596). The name is a pun on 'jakes', a chamber pot or privy, and on Homer's
     Greek hero of *The Iliad*. On the influence of Harington's translation of *Orlando Furioso* on
     Burnell's Marfisa, see Introduction, pp 59–61.

145 blind = secret, private, suggesting here brothels.

146 godly exhortation = a sermon, i.e., they sleep through a church service.

147 Throw out the house at th' windowes = make a great commotion, turn everything topsy-
     turvy.

HUBBA [*within*] Give way there!

FREDERICKE What lusty Gentleman's that? 95

SERVANT Mad Captaine *Hubba*, and as lusty a
    Virago[148] with him.

      Enter Hubba and Marfisa in an Irish Gowne tuck'd up to
       midlegge, with a broad basket-hilt Sword on, hanging
        in a great Belt, Broags on her feet, her hayre
         dishevell'd, and a payre of long neck'd
          big-rowll'd Spurs on her heels.[149]

HUBBA Come my brave *Marfisa*,
    You are but just now come to Towne you say?

MARFISA That you may well perceive sir, by my spurs. 100

FREDERICKE Here's handsome Cheese and Butter, and a Sword.

HUBBA They're a payre of excellent ginglers,[150] but pray
    Tell me: did you ride sideling,[151] or like a man?

MARFISA Howsoever, there shall ne'r a *Dane* ride i' my Saddle.

HUBBA What? not i' the way of honesty? as you love me, 105
    Say not so; I hope you'll be pleas'd to thinke of my service.

MARFISA I sho'd rejoyce to be well pleas'd i' th' way
    Of honesty: Yet, your faire words shall not
    Deceive me. As first try, then take on liking.

HUBBA But, with your favour I thinke't were better try: 110
    Least you sho'd chance repent too late hereafter.

MARFISA You will not put me sir, to use my Sword: *Puts hand to her sword.*
    If you doe, you must first begin at that.

FREDERICKE I thinke she meanes to make him marry her
    Perforce; I shall have my part o' th' Maske here. 115

---

148 Virago = a man-like, heroic woman, hence an Amazon.

149 Enter ... on her heels: The first apearance of Burnell's 'Irish' Amazon, Marfisa, named after
    an Amazon in Ludovico Ariosto's Italian epic *Orlando furioso*. Irish gowne = also known as
    the Shinrone gown, tight-waisted dress with voluminous skirts and wide sleeves; basket-hilt
    sword = sword with a hilt which provides a defence for the hand, consisting of narrow plates
    of steel curved into the shape of basket; broags = brogues, a rough shoe of untanned hide,
    associated with the Irish; big-rowll'd spurs = spurs with large rowels, i.e., large circular spikes
    at the back. This is battledress (see 5. 313–14 stage direction) and contrasts with the rest of the
    Amazons who appear '*attir'd like women onely*' (below 3. 140–1, stage direction,). For detailed
    discussion of Marfisa, her costume and this scene, see Introduction, pp 56–64.

150 ginglers = jangling spurs. In keeping with the rest of this exchange, the 'payre' carries innu-
    endo.

151 sideling = side-saddle.

HUBBA Pray Lady, take patience along with you;
    I am fairely yours.
FREDERICKE You had (on my knowledge)
    But need to say so, if she be in earnest.
MARFISA Then leade me to some honest place, where I may   120
    Unspurre, untucke my Gowne, wash, and so forth —— ——
HUBBA Most willingly, my faire *Marfisa,* thou sha't
    Have a looking-glasse too; I ever tooke
    A strange liking to thee, since first I saw
    Thee fight i' th' battle like a Lyonesse.   125
    Y'are Cossen-german to th' Lady *Fatyma?*[152]
MARFISA Her selfe dare not deny it, sir.
HUBBA I doe not   *Goes about her.*
    Onely marke your sweet face, but all things else
    About you. Y' have a fine legge. The fashion   130
    Of this Gowne, likes me well too; I thinke you had
    The patterne on't from us, as we from *Ireland.*[153]
MARFISA That I know not, but am sure a handsome woman
    Lookes as well in't, as in any dresse, or habit
    Whatsoever.   135
HUBBA So it seemes by thee, my
    Beautifull Mistris: For by that name, I must
    Stile you henceforth. Come, let your loving squire
    Conduct you.
MARFISA On before, I'll follow.   *Exeunt ambo.* 140

Lowd   *Enter Reyner, Landgartha, Valdemar, Scania, Elsinora,*
Musicke.   *Inguar, and Fatyma. The Ladies*
        attir'd like women onely.

REYNER My Queene and I, *Valdemar,* are much bound
    To thy free *Genius,* for this thy second Maske[154]
    After our nuptials; She more: but most
    Of all, thy owne Lady. For, it's for her sake
    Thou so affect'st both us.   145

152 Cossen-german = strictly speaking, this means first cousin though it is sometimes used to indi-
    cate a more distant relationship.
153 Ireland = the only reference to Ireland in the play text.
154 second Maske = implies either that a first masque has previously been staged for the wedding,
    or, picking up on previous references above, that the preceding scene was actually an anti-
    masque, now brought to order by the arrival of the royal party.

SCANIA I could not wish
    To 'a' met a kinder man.
LANDGARTHA His kindnesse makes
    You oft asham'd, you say; nor wo'd I have
    The King so over fond of me.   150
VALDEMAR You stand
    Confirm'd, Madame, in the pow'r your merits
    Hold, to charme his faculties to your obeysance.
LANDGARTHA You deliver that, sir, to picke a thanke from
    My Sister; at whom you point in that language.   155
SCANIA I doe beleeve he does: which yet, must be
    Conceiv'd onely to proceed, from his ill-plac'd
    Affection; not my desert to answer
    His; much lesse your perfections: being
    But a poore Pigmie, compar'd to the greatnesse   160
    Of the worth in you.
REYNER This friendly Complement   *Heere they take their places,*
    We will passe over: and now *Valdemar,*   *but the King and the Queene*
    To apt our aprehensions the more   *under a Canopie.*
    To the true understanding of your Maske: 165
    You may tell us somewhat of your scope in 't.
VALDEMAR That is sufficiently inform'd i' the thing
    It selfe; though lame it be. The matter (being
    All propheticall) I found in an old
    Worme-eaten Booke, in the Lady *Elsinora's*   170
    Library.[155] And I sho'd wrong your judgements;
    And my owne labour, though of little value,
    By staling[156] of it before hand.
FREDERICKE It's a fine tale;
    And cannot but please, unless it meet such minds,   175
    As are not to be pleas'd.
ELSINORA There is no Fustian,[157]
    Non sense, Winde, or fopperie in't.

---

155 Lines 168–71: Valdemar claims the authority of a prophetical text discovered in Elsinora's
     home for the content of his masque. This is reminiscent of Burnell's title-page which like-
     wise claims that he has dramatized 'an Ancient Story'. The library location suggests Hamlet's
     castle, Elsinore; the text suggests Geoffrey of Monmouth's twelfth-century *Historia Regum*
     Britanniae [The History of the Kings of Britain], primary source for the subject of Valdemar's
     masque, the Brutus myth. See Introduction, pp 49–51.
156 staling = making it stale.
157 Fustain = a coarse thick cloth, hence bombast, inflated speech. Elsinora's lines echo the crit-
     icism of overblown plays in Bermingham's dedicatory poem.

REYNER It matters not

What some odd envious foole sayes; that grieves most   180
At th'goodness of what he disprayses: and wo'd
Be glad 't were worse. We despise affected stuffe:
Or a strayn'd kind of Eloquence; being the smoake
And fruits of a vaineglorious, and an empty braine,
No flattery dwels we know in this. Let it begin.   185

The Maske.   *First enter six Satyrs*[158] *and dance a short nimble anticke*[159]
to no Musicke, or at most to a single Violine:
at the end of which enter Phœbus[160] *with*
Bow and Arrowes.

PHOEBUS Away unmanner'd deities though hope

Rayse you unto this mirth, for *Troy*: Your scope
In 't (form'd at the counsell of the higher gods)
Makes not the issue of their Periods,
So fortunate as you doe now suppose   190
(In your inferior knowledges) to dispose
For *Hectors*[161] safetie: whom *Aracides*[162]
(Madded for his lov'd *Menetiades*)[163]
Flyes to destroy. Nor can the *Fates* divert,
But that fierce horrid man, will soon convert   195
All unto sad detruction; unlesse
We the pryme gods and demi-gods suppresse
His force, not otherwise to be resisted,
Get you away from thence then: and instead
Of friskings, in these pleasant vales of *Ide*,[164]   200

---

158 Satyrs = woodland gods or demons, part man part goat, companions of Bacchus.

159 anticke = grotesque, comic dance.

160 Phoebus = Apollo. god of the sun, prophecy and poetry, guardian of Troy.

161 Hector = eldest son of Priam, king of Troy and the foremost Trojan warrior. His defeat by Achilles and Priam's subsequent retrieval of his body for burial are the climax of Homer's *The Iliad,* Books 23–4.

162 Aracides = descendant of Aiakos, son of Zeus, i.e., Achilles, grandson to Aiakos and the foremost Greek hero.

163 Menetiades = descendant of Menoetius, i.e., Patroclus, beloved companion of Achilles, killed by Hector. Patroclus' death brings Achilles out of long retirement to kill Hector in the climactic battle of champions, Homer, *The Iliad*, Book 24. It is notable that, in spite of Elsinora's protestations to the contrary (3. 177–8 above), the masque does indeed demonstrate a 'strayn'd kind of Eloquence' (3. 183).

164 Ide = Mount Ida, home of the Olympian gods.

Expose your aydes (to th' utmost can be try'd)

For *Pyram* and his issue[165], ne'r till now   *Exeunt Satyri, and enter*

In danger of an utter overthrow.   *Pallas*[166] *with Helmet, Shield*

PALLAS Fine youth, ne'r shorne. Thou brandisher of darts *and Lance.*

That with thy Bow slew'st *Python,*[167] thy best parts   205

Thou now must urge against me 'n single fight:

Till I have vanquish'd, or a shamefull flight

Compell'd to thy swift feet; nor shall thy deere

Beloved *Hector* scape my nobler Peere,

Divine *Achylles*; for his lov'd friend slaine,   210

Chiefly by thee.[168]

PHOEBUS O let me not in vaine

(Most chast and warlike Mayde) implore thee now

For *Hectors* rescue that so manie a vow

Payde me i' th' thighes of sacrifized Beeves,[169]   215

And not to me alone: For, my soule grieves

To thinke of his losse. Nor do's it fit thee

(As wholy bent upon impietie)

To mixe unguilty with the guiltie bloud.

Let it suffice, a vertuous Queene withstood   220

(*Penthesilea*[170] most renown'd) to her

Lives losse, the Champion thou dost most preferre,

---

165 Pryam and his issue = the children of Priam, king of Troy, more specifically the future of his son Aeneas, founder of Rome and hero of Virgil's *Aeneid.*

166 Pallas = Pallas Athene, goddess of war and wise counsel. It is very likely that the actors playing Marfisa and Hubba doubled as Pallas and Phoebus during their 'absence' from the masque.

167 That with thy Bow slew'st *Python* = Apollo killed Python, the monstrous serpent of Delphi, and transformed its former home into a shrine to his honour, the famous Delphic Oracle. There is a clear resonance both with St Patrick's banishment of snakes in Ireland, and with the account of Ragnar Lodbrok's [Reyner] slaughter of the monstrous serpents in Saxo Grammaticus. See Introduction, pp 40–4.

168 Lines 206–11: The gods will now do battle through their human champions. Hector, Phoebus' favourite, must die at the hands of Achilles, Pallas' favourite, in revenge for the killing of Achilles' beloved Patroclus whom Hector killed with Phoebus' help.

169 a vow ... Beeves = holy vows accompanied by sacrificed cattle.

170 Penthesilea = The story of the Amazon queen Penthesilea is recounted not in Homer's *Iliad,* but in the sequels – Arctinus of Miletus' lost *Aethiopis* (*c.*7th century BC) and Quintus de Smyrna's 4th-century AD *Posthomerica* – which form part of the Epic Cycle which narrates the fall of Troy. Penthesilea enters the Trojan wars just as fighting resumes after Hector's funeral. She does battle with Achilles; he kills her but when he removes her helmet and sees her face, Achilles falls in love. Perhaps the most famous of the Amazons, Penthesilea appears in Jonson's *The Masque of Queens* (1609) and is the fifth of Heywood's *Nine the Most Worthy Women* (1640), but is notably absent from Landgartha's battle speech above (I, 121–59).

With many other worthies: many more
Of *Pyrams* faire sonnes, slaine by him before.[171]
Which now let satisfie thy wrath; decline   225
Thy further vengence on the just, and thine
Owne feast Companion, me: For, the blest gods
Ought not to be (among themselves) at oddes.   *Exit.*
PALLAS He's gone: but by his pow'r shall no way thwart,
The *Fates* pronounc'd harsh-doome, shot at the heart   230
Of his devoutest, and brave friend. Here comes   *Enter Achylles.*
Peleïdes[172] to strike the blow, that summes
His happinesse, to obey my sterne Commands;
And can doe more then all the *Grecian* bands.

Enter Hector whom Achylles encounters in a dumbe show[173] by way
of a Dance and (Pallas assisting) killes: then exeunt Pallas
and Achylles. After which the Nymphs of
Mount Ida sing this following Song in
foure or five parts, to a pleasing
Tune.

Song.   *Though* Hector *now be dead, his name*   235
         And memory shall last, while fame
         Sounds her low'd Trumpet, lov'd, admir'd;
         By his example shall be fir'd
         To acts heroicke, future ages:
         And Prophets (sacred in their rages)   240
         Shall by his vertues be install'd;
         And he by all a worthy[174] *call'd.*

Hectors *body is taken away about the middle of the Song:*
after the end of it, Enter Phœbus and Pyram.

171 Pyrams faire sonnes = Mestor, Lycaon and Dryops, as well as Hector, were slain by Achilles.
172 Peleïdes = descendent of Peleus, i.e., his son Achilles.
173 dumbe show = a mime interlude, cf. Shakespeare, *Hamlet* 3.2.134. See Dieter Mehl, *The Elizabethan Dumb Show: The History of a Dramatic Convention* (London: Methuen, 1965).
174 a worthy = the Nine Worthies, first collated in the 14th century, were exemplary figures who embodied the ideals of medieval chivalry. The list consisted of three good pagans: Hector, Alexander the Great, Julius Caesar; three good Jews: Joshua, David, Judas Maccabeus and three good Christians: King Arthur, Charlemagne and Godfrey of Bouillon. The comic performance of 'The Nine Worthies' in Shakespeare, *Loves Labours Lost* 5.2 satirizes their popularity in Renaissance schools and pageants. On Thomas Heywood's female 'worthies', see Introduction, pp 58–9.

PHOEBUS Much honour'd and deere old man, did'st not heare,
    How the *Idalian* deities forbeare
    Not (sacred loving *Nymphs*, and griev'd like thee)   245
    To chant a mirthfull pleasing melody?
    Glad for the future glory of thy sonne,
    Reason sho'd governe: and a faire fame wonne,
    Is of mans humane life the chiefest part,
    Chiefest in *Hector,* and shall not depart   250
    For thy for-ever-most fam'd house: For, know
    Th' gods on thy line (of *Dardanus*)[175] will bestow
    The largest Empyres; which to thee I'll now
    Show for thy comfort: that thou sho'dst not bow
    (Too much dejected in thy minde) to what   255
    They in their Counsels doe predestinat.
PRYAM Heavens brightest eye, I'll doe what lyes in me,
    To obey thy will, and in my sowre destinie.
PHOEBUS My tale in two parts, I doe thus impart:
    A Prince from *Troy* hereafter shall depart,[176]   260
    When *Troy* takes end (as all dominion
    Of mortals must:) whose chance will fetch him on
    The *Lybian* shores, and upon *Latium* next.
    Before which time and after, though oft vex'd
    By the high-minded *Juno,* for her hates   265
    Conceiv'd against the *Troians*: Yet, the *Fates*
    Have destin'd him that throne of *Latium,*
    Marrying the daughter of its King. From him
    (The Royall seate first chang'd to *Alba*) shall
    Descend two Princes, twins; for which, a fall   270
    Their mother takes from *Mars,* a votresse she,
    Compell'd unto that state. Impietie
    In an ambitious kinsman, to be drown'd
    Sends both the Infants: who (sav'd by chance) are found

175 Dardanus = founder of Troy and ancestor of Priam.
176 Lines 260–80: Phoebus begins by prophesying the fate of Aeneas in a very condensed retelling
    of Virgil's *Aeneid*. Priam's son, Aeneas, escapes at the fall of Troy and, in spite of Juno's best
    efforts to prevent him, travels first to Carthage ('*Lybian* Shores') and then to Italy (*Latium*) to
    found the Roman Empire. He marries the king of Latium's daughter, Lavinia; they have a
    son Silvus and rename *Latium* as Alba Longa. Aeneas is thus ancestor of the 'twins', Romulus
    and Remus. Their mother, the vestal virgin Rhea Silvia, became pregnant by Mars. Her
    ashamed family, not believing that they were fathered by a god, sent the babies to be
    drowned. They were famously rescued: first suckled by a she-wolf, then brought up by shep-
    herds, they eventually went on to found Rome.

Of a she-woolfe, and nourish'd with her Teats;   275
Till by a sheepheard found, and by brave feats
Made know'n to be themselves, they build a Towne
Which shall be call'd *Rome*; and shall wear the Crowne
Of the worlds Monarchy, hundreds of yeares.
This is the first part of my tale.   280
PRYAM My feares
And sorrow (which till now I did suppose
Could not be done) th'hast heal'd. Disclose
The other part (deare god) that's left untould.
PHOEBUS Which (in no obscure terms) I doe unfould: 285
A Prince call'd *Brutus* (of the *Troian* race)[177]
Third to the first spoke of, being in the chace
Of wild beasts, by the unlucky fate he kils
Silvius his Father, with the shaft he drils
At other game: Which fact, so much doth bend   290
The *Latines* against *Brutus*, him they send
To sad exile. Who, (after a time) arrives
At a brave spatious Iland (that derives
Her name from white rocks, being a little world[178])
With other *Troians* before met, and hurl'd   295
Too on misfortunes. A town call'd new *Troy*
He builds here th' Land cals *Brutaine*: doth enjoy
The whole as King; and his posteritie
For many ages, shall raigne there, as he.
Sometimes (in pow'r and plentie) conquering   300
The neighbor Nations: sometimes these (for nothing
But 's subject unto change on earth) afflict
Againe *Troy's Brutaines,* in their owne district.
Of which a certaine people, and call'd *Danes*
(*Cymbrians* by some) will prove their worst of banes.   305
But shall be beaten backe; not without paine.
At length (in processe of much time) shall raigne

177 Lines 286–322: In the second half of his prophecy, Phoebus recounts the fate of Brutus,
another legendary prince of Troy, following Geoffrey of Monmouth's twelfth-century
Historia Regum Britanniae. Great-grandson of Aeneas, grandson of Ascanius and son of Silvus,
Brutus is exiled for the accidental killing of his father. He travels from Alba Longa (formerly
Latium) to Albion where, under Diana's direction, he settles, renaming it 'Brutaine' (Britain).
During his long reign Brutus protects his borders from the Danes (Cimbri) and founds a new
Troy on the Thames, now London. On the significance of Burnell's use of the Brutus myth
to claim Reyner and Landgartha as ancestors of the Stuart kings see Introduction, pp 49–51.
178 Iland that derives … white rocks = Albion, from *alba*, meaning white; i.e., England.

In this faire Ile, a Prince (one way descended
Of *Troian* race: I' th' other side extended
Up by the Royall bloud of *Danes,* unto   310
A warlike King call'd *Reyner,* that shall wooe
And wed a Lady Amazonian,
Landgartha nam'd) which Prince shall be the man
(Having his subjects in their loves combyn'd;
Who shall to evils onely be confin'd   315
By their owne sad dissentions, being of all
Earths men, the properest and most martiall)
To exalt thy bloud. He shall (by 's right)[179] enjoy
The Land of *Danes*; and in this place where *Troy*
Now stands, shall Conquer, and build it againe.   320
Will also conquer *Greece,* and there restrayne
Th'impieties of wicked men. Thus, *Fate*
I have layd ope' to thee, to consolate
Thy selfe and sad Queene; Now I must away:
For, from the gods I've made too long a stay.   *Exeunt ambo.* 325
VALDEMAR Your Majesties have now seene all; even as
 I found recorded in the foresayd Booke:[180]
 How true heaven onely knowes. Yet, all may prove true
 (Being not impossible) if men be wise.
REYNER And not destroy themselves, as it's there spoke.   330
 Our part on't has hit right; and so may that.
 And now *(Valdemar)* to requite thy love,   *All rise.*
 My Queene and I will make your Maske compleate,
 By being your dancers.   *Enter Hub[ba] & Marf[isa] without her*
HUBBA I must first beg your   *sword, & her Gowne untuck'd.* 335
 Pardon, to leade the measure, sir, for I have
 Brought a fine friendly dancer with me; and
 We will to foot it ——— ——— ———
REYNER *Hubba,* thou alwayes comm'st in pudding time.[181]
LANDGARTHA Let's stand; I long to see *Marfisa* dance.   340
 Here Hubba and Marfisa Dance the whip of Donboyne[182] *merrily.*

---

179 by 's right = Reyner's blood birth-right to rule is once again stressed but here it is adjacent to
  claims of right by conquest. On the sources for Reyner's future conquests in England, Ireland
  and continental Europe see Introduction, pp 40–1.
180 'foresayd Booke' = see 3. 170–1 above.
181 pudding time = the time for pudding, hence a lucky, propitious moment.
182 whip of Dunboyne = a country dance from the Boyne area of the Pale. For further discussion of its origin and literary resonances, see Introduction, pp 61–2.

REYNER This was excellent. We shall but shame our selves,
　　In following of you. Come let us begin.

　　　Here they dance the grand Dance in foure Couple, Reyner and
　　　　　Landgartha, Valdemar and Scania, Fredericke
　　　　　　and Elsinora, Inguar and Fatyma.

REYNER So, Cousin, we have made you some amends,
　　For your part of the Maske: and now you shall
　　(Being so kinde a husband) conduct your Lady　　　　　　345
　　Unto her Chamber; and there use her kindly
　　Too as she deserves. Our Aunt and Cousin may
　　(After all this noyse) also retyre; and say
　　(In solitude and silence) th' many prayers
　　They have omitted all the day. As for　　　　　　　　　350
　　The Queenes grace: she must give me leave,
　　To usher her to bed.
LANDGARTHA Must.[183] That, in such
　　A servant, were too peremptory. But
　　If you plead your title King; I'll answer　　　　　　　355
　　That I know how to fight: and have ere now
　　Stoop'd[184] a too hasty Prince. Therefore, good sir,
　　You are best speake me faire; or I may put you
　　Beside your sweet hopes;
　　And give you somewhat of the sowre to taste.　　　　360
REYNER That, and to kill me, were all one: For which,
　　I now (and ever will) humbly intreat,
　　As a poor suppliant with you to treat.　　　　　*Exeunt omnes.*

183　Must = on Landgartha's sensitivity to the language of service versus the language of freedom,
　　see Introduction, pp 55–6.
184　Stoop'd = brought down, conquered.

The fourth Act.

Enter Reyner musing at one doore, and Hubba to him at the other.

REYNER Is *Inguar* yet return'd from th' Fleet?
HUBBA Not yet sir.
REYNER Let him be quickly sent for then: be gone.   *Exit Hubba.*
    A poore gentlewoman, an ordinary
    Noble mans daughter, to have catch'd me thus;   5
    Whom *Cesar* would rejoyce, to have made his sonne,
    Some horrid plague confound her modesty,[185]
    And her for me, for now I care not for her;
    Though I dissemble it; because I dare not
    (She is so damn'd valiant) doe otherwise   10
    Till I have got from hence: For she (being
    So belov'd too of the *Norwegians*) might
    Cut short my life and passage. But yet, *Reyner*,
    Thinke how exceeding worthy she is of love;
    And of a Prince: thinke of her vertue, doe: 15
    Thinke of her beautie, myldness, vallor, and
    What else: no, no, I will not; will not love her:
    For I have tooke enough of what I most lov'd;
    Which, I confesse could not but please my Palat[186]   *Enter Vald[emar].*
    But here comes *Valdemar,* who like an Asse   20
    Still dotes on his wife, I'll not therefore trust him.
VALDEMAR Your resolution to be gone for *Denmarke,*
    Men doe admire;[187] and I must tell you, sir,
    (Seeing you will needs be constant, in so bad
    A purpose) some doe feare your projects are   25
    Ignoble. I then (as one that lov'd you once;
    And will doe still, unlesse you forfeyte your selfe)
    Wo'd be your adviser, if you dare take advice.
REYNER Y' are too sawcie;[188] and what I have resolv'd on,

---

185 modesty = self-control, temperateness.
186 Palat: Reyner in this act takes on a number of attributes previously associated with Frollo, cf.
    Frollo speaks of using the Amazons for his 'private pallat' (1. 59).
187 admire = wonder at.
188 sawcie = (saucy) insolent, impertinent.

I will not alter. Must we be curb'd by you,   30
In tendering the welfare of our subjects?
Shall *Denmarke* be still forgotten?
VALDEMAR That colour
Dyes but very poorely; though you stalke with it.[189]
The fall of your obstreperous passion, to   35
Your Queene (sir) people take notice of: though she,
Poore Lady, (asham'd to be deceiv'd or scorn'd)
Say nothing of it; restrayn'd too, by her love
To you. But, we that are your Countriemen
(Whom you mainely dishonour in't) can have   40
No such patience.
REYNER Our affection to our
Lov'd faire Consort (though you be pleas'd to doubt it)
Will not be question'd, but by your slanderous tongue.
VALDEMAR You cannot sir. Nay shall not, maske your blacke[190]   45
Intentions so from me; they doe appeare
Too many. And she whom you most wrong, is more
Then worthy of you; had you but the wisedome
And grace to thinke so still. But be assur'd
(When she is rid o' th' burthen she now carries)[191]   50
She'll be reveng'd at full for her dishonour;
And snatch the Crownes you wear from of your trech'rous
Temples.
REYNER You will not play the Traytor, in
Conspiring with her?   55
VALDEMAR Though I sho'd not, sir,
You need not doubt but *Harrolld*[192] will; who thinkes
His right to *Denmarke*, as good as yours to *Norway.*
REYNER That Christian dog's head and yours too, had beene
Chopt off 'ere this, had I not been a foole.   60
VALDEMAR If you durst (you make me now beleeve) that had
Beene so. But I'll make shift to save one of 's;   *Enter Ing[uar]*
And thinke you'll hardly save your selfe from t'other.   *& Hubba.*

---

189 That colour ... stalke with it = even though you tell it with conviction, your story does not
    conceal the truth.
190 blacke = the colour first associated with Frollo (e.g., 1. 38, 158) here shifts to Reyner.
191 When ... burthen she now carries = when she gives birth. This is the first we hear of
    Landgartha's pregnancy.
192 Harrolld = Harrold, i.e., Harold 'Klak' Halfdansson, also known as Herioldus II (*c*.785–*c*.852),
    was twice king of Jutland (812–14 and 819–27) and famously converted to Christianity while

REYNER You may doe what you list; and so will I.

    Are all the Shipping ready?   65

INGUAR They are sir, but ——————— ———

REYNER Come, spare your breath; I know what you wo'd say.

HUBBA Wo'd all the Cables and Sayles were burnt:

    You brought us hither with the hazard of our lives,

    To gaine this kingdom for you; and now you have it,   70

    You'll wisely gi' 't away; an fetch 'em all

    Upon our backes.

REYNER Who made you a Counseller?

    There's your reward.   *strikes him.*

HUBBA I shall take more then this   75

    Ere long if I sticke to you.

VALDEMAR You doe well

    To practise before hand.

REYNER Traytor, doe you upbrayd us?   *Offers to draw,*

INGUAR I beseech you sir, to suppresse your passion;   *so does Vald[emar]*   80

    And not to rayse a tumult here: knowing   *& Ing[uar] steps in.*

    How truely-loyall the Prince *Valdemar,*

    Has ever beene to you, sir, and now pleads

    Strongly against himselfe; in seeking to

    Detaine you, with your gracious noble Queene.   85

VALDEMAR He accounts his friends, his neerest enemies.

REYNER We take heaven to witnesse, we are wrong'd.

    But peace; here she comes.   *Enter Land[gartha] with Childe*[193]

LANDGARTHA Will you needs be gone, sir,   *and Scania not so.*

    And leave me thus?   90

REYNER It is but two houres sayling,

    In a faire day; and we shall soone be backe.

LANDGARTHA I doe not use to weepe: But now I must;   *Weeps.*

    My heavy minde fore-speakes some future evill.

    Death (which shall be welcome) I know's not farre from me.   95

REYNER [*Aside*] May the gods grant to hasten it.

SCANIA The time was

    When shee, sir, could with a nod 'a' forc'd your fancie,

    In a farre greater matter, then your stay

at the court of Louis the Pious in Mainz in 826. In Belleforest Harrold with the Emperor's
support, raises a rebellion against Regner not (as Burnell has it) while the King is absent in
Denmark, but while he is engaged in war raids in Ireland, Great Britain and Scotland, *Histoires
Tragiques*, p. 869. See also Introduction, pp 39–40.

193 with Childe = pregnant.

For some small time. 100
REYNER And shall againe sweete Sister,
    But the meere necessitie of our departure,
    Is such: that we must needs away, at this
    Very instant.
LANDGARTHA Then give me leave (deare sir,) 105
To share the worst may happen in your voyage.
REYNER So to indanger your life, we'd loose ours first,
    You shall by no means stirre, my only soule. Come:
    We will conduct you to your Chamber, and there
    Leave you (with your friends and mine) to be guided 110
    By your accustomed vertue, and strong heart. *Exeunt.*

Enter Cowsell and Radger.[194]

COWSELL O brother, brother, I know the very griefe on't,
    Will kill me out right, as dead as a Herring.
RADGEE O deare, loving brother. I shall fare no better,
    I'm sure o' that; wo'd I had never seene you. 115
COWSELL Besides brother, I tooke such an affection
    To the women, fine, courteous, honest cre'tures.
RADGEE And we to you brother, and to all the *Danes*.
    You came not to pray on 's but to deliver
    Us from the *Swedes*. 120
COWSELL We ought to love each other,
    Brother, being so neere neighbors, and friends.
RADGEE And so we doe, deare brother, all those are good and honest.
    Who wo'd 'a' thought his grace sho'd leave the Queene
    So abruptly, i' the latter end of her time too? 125
COWSELL Hard against our wils: but sayes, he'll soone be backe.
RADGEE I' th' meane time brother, and before we part,
    We are best take t'other cup.
COWSELL I thought to 'a'
    Made that now my motion brother, we shall 130
    Remember you in *Denmarke*.
RADGEE And when we
    Forget you brother, may the gods forget us.
    Ho! drawer,
ROLFO [*Within,*] Anon anon sir. *Enter Rolfo.* 135

194 See note 97 above.

RADGEE Honest *Rolfo*, one flaggon more of that
    You gave us last, the very same I charge thee,
    Without tricks or mixture.
ROLFO By *Jove* sir, you shall:
    What? Doe you thinke I'll use you like a stranger?   140
COWSELL Prithee kinde *Rolfo*, let not us be forc'd
    To knocke agen.   *Exit Rolfo.*
RADGEE Captaine *Hubba* (as I
    Conceive brother) goes not along with you;
    I met him spurring to our house, as I came.   145
COWSELL The Princess *Scania*, by much intreatie
    Got leave of the Lord *Inguar*, his Coronell,[195]
    To stay onely two dayes; and he is gone
    A visit to his Mistris.   *Enter Rolfo.*
RADGEE Welcome *Rolfo*.   150
    Come, give it me: for we shall need no glasses. *They drinke at the Lines.*[196]
    Here worthy brother, halfe to your good journey .
COWSELL Let me see brother, (*Peeps into the pot*) you have drunke the full halfe

—————

    Here *Rolfo* fill't agen.   *Exit Rolfo.*
RADGEE O sweet brother, that you co'd stay all night,   155
    I sho'd never be weary of your company.   *Enter Rolfo.*
COWSELL Nor I of yours brother, and now from the deepe
    Bottome of my heart to th' wide mouth of my stomacke
    I speak it dearest brother, here's a whole one,
    To our next merry meeting ——— ——   160
RADGEE Quickely *Rolfo,*   *Exit Rolfo.*
    Fetch it, and be honest. O sweet brother,
    That I co'd imbrace you thus for ever, ever.   *They imbrace.*
COWSELL I must kisse at parting.   *They kisse.*[197].
ROLFO Y'are a couple of th'arrantest[198] kind gentlemen.   *Ent[er] Rolf[o]* 165

195 Coronell = colonel.
196 *They drinke at the Lines* = i.e., they drink as the lines are spoken.
197 Lines 163–73: reports of the Irish habit of kissing and over-familiar greetings are found in
    English writings on Ireland, see Sheila T. Cavanagh, '"Licentious Barbarism": Spenser's View
    of the Irish and *The Faerie Queene*', *Irish University Review*, 26:2 (1996), 268–80. Gerald of
    Wales' apocryphal report of the Irish nobility who had travelled to Waterford in 1185 to offer
    the kiss of peace to Prince John and instead had their beards pulled had recently been resur-
    rected, 'The Conquest of Ireland' in *Historical Works of Giraldus Cambrensis*, pp 165–324 (315);
    Edmund Campion's 'A Historie of Ireland', II, I, p. 68 in Sir James Ware (ed.), *The Historie
    of Ireland* (Dublin, 1633).
198 arrantest = most notorious, downright (usually of rogues).

RADGEE Give me the pot: I ne'r drunke i' my life
    With more sorrow, and a better desire. ——— ———
COWSELL Here, take Money *Rolfo*, my brother payd last,
    I must kisse thee too *Rolfo*,
ROLFO [*Within,*] Rogue.   170
    Anon, anon, sir.   *As they kisse*
RADGEE Nay, *Rolfo*, for all
    Your haste: I must (for my brothers sake) take
    Off that kisse, from thy now sweet (though greasie) lips.   *They kisse.*
COWSELL And now farewell, but not for ever, my dearest   175
    And best of friends.
RADGEE We'll part at t'other Taverne.
COWSELL Then arme in arme let's march, most worthy brother.   *Exeunt.*

Enter Hubba and Marfisa.

HUBBA I could not otherwise chuse, Mistris (though
    Your distrust of my unfayn'd affection,   180
    Kept me thus long from injoying, what I
    Most desir'd in a noble way) but come
    (Urg'd by that love, that ever shall remaine
    With me, wheresoe'r I goe) to tender
    The duty of a servant, in taking leave   185
    Of you, before my suddaine departure.
MARFISA It's indeed too suddaine: and I doe now
    Repent the not imbracing, what I was not
    Enough good to accept, your love. For, I confesse
    Though somewhat late, I lov'd you more then you   190
    Did me; and ever shall unlesse the fault
    Be onely yours, in proving (which I doe
    Not yet suspect) a changling. I shall for
    My part, punish severely in my selfe,
    Th'offence of not being yours, by a continu'd   195
    Sadness and griefe, till once agen I see you.
    HUBBA And though I have beene too much noted for
    My mirth (which yet, was never sawc'd with spite,
    Or other bad condition:) I promise
    (For my misfortune in thus missing of you)   200
    Not to laugh once (unlesse against my will,
    At some unlucky chance) till I possesse
    The treasure I most covet.

MARFISA That (if you
    Meane me) shall be yours when we meete next, and   205
    Safely kept for you, untill then. I' th' meane time,
    I shall charily[199] preserve (though but a poore
    Satisfaction for you) your image in
    Th'interior of my minde.
HUBBA Which overpay's,   210
    With much advantage, all my services.
MARFISA 't was a strange resolution of the King,
    To leave his Queene, she being so much against it;
    And he so strangely fond of her at first:
    Which she deserv'd, being a Lady the world   215
    Cannot match.
HUBBA He is these thirtie houres in *Denmarke*:
    Where if he prove unkinde to her, that cannot
    (In true judgement) condemne others, that like not
    Such proceeding.   220
MARFISA He had neede be circumspect
    In what he do's; or he may soone repent it,
    And perchance,
    When matters prove past remedy to him,
    Yet, while I find you sound: no alien faults   225
    Shall make me hate, what once I so affected.
HUBBA Resting on that assurance, I must now
    Crave the kind favour of a parting kisse.
MARFISA That you shall have [*they kisse*] and half a dozen more,
    When you come to your Ship: For, so farre I   230
    Will with you; and wo'd along to *Denmarke*, but to try
    If I may build upon your constancie.   *Exeunt.*

Enter Harrold and Eric.

HARROLD It's now but need, we both looke to our selves:
    Or we may pay the forfeyt of our slackenesse.
    (With the losse of both our heads) upon a Scaffold.   235
    For, *Reyner* having cast the faire *Landgartha*
    Off, (of whom he was not worthy:) and by
    A dreadfull precipice, fall'n from much goodnesse:
    He will not stop at his first fault. But (hurri'd
    By the guiltinesse of his Conscience)   240

199 charily = carefully, cautiously.

Runne headlong downe the hill, upon the rocke
Of dangerous mischiefe; to which he's now ingag'd.
ERIC She is a Lady of so stout a heart,
 That when she finds him base (although she lov'd him
 Exceedingly) she cannot but be reveng'd   245
 For her repudiation, and disgrace.
HARROLD And may prove our strong friend to ruine him;
 That has threatned (and that not privatly)
 To rid himselfe on us.
ERIC And will, if he can: 250
 You may by his death then, that wo'd be yours,
 Settle your selfe securely in his kingdomes,
 By matching and partaking now with her.
HARROLD Brother, the man whose deitie we adore
 (And who to give us rest, still liv'd without it)   255
 Can witnesse for me, could I but perswade
 My minde by any probabilitie,
 't were possible, for me to live in peace here,
 And not to have my throat cut: although my right
 Unto the Crowne of *Denmarke* be apparant,   260
 My title while I slept or wak'd, sho'd sleepe;
 As when King *Reyner* liv'd a vertuous kind man.
 For I delight not in th'expence of bloud;
 Though I feare not to spend my owne in a
 Just cause. But seeing all rest is deni'd me: 265
 As the strong law of nature binds, I must
 Shift for my selfe, the best I may. Which shall not
 Be effected by base trechery, or murder.
 Nor doe I chiefly yet meane to rely
 On th' brave *Landgartha's* assistance; whom the   270
 Love of a wife, and hope of reconcilement,
 May urge beyond all spirit of revenge.
ERIC What is't you meane to plot then for our safetie?
HARROLD We'll to the pious Christian Emperor,
 Lewis the *Debonaire*;[200] who (as you know)   275
 Do's oft solicite me to plead my right
 To th' Crowne, by dent of sword; that being the best
 (Nay onely) Patent,[201] *Reyner* has to show for 't.

---

200 Lewis the Debonaire = Louis the Gracious or Gentle, better known as Louis the Pious (see
 2. 134–41).
201 Patent = a document stating the right to property or title.

Though he from's father got it: which doth lessen
Much his guilt.   280
ERIC It's not his guilt that now most troubles him;
But by more sinne to guard it.
HARROLD Twelve thousand
Expert Souldiers (that lye neere here, o' th' borders
Of *Germany*) I may have when I list;   285
To adde (with all speed) to our owne sure friends.
And unto others that will fall in troopes,
From now dishonour'd *Reyner*, for his base
Adultery intended with *Vraca*,²⁰²
To strengthen himselfe against his wife and me.   290
ERIC Unheard of madnesse, so vilely to betray
(And to's owne ruine) a poore and vertuous Lady;
That but for him, and his damn'd shamelesse lyes,
Had never marry'd any. Being withall
(As 't is reported) most extreamely faire,   295
Farre, farre beyond the other.
HARROLD Such are the follies
Of humane nature, when it is forsaken
Of him that made it:²⁰³ But we'll now make use on't.
ERIC You sho'd be suddaine, least we be layd hold on;   300
And to take him unprepar'd.
HARROLD When night ascends
Her sable charyot, we will both of us
(Mounted on our best horses) post away;
And be (I hope) ere we be miss'd, pass'd danger.   305
Come, let us therefore in, and loose no time:
Which, in necessitie's a fatall crime.   *Exeunt.*

---

202 Vraca = listed in Dramatis Personae as Frollo's daughter. Vraca and her part in the action are
essentially invented by Burnell; in Belleforest, Regner's second wife remains anonymous and
absent. On possible sources for Vraca in the Ragnar sagas see Introduction, pp 42–4. Vraca
has been read as an allegorical figure for both the New Protestants in Ireland and for Scotland,
see Catherine Shaw, 'Landgartha and the Irish Dilemma', *Éire-Ireland*, 13:1 (1978), 26–39.
203 him that made it = i.e., God. Harrold's Christianity is again highlighted.

The fifth Act.

Enter Valdemar and Inguar.

VALDEMAR You are happy beyond expectation
    In your Embassage:[204] for all men did conceive
    (And very probably) the Queene would ayde
    With th'utmost of her pow'r, *Harrold* in his
    Designe for *Denmarke.* But the noble Lady,   5
    (Although in outward show, she have not granted
    What you demand) I know (such is her vertue
    And loving nature) is comming in her minde,[205]
    Now to assist your most ungracious King.
INGUAR For which in chiefe he is to you beholding;   10
    Though he deserv'd it not, at his departure.
    But now, Contrition has wipt off his guilt,
    Though not the punishment, before the gods.
    Nor is there any hope left us on earth,
    But what we now may gaine here by your meanes.   15
VALDEMAR Had you but beene a witnesse of her griefes,
    (Able to rive[206] a heart of steele) you had
    Melted (as we almost did) into teares:
    Especially when she heard of th'infamous
    Marryage, with *Swealands* daughter (told her by   20
    A whispering flatterer:)[207] how then she tore
    Her golden hayre, and us'd such cruelty
    On her faire limmes, which had wellneere ended her
    (Notwithstanding what we could doe to hinder't:)
    Cursing the time when she e'r saw a *Dane*;   25
    Not for her husbands renogading[208] most*:*

---

204 Embassage = embassy.
205 comming in her minde = i.e., she has already made up her mind to come to Reyner's aid.
206 rive = tear, rend.
207 Lines 19–21: Landgartha learns of the Reyner's marriage to Vraca from a third party rumour.
    Burnell here makes it clear that Reyner's marriage is bigamous; Reyner has not asked
    Landgartha formally for a divorce as he does in Belleforest, *Histoires Tragiques*, p. 863–4 and
    Saxo Grammaticus, *History of the Danes*, p. 281.
208 renogading = abandoning faith.

But the losse of her virginitie, and foule
   Disgrace.
INGUAR We heard of all: Yet were compell'd
   By strong necessitie (perforce) to build   30
   On her heroicke goodnesse, and your worth.
VALDEMAR 't was well conceiv'd; and better put to tryall,
   That compulsion may worke peace agen.
INGUAR Here the divine Lady comes (her selfe) unto us.

     Enter Landgartha, Scania, Elsinora, Fatyma, & Marfisa
       in womans apparell with Swords on.

LANDGARTHA Although (Lord *Inguar,*) your soveraigne, and my   35
   Unkind husband, were rather to expect
   Sharpe warre and hate then any ayde from me
   In his distresse: having (as farre as 't lay
   In him) disgrac'd me by his flight; and as
   I'd us'd false play with others: yet, my love   40
   To him (deepely engraven in my heart.)
   Joyn'd to my owne innocence and merit, has
   (As all may see) got the upper-hand; and stopt
   My once intended course of strict revenge;
   Though he enjoy another wife, now the Mistris   45
   Of what is mine by bond.
INGUAR Most gracious Queene,
   I can say nothing, to excuse his guilt;
   Or lessen it: but that your vertue shines
   The brighter for his deepe ingratitude,   50
   Which now's the greatest Corrosive[209] to himselfe,
   And cause of all his evils, by the losse
   Of in a manner all was his before:
   And that his act, has render'd both of you
   Famous to all the world, in different manners: 55
   You as the glorious mirrour of all worth,
   But him (with grief I speake it) for's offence.
SCANIA Which now (deare Madame) as it is repented,
   Exacts your mercy more then punishment.
ELSINORA To prove a lasting Pyramid to all   60
   Succeeding, times, of such a noble act.

209 Corrosive = consuming grief.

VALDEMAR It can yeeld you no benefit to ruine
    Him and his poore subjects, being also yours;
    And in their loves, they're yours.

FATYMA Much more then his   65
    I doe beleeve.

INGUAR Madame. I can depose[210] it.   *To Fatyma.*
    And that they 've ever deem'd it their chiefe glory,
    To have had her for their Queene; their hearts he lost,
    When he lost her: nor is there ought can rayse   70
    The minds o' th' few, that now sticke to him, but her
    Strong assistance, and the try'd vallor of the
    Norwegian Ladies, that before
    Gave us the victory against the *Swedes*.

LANDGARTHA King *Reyner* and your selfe (Lord *Inguar*) have 75
    Too many friends here, to be deni'd in what
    Our pow'r may stead him, or you demand.
    And I'm the more induc'd to pardon his fault,
    That I acknowledge my selfe faultie too
    (And which my heart has oft accus'd me for,   80
    With no small griefe) in granting that to him
    Under the flattering title of marryage, which I
    Resolv'd ne'r to 'a' lost; and which he durst not
    Seeke to have forc'd from me. But it's now past helpe.

SCANIA There's one way yet left (Madame) to helpe all.   85

LANDGARTHA He then transported, by his fierce desire,
    Which slav'd him: by craft (I'll give it no worse
    A name) did that wrong to my modestie,
    Which I (being not so deepe in passion)
    Might well have hinder'd; and by yeelding to it,   90
    Have given scope for others to condemne me.

INGUAR Which none can justly doe: For, I'm assur'd,
    Madame (though you have cause not to beleeve it)
    That his intents to your grace, were sincere
    At first, as now they are: and therefore (deare Queene,) 95
    You are to meete his past ill, with your goodnesse.
    Which, if you doe not speedily: there will be
    No time, nor meanes hereafter, left for you
    To exercise your vallor in this cause.

LANDGARTHA When we behold our neighbors house on fire, 100

---

210 depose = bear witness to, vouch for.

The Proverbe sayes we ought looke to our owne:[211]
This you conceive; and I suppose you are
Inform'd by these that love you, that we have
As many valiant men and women, in
A readinesse, as may, if heaven be pleas'd   105
(For we are pleas'd in't) reinthrone your King;
And chase those rebels that now urge his flight.
Let then my brother (the Prince *Valdemar*)
And you, make all the haste you can before us;
With newes of our approach. And, one thing more   110
I must intreat you doe for me: which is
To deliver this Letter, unto him that
Caus'd my sorrow; and left me great with child.
Which fruit of his, he shall soone looke on, young
Frideslaus.[212]   115
VALDEMAR He sho'd 'a' stayd, to have got
      Such another.
SCANIA In honesty, he could
      Have done no lesse.
INGUAR Your graces Letter, I hope   120
      Within these three houres, he shall reade at furthest.
VALDEMAR You'll give me leave to goe before, to provide
      A lodging for you?
SCANIA Yes: for I meane to be
      Your bedfellow to morrow night.   125
VALDEMAR And I shall strayne my selfe, to bid you welcome.
INGUAR The King will doe as much too, for your Highnesse.
LANDGARTHA [*smilingly*] Fy, not so soone man; that were a shame indeed,
      People wo'd then say, that I went to aske it.
      Nor does he neede me; having one (at least)   130
      Already to keepe him warme.
INGUAR He thinks of none,
      But your Grace.
VALDEMAR We must be now abrupt in our
      Leave taking.   135

211 Lines 100–1: 'Your own property is concerned when your neighbour's house is on fire',
    Horace, *Epistles*, 1, 18, 84).
212 Frideslaus = Friedlef, their son, according to Saxo Grammaticus. His name invokes Fridleif I
    and II, earlier kings of Denmark, who appear in Saxo Grammaticus. Both Saxo Grammaticus
    and Belleforest note that Lathgertha and Regner also had two daughters whose names have
    not survived, *History of the Danes*, p. 281, *Histoires Tragiques*, p. 870.

LANDGARTHA Be gone. *Scania,* fare you well, *Inguar,* may all
    The gods be your guides.   *Exeunt ambo.*
LANDGARTHA And now *Marfisa.*
    Silence declares with you, how gladly your heart
    Consents, to goe for *Denmarke.*   140
MARFISA I meane to doe
    Your Majestie some service there, now that
    You measure my affection by your owne.
SCANIA But what, if you come to weare the Willow garland,[213]
    By the inconstancie of Captaine *Hubba*?   145
MARFISA Not (doe as the Queene did) forgive the offence.
FATYMA No lesse then 's life would satisfie your anger.
MARFISA Doe you make doubt on't?
ELSINORA I beleeve him honest.
LANDGARTHA What is your owne opinion? *Marfisa*   150
MARFISA I still suppose the best.
LANDGARTHA Then wayte upon
    My cousin *Fatyma*: and both of you make haste
    To summon with all speede (on paine of death)
    All our troops (both men and women) in *Ansloy,*   155
    Saltsburge, and thereabouts.[214] Our Sister and Aunt
    Shall to the neerer quarters; whilst I prepare
    Here all things requisite for our departure.
    And as we once made no small haste to meete
    King *Reyner,* when he brought us ayde against   160
    Our foes: let's doe the same in gratitude
    (And with more honour) now, in assisting of him.
    Those which we leave, will keep safe here. Away.
FATYMA The trust impos'd on us, we'll not betray. *Exeunt omnes severally.*

A march.   *Then enter Harrold, Eric, and*
                          Lothaire[215] *arm'd.*

213 Willow garland = symbol of being forsaken; cf. Desdemona's song in Shakespeare, *Othello*
    4.3.39–56.
214 Ansloy = Anslo or Obslo, now Oslo; Saltsburge = Salzburg. The mention of Salzburg may
    be a reminder of the pan-European history of the Amazon empire and/or an attempt to link
    Landgartha's Amazons to the contemporary Anne of Austria (1601–66), the powerful queen
    consort of Louis XIII of France, see Ian Maclean, *Woman Triumphant: Feminism in French*
    Literature, 1610–1652 (Oxford: Clarendon Press, 1977), pp 64–87, 220–32.
215 Lothaire = Lothair I (795–855), eldest son of Louis the Pious. He was appointed co-ruler with
    his father in 817. Shaw identifies Louis the Pious and Lothaire as figures for Archibald
    Campbell, duke of Argyll, and William Kerr, third earl of Lothian; both leaders of the

HARROLD We must make haste Lord *Lothaire,* (now that by   165
    The helpe of heaven, for which we chiefly move:
    And the assistance which your Lord and ours,
    The noble Emperor *Lewis,* true inheritor
    Of his great fathers vertues did afford us,
    We are ascended to what is our right,   170
    Being thereto lifted by your manly worth too)
    To make all sure, by joyning our last issue
    With *Reyner,* ere the brave *Landgartha* come
    (Whom he once more thinkes to deceive:) For, where
    Shee leads, all goes to wracke i' th' other side.   175
LOTHAIRE It's strange so stout a minde as hers, sho'd ever
    Yeeld love or obedience to a man that has
    So basely dealt to her.
ERIC She squares all her
    Actions by the rule of goodnesse, not   180
    Of passion; and thinkes this deede of hers,
    A very gratefull offering to her gods,
    Yet, we doe hope to send (before she land here)
    Her husbands rancke soule, to great *Belzebub.*[216]
HARROLD Then let's march on with speede; and trust our cause   185
    To him, that only gives life by his lawes.   *Exeunt a march.*

        After the march, Enter Reyner and Hubba.

REYNER Heare you no newes from *Inguar* (*Hubba*) yet?
HUBBA Not a word: But a ship is now on entring
    In at the haven; and we hope it's his.
REYNER No, no. We are of all the world forsaken,   190
    But most of heaven: For, we have deserv'd it,
    And our repentance now comes too too late.
HUBBA I doe beseech you sir, not to yeeld to
    Such weake, unmanly diffidence.
REYNER We wrong'd   195
    Thee (*Hubba*) too; and now thy loyaltie
    And kindnesse wounds our soule deeper, then if thou hadst
    Prov'd false, all turnes to my confusion.
HUBBA It was your passion and not you, strucke me, sir.

contemporary Scottish opposition to Charles I, 'Landgartha and the Irish Dilemma', pp 35–
6.
216 Belzebub = Beelzebub, a chief devil; Eric introduces the Christian pantheon to the play.

REYNER Would I were quickly dead, or never borne,   200
    To see the evils which I have occasion'd,
    And must needs feele, if I but live a while.
HUBBA Your noble Queene *Landgartha,* will I doubt not
    (If i'th' meane time sir, you doe what lyes in you,
    With patience) soone rid you of those feares;   205
    And State you as before; and in her love too.
REYNER I ne'r shall see that *Halcyon* day[217] againe,
    To see her, *Hubba,* though you all suppose
    The contrary; and caus'd me send to move
    Her goodnesse. She is too magnanimous   210
    Ever to looke at such a wretch as I am,
    That deceiv'd her once so foulely.
HUBBA. You'll finde
    Your selfe deceiv'd, I hope sir, in that ere long.
REYNER Had I but faithfull prov'd to her, as she   215
    Deserv'd (thou know'st it *Hubba,*) I might then
    'a' playd at stoole-ball[218] with young children, or
    Have wasted time more idley, if I'd listed;
    And have my estate multiply'd to many
    Kingdomes. Now, thou seest, we are not worth one   220
    Province, Stricke me heaven.   *Enter Valdemar and Inguar.*
VALDEMAR Honest Captaine, I
    Am glad to meete you alive.
HUBBA Your Highnesse poore servant.
INGUAR The King walkes strangely sad.   225
HUBBA He's not himself: and therefore, whatsoever
    Newes you bring; y' had neede use your accustomed
    Discretion in the relating of it.
REYNER You are both as welcome hither, as my
    Distraction will give me leave to bid you.   230
VALDEMAR I never knew you (sir) too much exalted
    At flatt'ring Fortunes smiles, or when you Conquer'd:
    And (now she frownes) you still ought to preserve
    A valiant indifferencie.
REYNER Healthy men   235
    Know how t'afford good counsell unto others,

217 Halcyon day = tranquil, peaceful days from the myth of the Halcyon, a species of kingfisher,
    which was said to build its nest on the seas in winter, magically calming the waves.
218 stoole-ball = early bat and ball game using a stool as a wicket.

Whose forces being too weake, to beare the blowes
Of their diseases, yeeld and languish under
The waight that's insupportable.

INGUAR The weaker   240
Their minds are, the more they yeeld; beyond
Necessitie: and thereby become chiefe Actors
In their owne Tragedies.

REYNER I know you speake this,
To prepare my minde, for the bad newes you bring.   245

INGUAR Your vertue will now most consist, in not
Being over joy'd, when you read this Letter,
Written and sent by her, that sayes she loves you.

REYNER Let me see 't. I know the hand, it's hers,
O let me, let me kisse it, kisse it still,   *Kisses the Letter.* 250
And not presume to looke what it contaynes,
To plague my guiltie conscience.

VALDEMAR Reade and be rul'd.

Reyner opens and Reads.

If this my second duty, may prove as happy in the recovery of thy
kingdomes, as my first was against a Tyrant; yet honouring thee   255
with the victory: I shall account my travell well bestow'd. Make head
bravely (as wisedome permits) against the enemie: for I am comming
with all speed, to let him know, that Landgartha *(being thy Queene*
and only lawfull Wife) is a warrior: and will prove so to his prejudice,
and thy advantage: having from her heart (notwithstanding thy   260
unkindnesse) absolv'd thee of all the wrongs thou did'st her.
Landgartha.

REYNER A gracious language! O you gods defend me,
From turning altogether foole at this. For, my
Frayle vessell is not able to contayne,   265
The forcible excesse of this sweet comfort.
My soule results so strangely; mounts, mounts up,
That I have much adoe, to keepe from dancing:
My nimble spirit elevats my body,
And my very life (I thinke) will now with joy   270
Forsake me, fly away.

VALDEMAR Be not in extreames,
So like a meere franticke.[219] Pray recall your wits,

---

219 franticke = madman, lunatic. Once again, as in Act 3, Reyner is associated with illness and

Before she comes you may loose all; your selfe, and us.
REYNER Excuse me, worthy Cousin, you feele not   275
    The force of my impulsion. Yet, I confesse
    I'm (but as others are) a poore weake man;
    Subject to many changes 'gainst my will.
INGUAR Collect your selfe, were 't but in obedience   *Enter scout.*
    To your wise and noble Queene. What newes with you?   280
SCOUT That *Harrold* and his brother *Eric,* with
    A mighty pow'r of *Danes* and *Germans,* march
    Hither with speed, doubtlesse to force a battle.
INGUAR Which we must decline, till our best souldier
    Come: and then we are for 'em.   285
VALDEMAR Lead us from hence,
    To guard your works;[220] and doe not now forget
    (Your wish'd ayde being so neere you) your old vallor;
    And judgement to command.
REYNER I hope we shall not.   *Exeunt.* 290

A march.   *Enter Harrold, Eric, Lothaire, and one*
                      or two more, with Battle-axes.

HARROLD Our foes have fortifi'd themselves so strongly,
    With Waggons, Carts, huge tymber, and deepe trenches:
    As 'tis impossible almost to force 'em.
ERIC Which if you doe not, you'll finde it a worse taske,
    To quayle *Landgartha*; whose fleet's now at sea;   295
    Nay hard on landing.
LOTHAIRE Th' present attempt will not
    Perchance, prove so dangerous, as to th'eye
    It seemes; if we valiantly ingage
    Our selves in th'onset.   300
HARROLD Let us boldly on then;
    And to conclude what hitherto, we have
    So prosperously achiev'd. I will beginne:
    And die, rather then loose what I have wonne.   *Exeunt.*

Allarums,   *A while after which is begun, enter Reyner*
                 and Valdemar with Battle-axes.

    extremes of emotion.
220 works = fortifications.

REYNER All's lost beyond recoverie, they are broke   305
    Upon us in, and fight like hungry Lyons,
    Tearing our men to peeces, that now leave,
    In foule disorder.
VALDEMAR Doe you (whil'st I charge up,
    To give some stop unto their furie) rally   310
    And hearten yours, the best you may. For, if
    We can hold out, but one full houre: the noble
    Landgartha (that with speed incredible,
    Has almost landed all her forces) will be
    With us, to mend all agen.   315
REYNER She shall never meet me flying.   *Exeunt. allarums.*

> *Enter Landgartha, Scania, Elsinora, Fatyma, and Marfisa:*
> *The foure Ladies, like Amazons. Marfisa with her*
> *Gowne tuck'd to th' midleg, spurs, &c. As*
> *in the first of the third Act; Battle-*
> *axes withall.*

LANDGARTHA You heare this Musicke, Ladies, and perceive
    What need our friends have of our swift assistance.
    We are not therefore now, to insist upon   *Here the Allarums*
    A tedious consultation; or on words   *sound as a farre off.* 320
    By me deliver'd, to encourage those
    Whose worths I know already.[221] Doe you Aunt
    (Assisted by *Fatyma* and *Marfisa)*
    Lead halfe our Armie: and wheele round about
    (With speed and silence) to charge strongly home,   325
    Upon our enemies backes. My sister and I
    Will to our Husbands, that are hardly prest;
    Their men all routed, and a number slaine.
    Farewell, I hope that we shall meete againe.   *Exeunt severally allarums*

Allarums.   *Then enter Reyner at one doore,*
                and Harrold at the other.[222]

REYNER Stand Traytor!   330
HARROLD Thou usurper, I will stand;
    And could afford you other glorious titles:

221 Lines 317–20: The urgency here contrasts with the rhetorical battle speeches of Act I.
222 The stage direction seems to promise the expected single combat between the men, but this
    is quickly displaced when Landgartha appears. See I, 297 above and Introduction, p. 38.

But that I meane not (having met you) to
Waste time in words, untill your foolish sweet-heart
(Whom you wo'd still deceive) come to your rescue.   335
But now, I hope you never shall enjoy her,
You know how.

REYNER You shall know somewhat from me, howsoever.

Here they fight, and Harrold beats Reyner under him; on which
Landgartha enters, beats in Harrold and returns.

LANDGARTHA Is it you? I were not beholding, to   *Land[gartha].*
    Have done this for you now. Goe, look to your selfe & people. *Exit.* 340
REYNER Deare heaven, where am I? or, is this a dream?   *Reyner rises as*
    It was *Landgartha* sure. O no, it was not,   *she beats in Harrold.*
    That glory and great miracle of the world,
    Could not afford such grace to me, the meere
    Fall'n dregs of villanie. But yet, 't was she,   345
    The figure of her heavenly face, was once
    (And still is) so imprinted in my soule,
    As 't is impossible I sho'd forget her,
    Therefore you gods, heape all those mountaynes on me,
    Which the impious Gyants lifted against you,[223]   350
    Or sincke me downe into the very Center,
    That I may ne'r behold her any more,
    That is so like you, both in shape and goodnesse.
    For, both I have contemn'd and my most base
    Ingratitude, never appear'd at full;   355
    Till now. O *love*, pownd pownd me with thy thunder,
    For, my confusion is the worst of torments. *Enter Scania and Valdemar.*
SCANIA The King's in danger; and we had need make haste
    To disingage him.
VALDEMAR That's done (I hope) already.   360
REYNER Welcome deare Sister, I am asham'd to looke
    You in the face.
SCANIA We heard (sir) you were in danger.
REYNER I was: But now may (when I list) goe take
    A nap. Wo'd the infernall dogs[224] would teare   365

---

223 the impious gyants = the Titans, see 1. 182 above.

224 infernall dogs = Cerberus the many-headed dog that guards the gates of the Underworld and
    has an appetite for living flesh.

My limbs to callops:[225] or adde some worse torment
    Unto my minds affliction.
SCANIA You neede not
    Afflict your selfe so much, for ought we see:
    For, now the wheele is turn'd to your advantage;   370
    My Sister is friends with you too, sir.
REYNER She sav'd
    My life, when I was downe; and ready to
    Receive the last (and mortall) blow. But then,
    Gave me so sad a looke, O loving Sister,   375
    That life which is her gift, if I must keepe
    In her displeasure, is much worse then death.
SCANIA Sir, if you will be rul'd by me, you must not
    Expresse too much, those vehement affections:
    For, she's acquainted but too well already,   380
    With your sad passion, and the continuance of it.
REYNER Seeing you (deare Lady,) in love and wisedome,
    Esteeme that my best course: I shall be dumbe
    As night, calme as the calm'st evening after
    A stormy day.   385
SCANIA Let's follow, where she went then.   *Exeunt.*

Enter Harrold and Eric.

HARROLD After our losse and watching these two nights,
    I cannot brother (the toyle of our journey,
    Lying so heavy too, on my tyr'd body)
    But sleepe a little, though it be dangerous.   390
ERIC My neede's no lesse; a little sleepe will serve.
HARROLD Let's take it here then, the place being solitary.

They sleepe, and a sweet solemne Musicke of Recorders is heard, then enter an Angel.

ANGEL Heaven has decreed, another day
    Shall gaine what you have lost. Your way
    Take both (as you were forc'd before)   395
    Unto the pious Emperor.
    One of you shall be King:[226] whose seed

225 callops = collops, pieces of meat.
226 Lines 390–403: The angel's 'prophecy' mirrors the history of the Christian mission in the
    North narrated by Adam of Bremen in his eleventh century *Gesta Hammaburgensis Ecclesiae*

Shall be so too, untill't all bleed.
Then (when that issue is extinct)
Norway and Denmarkes whole precinct   400
Shall be rul'd by Landgartha's line,
And Reyners. Her the power's divine
Will (for her Morall vertues) turne
A Christian, ere she come to th'Urne:
Yeeld faith to this: For, without doubt,   405
What I have sayd shall come about.   Exit Ang[el] then Eric stirs
ERIC. Sir, you sleep exceedingly soundly: Pray wake.   and wakes Har[rold]
HARROLD I now am fresh enough; Come let's be gone.
ERIC Dream't you nothing, while you slept?
HARROLD No, did you?   410
ERIC Me thought I heard a most heavenly Musicke;
    And that an Angel did appeare: and wish'd us,
    Betake our selves again to th'Emperor,
    That what we lost, another day sho'd purchase;
    And that the faire Landgartha (as the reward   415
    Of her Morall vertues) would be made Christian,
    Before she di'd.
HARROLD Though we afford no credit
    Unto such dreames:²²⁷ Yet we must steere our course
    That way; there being (after so great a losse)   420
    No comfort left, where our foes are so strong.
ERIC Heaven will in time (I hope) revenge our wrong.   Exeunt.

                    Enter Cowsell and Radgee.

COWSELL Come brother Radgee, it is now concluded,
    We shall never part agen.

227 Lines 415–16: the Christian Bible has numerous warnings against the dangers of accepting

        Pontificum (Deeds of Bishops of the Hamburg Church) and repeated in the *Chronicon Roskildense*
        [Roskilde Chronicle] (*c.*1137–8). In this account, Harrold's brother Erik succeeds him at his
        death and he is in turn succeeeded by his son 'Eric the Child' who is first antagonistic towards
        but later converts to Christianity. The (unsourced) claim that Landgartha converts to
        Christianity is repeated and enhanced in an anonymous early nineteenth-century account of her
        life, *The Storie of Faire Landgartha, Queene of Norway* (London, 1827), also collected in Lady
        Charlotte Bury, *Journal of the Heart* (London, 1830), pp 99–128. This dream-vision does not
        occur in Burnell's sources but his invention responds to the appearance of St Patrick's guardian
        angel while Patrick sleeps just before he expels the serpents in Shirley, *St Patrick for Ireland*, 5.3.
227   Lines 415–16: the Christian Bible has numerous warnings against the dangers of accepting
        dreams as prophesies, e.g., Ecclesiastes 5:7: 'For in the multitude of dreams and many words
        there are also divers vanities: but fear thou God'.

RADGEE O deare brother,   425
    I never had a good day on't (much lesse
    A good night) since (being barr'd the comfort of your
    Sweet conversation) you parted from me.
COWSELL Nay brother, I can howle the same sad Madrigall
    Too: For looke you brother, (we were all so frighted   430
    By those fat-foggy²²⁸ *Germans* (who men say
    Are nothing but flesh and belly:) that we durst
    Allow no time for mirth and drinking.
RADGEE Very
    Strange that brother. For, they say themselves are   435
    Exceeding good fellowes.
COWSELL Just of that seize.
RADGEE I'll tell you more what I heard spoken of 'em,
    Brother, they're sowre: and never worth the trusting,
    Or honest i' their bargaines, untill they   440
    Be drunke, or at least halfe drunke.
COWSELL That's as true,
    Brother, as that you and I drunke halfe a score
    Flaggons yesternight a peece. The North winde
    Is not so bitter in a morning, till he   445
    Has tooke a buttrum,²²⁹ or his Wine.
RADGEE And then,
    Makes as good Musicke, as a Bagpipe when it's
    Full blow'n. What doe you thinke of the *Swedes*? brother.
COWSELL They are not (yet) altogether so good drinkers,   450
    As th' *Germans* are: but well fall'n to 't of late.
    Which makes me suppose, brother, they'll be beaten
    Out too. For besides, the King will no more kisse
    The Queene *Vraca,* as 't is spoken: But sticke
    To's owne old Camrade, being indeed the fairer.   455
RADGEE Yet, in my opinion brother: his Grace
    Being marry'd to both, sho'd doe exceeding well,
    To keepe both still: Sleepe betwixt both 'a' nights:
    And imbrace both by turnes. What say you brother?
COWSELL What? But to concurre with you? and for many   460
    Good, and convincing reasons. 's for example:
    The King being kept so warme on both sides, by
    Two such delicate cre'tures, 't were impossible
    He sho'd catch cold; I, or perchance be troubl'd

228 fat-foggy = bloated and fat.   229 buttrum = butt or cask of rum.

With Coughs, Scyaticas, or other bone-ach; 465
And to have *Swealand* and *Norway* at command,
Were a matter of no small importance,
You conceive me, brother.
RADGEE[230] Few wise men better
In part. But, stand aside: themselves are comming. *Florish.* 470

Enter Reyner, Landgartha, Valdemar, Vraca, Scania, Inguar, Elsinora,
Fatyma, Hubba and Marfisa; the Norwegian Ladies
in womans apparell, with Swords on; Marfisa
with her Gown untuck'd and sword on.

INGUAR You will not (gracious Madame) thus deceive
    The expectations of your poore, and loving
    People: whose whole hopes, comfort, safetie (nay all
    We can for the present, or hereafter call ours)
    Are but benefits deriv'd from the fountaine 475
    Of your warme bountie; at whose goodnesse yet
    We most rejoyce. Doe not then (deare Empresse,) strike
    Sorrow to our lately bleeding hearts; that still
    Pant (and not slowly) by our former feares;
    And the sore stripes we tooke: Which, but for you, 480
    For ever were incurable; and now
    By your forsaking of us, will fester worse
    Then before.
LANDGARTHA That you neede not feare, Lord *Inguar*.
    For, I shall ne'r be wanting in my care, 485
    And love unto this Nation. Leaving here
    The best halfe of our Army, now behinde us;
    To prevent all future mischiefes.[231]
INGUAR Our dishonour
    In your departure, we shall ne'r recover. 490
REYNER My offence (which now's my worst affliction,
    With what it does occasion) all may see,
    Tooke origen and issue, more of humane
    Fraylitie, and foolish pride: then want of love
    To you; or of desert in you, to merit 495

230 In the original the speech is erroneously given to 'COWSELL'.
231 Lines 481–5: Landgartha's response counters contemporary resistance to Wentworth's 'Irish'
    army, particularly those in England and Scotland who viewed it as a potentially invasive rather
    than defensive force. See Introduction, pp 21–5.

A better and more pow'rfull man then I am;
Th' worlds onely Monarch, if there were but one,
For which, I (without your mercie to restore me
Once more unto your heart, as to my kingdomes)
Must spend my dayes (which shall not then be many)   500
Like to a sickely beast without a soule.
LANDGARTHA My heart shall still receive you: But, on my word,
Th' rest of my body you shall not enjoy, sir,
I now am gaunt[232] you see,
All though you must not have a feeling of it;   505
And if I doe play false, my belly will show't
Questionlesse: For, I am fruitfull if
I sho'd be touch'd.[233]
VALDEMAR Although but weakely, Madame.
LANDGARTHA It may be so.   510
SCANIA The Kings grace now pleads mercie,
Love, and repentance: and seeing there's no feare
He sho'd offend you any more, we all are
Sutors for him; and will become his sureties.[234]
LANDGARTHA I love him still I doe confesse: because   515
I gave him that, no other ever had
(Or shall have) from me; and mercie I have show'n
In my assistance. But, the wrong he did me
As I was his wife, being irreparable:
I will in Iustice punish, in not paying   520
To him (unfaithfull) the duties of a wife.
For, having often prov'd the way of falshood,
He may walke in't agen; and as before,
Without all kinde of scruple or remorse.
SCANIA[235] We'll all be bound, he shall no more leape o'r   525
The hedge: for, if he sho'd: We that doe now goe
Joyntly for him, wo'd then prove worse then varlets,[236]
To torment him.

232 gaunt = thin, i.e., no longer pregnant.
233 Lines 503–5: Landgartha's extraordinary fertility echoes that often imputed to Irish women
   by English commentators, see, for example, Spenser, 'View' in Ware (ed.), *The Historie of
   Ireland,* p. 38.
234 Sutors … sureties = we will all act as suitors for him (i.e., plead his case) and act as a bond for
   his good behaviour. Scania here echoes Landgartha's insistence on legal clarity.
235 SCANIA: The speech prefix is missing in the original; it is necessary to make sense of the
   exchange. It has been added in MS only in the Houghton copy.
236 varlet = male servant, also has the sense of male whore.

ELSINORA Come, leave your anger, and
    Be rul'd by those that love you.   530
VRACA I shall yeeld
    Up willingly my clayme to you, that best
    Deserve him.
LANDGARTHA Your clayme is nothing: and your
    Possession is but meere intrusion   535
    On what's anothers due, if she were pleas'd
    To challenge it; I'll say no more, because you are
    A woman.
VRACA I thought what I did was well done;
    And therefore in my minde at least am free,   540
    Being often told the lawfulnesse, by all.
LANDGARTHA By those that measur'd the length of their conclusions,
    By the crooked line of your affections.
    But as I kill'd your father (that had rather
    Then th' worth of your great dowry, have made me   545
    His second wife)[237] I could with farre more ease
    (As all the world can witnesse) be reveng'd
    On you, and this your kinde friend: but that I wav'd
    Him for my husband, that despis'd me as
    His honest Mate; and wo'd 'a' lov'd me for   550
    By-blowes.[238] Therefore, enjoy him still: for, I suppose
    You are a Hen, that must be trod.[239]
VRACA That's more then you know; or I hope shall finde.
REYNER She shall ne'r enjoy me; nor has not
    Of a long time I'll sweare, if that will serve.   555
LANDGARTHA It shall not (sir) beleeve it. Yet, ne'r feare
    You shall be arm'd i' th' front[240] by me; which is
    A wrong this other Lady cannot doe you,
    If she wo'd.[241]
VRACA I'll leave that now for you, that have   560
    The abler bodie.
LANDGARTHA And you the frayler minde.

---

237 your father = i.e., Frollo.
238 By-blowes = a side blow not aimed at the legitimate target, therefore extra-marital affairs and, by extension, illegitimate children.
239 a Hen that must be trod = i.e., copulated with. Cockerels 'tread' the female while mating, sometimes inflicting serious injury.
240 arm'd i' th' front = cuckolded, given the horns associated with infidelity.
241 i.e. only Landgartha can cuckold Reyner as only she is his legitimate wife.

But if you chop words²⁴² with me thus, or insult:
I may (for a farwell) cracke your birds necke,
Before we part.   565

VRACA I must not stand so neere   *She steps behinde Reyner, and holds*
    You then.   *him betwixt Langartha and her selfe.*

REYNER Nor I prove any safeguard for you.   *Steps from betwixt them.*
    But sho'd take part with her, whom I love best;
    And has best right unto me.   570

VRACA That you say
    To flatter her, and for meere feare. But if
    I had you in private, I know what you
    Wo'd sing; and play too, if I sho'd but yeeld.   *Land[gartha] runs at her,*
                                                     and Elsinora steps in.

ELSINORA What doe you meane?   575

LANDGARTHA That I will ne'r have him,
    That is resolv'd.

ELSINORA Your resolution
    (I must say) in that, is worse then madnesse.

LANDGARTHA I'll not quarrell with you, Aunt. Yet, doe admire²⁴³   580
    A Lady of your know'n modestie, should be
    So farre mistaken, and in such a cause.

ELSINORA It's you that are mistaken: I confesse
    I was at first an opposit²⁴⁴ in your love
    Unto the King: but, seeing you would needs   585
    Yeeld (then) your virgin Forte unto his Highnesse:
    I now wo'd have you take what wives doe use;
    And let me still live chaste, that doe professe it.

SCANIA My Aunt sayes more (to me I am sure she did:)
    All ought to live according their vocation.   590
    And not preposterously prove aliens to it.
    Nor will it serve to say he tore the bond,
    Now that he's sorry for't: For, still the generall good
    Must be preferr'd to all particular
    Merit; or that devotion that may   595
    By foolish zeale, prove a too great offence.

LANDGARTHA I must hear more opinions, ere I part
    From my strong purpose: therefore sir, adieu.
    Be merciful in chiefe, unto your subjects;

---

242 chop words = exchange or bandy words.   243 admire = wonder that.
244 opposit in = opposed to.

To allure their hearts, by love:[245] that being the tye   600
That will hold strongest; never can be broken,
Unless by fooles, or mad men. For, that partie
That sho'd tend to any mischiefe, 'gainst a good Prince:
Were first to kill all his subjects, being the Kings friends;
Or perish himselfe, by his fatall and bad   605
Purpose. Be just and vertuous, and you neede not
Feare poyson, poynards, or conspiracie.
To end: *Norway* shall be preserv'd for your young sonne;[246]
And as for me (though yours:) I'll end my life,
An honest widdow, or forsaken wife.   *Exit with Elsinora,* 610
VALDEMAR I must take leave too.   *Fatyma, & Marfisa*
REYNER Farewell, worthiest Cousin.
SCANIA You know the way to *Norway,* Sir, and if
    I might advise so wise a King to follow
    Us thither, and not slowly: that honourable   615
    Obligation would so bind your Queene
    (Being seconded by us your friends, and reason)
    That I beleeve what now she does denie,
    She wo'd then grant; especially, when she
    Perceives you constant in your vow'd affection: 620
    For this perchance she do's to tempt and try you.
    Nay, I am sure she do's; and that she will be
    Yours againe, if you persever in your love to her,
    In the meane time, I shall not fayle to prove,
    Your grace's faithfull, loving advocate.   625
REYNER In you the anchor of my trust lyes only fix'd
    Deare sister. I must follow your advise.   *kisses her.*

Exit Scania & Valdemar.

RADGEE O brother, brother: must we part at last?   *They imbrace.*
COWSELL No, no: get afore; I'll steale along with you.   *Exeunt Cow[sell]*
REYNER *Inguar,* Did'st thinke our hopes sho'd end in this?   *& Radgee.*
INGUAR It may prove better; and I hope it will sir.   630
REYNER Accursed *Fate* of man, of foolish man,

---

245 Lines 597–9: Landgartha cautions Reyner against tyranny, cf. Shirley, *St Patrick for Ireland,* f.
     B4r. 'I had rather hold my servant/By his owne love that chaines his heart to mine,/Than all
     the bands of state.'
246 sonne = i.e., Friedlef, see note 212.

That cannot prize a Jewell while he has it,
Till it be lost, and then his griefe is vaine,
Vaine and unprofitable, when no hope   635
Is left to finde it, which I feare's my case;
Our miserie the mirror's made, by which
We onely see our faults, our dangerous wounds.
Which likely then can never be recur'd:
Being Gangreene filthy sores, that doe Corrode   640
So farre into the very soule of man,
That they hale to sad desperation.
To which point I'm almost arriv'd, the Gemme
I lost, being so rich, as all earths Potentates
A richer could not boast.[247] Which if I finde not   645
(Strucke with my dire misfortune) my owne hand   *Exit with*
Shall send my spirit to the *Stygian* strand.[248]   *Ing[uar] & Hub[ba].*
VRACA And seeing I've walk'd astray, I will from hence:
By future good to expiate my offence.   *Exit in the middle.*

FINIS.

---

247 Lines 630–2: cf. *Othello* 5.2. 344–6 'of one whose hand,/Like the base Indian, threw a pearl
     away/Richer than all his tribe'. See also Proverbs 31:10 on the virtuous woman.
248 Stygian strand = the banks of the river Styx, the crossing to the Underworld.

EPILOGUE.

Scania (that spoke the Prologue) now delivers the
Epilogue, apparrelled as in the last Scene,
with her Sword and Belt in
her hand.

Though our Author cares not how his Play may take:
Yet, cause he purposes not to forsake
In his affection, any Worthy here;
He hath sent me 'fore the Court breake up, to appeare
For him agen; to see how it hath pleas'd:
For, notwithstanding he meanes to be eas'd;   5
For ever of th' like taske: Yet, from his heart
He wishes, you and he sho'd fairely part.
And this he more (for him) desir'd me say:
Where others spend a yeare about a Play
(Picking a sentence here, a word from thence)   10
This Tragie-Comedy with the expence
Of lesse then two Moneths time he pen'd: For he
's not too ambitious of the dignitie
Of a prime Poet; which he needs must know,
The Muses chiefe (*Apollo*) doth bestow   15
But very rarely. Himselfe he knowes too
Better i' th' Art then some that to be so
Thought worthy, maligne him. If this please you,
It's all he'll ask of *Hellicon:*[249] Adieu.

Some (*but not of best judgements*) *were offended at the Conclusion of this Play, in regard* Landgartha *tooke not then, what she was perswaded to by so many, the Kings kind night-imbraces. To which kind of people (that know not what they say) I answer (omitting all other reasons:) that a Tragie-Comedy sho'd neither end Comically or Tragically, but betwixt both: which* Decorum *I did my best to observe, not to goe against Art, to please the over-amorous. To the rest of bablers, I despise any answer.*[250]

This Play was first Acted on *S. Patricks* day,
1639. with the allowance of the
Master of Revels.[251]

249 Hellicon = mountain in Greece, home of the Muses.
250 On this afterword, see Introduction, pp 64–6.
251 Master of Revels = John Ogilby. See Introduction, pp 13, 25, 32.

List of emendations

[Prefatory Verses]
Eleonora Burnell Poems
Abbreviated forms lengthened atq to atque:
I, l.15 sciteque; II, l.8, atque; l.10, Brutaginaeque; l.11 quacunque
In Bod Malone 203 (2), the name 'Eleonora Burnell' is cropped.

Jo. Bermingham Poem
In Bod Malone 203 (2), 'Jo. Bermingham' and the last line of Bermingham's poem are
cropped.

Philippus Patricius Poem
Abbreviated forms lengthened atq to atque:
l. 3 votoque; l. 4 Ioniumque; l.5 suavisque; l.10 multorumque; l.12 symmetriaeque; l.18 cri-
minibusque

Prologue
l. 5: were] we e
l. 7: therefore] There ore

The first Act
ll. 72, 82, 283: stage direction moved from right hand margin to square brackets in text.
l. 23: launch'd] lanch'd
l. 118: off] of

The second Act
l. 84: stage direction moved from right hand margin to square brackets in text and ascribed to
Hubba, l. 84, for sense of scene.
l. 211: dispos'd it] dispos' itd
l. 220: full stop added at line end.
ll. 224, 249, 451, 454: stage direction moved from right hand margin to square brackets in text.
l. 295: grace's] grac's
l. 502: stage direction moved from right hand margin to square brackets in text and placed to
make sense of address.

The third Act
l. 16: Inserted new line. The original runs on to fit the page.
l. 17: Make] make. Stage direction moved from right hand margin to square brackets in text.
l. 22: Radgar] in original
l. 44: Brother] brother
l. 94: Give] give. Stage direction moved from right hand margin to square brackets in text.
l. 139: On] on. Inserted new line. The original runs on to fit the page.
l. 183: a strayn'd] astrayn'd

The fourth Act
l. 59: dog's head] dog-shead
l. 78: stage direction moved to l. 79 to make sense of action.
ll. 96, 135, 170. 229: stage direction moved from right hand margin to square brackets in text

The fifth Act
Title: fifth act] fift act
l. 128: stage direction moved from right hand margin to square brackets in text.
l. 385: Let's] let's. Inserted new line. The original runs on to fit the page.
l. 449: speech prefix: replace COWSELL with RADGEE
l. 525: speech prefix SCANIA added.

Appendix:
'The persons of the Play'

What follows is a brief summary of key sources for each of the characters listed. It includes an account of their appearance in (or in the case of 'invented characters' their absence from):

Saxo Grammaticus, *The History of the Danes, Books I–IX*, ed. Hilda Ellis Davidson translated by Peter Fisher (Cambridge: Boydell and Brewer, 1998) (*HD*)

and

François de Belleforest, *Le Quatriesme Tome des Histoires Tragiques: Partie extraictes des oeuvres Italiennes de Bandel, & partie de l'invention de l'Autheur Francois* (Turin, 1571) (*HT*)

as well as the place they occupy in a contemporary allegorical reading of *Landgartha* and a note of possible appearances in other early modern literary works. For further consideration of Burnell's access to and use of sources, see Introduction, pp 36–51. It is worth noting that Burnell significantly alters the names of the following characters from their sources: Frollo; Landgartha; Reyner. In the case of Landgartha, this becomes the accepted spelling of her name in later English drama and prose.

Frollo: Also Frø/Freyr/Fro: king of Sweden, ancestor of the kings of Uppsala and associated as the god Freyr with a fertility cult thought to involve human sacrifice. In Saxo Grammaticus Frø invades Norway, kills Regner's grandfather Sivard II and sets the Norwegian noble-women to public prostitution. Regner, king of Denmark, invades Norway to seek revenge; the wronged women, Lathgertha among them, assist him and Regner kills Frø (*HD*, I, p. 280, II, pp 55, 109). In Belleforest, Fro is hunted down and slain by the women (*HT*, 849). In Burnell's allegory, Frollo is identified with the Scots. A minor character named Frollo appears in Sir William Davenant, *The Tragedy of Albovine, King of the Lombards* (London, 1629), but bears no relation to Burnell's character.

Hasmond and *Gotar:* Invented characters. The names Hamundus and Hamund (father and son) and Gøthar (given to a Norwegian and a Swedish warrior) are found in Saxo Grammaticus (*HD*, I, pp 113–15, 212–14, 252–3). The character Gotharus appears in Shirley's Norwegian play *The Politician* (1655), believed to have been written *c.*1639, and possibly staged in Dublin. A machiavel advisor and politician, he engineers a wedding between his lover the widow Marpisa and the King in order to make their son Harald successor to the throne.

Landgartha: Also Lathgertha, Lagertha, Ladgertha, Ladgerda: shieldmaiden and first wife of Regner (see below). In Saxo Grammaticus, she is distinguished for her bravery among the Norwegian women who fight with Regner against Frø. Regner credits her with his victory, attempts to woo her and pursues her to her home in the Gaulardal valley. There he kills the bear and the hound that Lathgertha has set to guard her chastity, wins her and they have a son (Friedlef) and two daughters. After three peaceful years Regner leaves Lathgertha to put down a rebellion back in Denmark, falls in love with Thora, daughter of the king of Sweden, and divorces Lathgertha. She remarries after their divorce but nonetheless comes to Regner's aid and again secures his victory when he asks for her help to put down a rebellion by Harald Klak (see below). On Lathgertha's return to Norway, she abruptly kills her second husband in order to claim sole power. Lathgertha appears only in Saxo Grammaticus though his editor suggests that the figure is derived from *Hlaðgerðr* (Hladgerd) who appears in the sixth-century Halfdan sagas; on the goddess Thorgerd, indigenous to Lathgetha's home, the Gauderdal valley; on a possible Frankish tradition of a warrior maiden Leutgarde and more generally on the iconography of the loose-haired Valkyries (*HD*, I, pp 281–3, II, pp 151–2, 154–5). Belleforest omits all mention of a second husband and establishes his 'Landgerthe' as a quasi-saintly model of northern loyalty and chastity (*HT*, 875). In Burnell's allegory, Landgartha is identified with the Old English in Ireland. Lathgertha is also the subject of Joshua Barnes' manuscript masque 'Landgartha, or the Amazon Queen of Denmark and Norway'. Written to celebrate the marriage of Anne, daughter of James, duke of York (soon to be James II) and Prince George, son of Christian V, king of Denmark and Norway, in July 1683, the masque was neither performed nor published.

Scania: Invented character, one of the Norwegian Amazons and thus identified in *Landgartha* as Old English in Ireland. Scania was the Roman term for what is now the Southern tip of Sweden; until 1658, Scania was part of the kingdom of Denmark. During the Lathgertha episode in Saxo Grammaticus, Regner puts down a series of rebellions involving the people of Jutland and Scania perhaps giving a source for the name (*HD*, I, pp 281–2).

Elsinora: Invented character, one of the Norwegian Amazons and thus identified in *Landgartha* as Old English in Ireland. Helsingør is on the east coast of Denmark across a narrow strait from Scania; here the English spelling Elsinore follows Shakespeare's name for the fifteenth-century Kronborg castle in Helsingør, the location of *Hamlet*.

Fatyma: Invented character, here indicating the Eastern connections of the Amazon Marfisa/Marpesia (see below). In Burnell's allegory, she is closely identified with Marfisa and thus Old Irish interests. Fatyma/Fatima is the doomed daughter of Prince Mirza and grand-daughter of Abbas, king of Persia, in both Sir John Denham, *The Sophy: A Tragedy* (1641), and Robert Baron, *Mirza* (1655). A Fatima also appears in Sir William Lower's *The Nobel Ingratitude* (1659), a translation from Philippe Quinault,

Marfisa: Based on Marfisa, the Amazon warrior who first appears in Matteo Maria Boiardo, *Orlando inamorato*, and is further developed in Ludovico Ariosto, *Orlando Furioso*, translated into English by Sir John Harrington (1591). She appears nowhere in either Saxo Grammaticus or Belleforest. Separated from her twin brother Ruggiero when a child, Marfisa becomes queen of India and fights for the Saracens. She later converts to Christianity and fights for the Holy Roman Emperor, Charlemagne. Unlike Bradamante, the Christian Amazon figure who eventually marries Ruggiero, Marfisa retains her Amazon identity to the end. Her name and Eastern connections suggest links with Marpesia (also Marthesia), legendary queen of the Amazons. In Burnell's allegory Marfisa is identified with Old Irish interests. The strength and steadfastness of her character is a direct riposte to the corrupt and ruthless Norwegian Queen Marpisa in James Shirley, *The Politician* (1655), believed to have been written c.1639, and possibly staged in Dublin.

Fredericke and Wermond: Invented characters. No Frederick appears in Saxo Grammaticus, though Valdemar II, to whom the *HD* is addressed, invaded the territory of Frederick II of Germany. Wermond may invoke the tale of the Danish king, Vermund, whose son Offa brings about peace by a duel, a tale also told in Anglo-Saxon chronicles (*HD*, II, p. 67).

Reyner: Also Regner/Ragnar/Regner Lothbrog/Ragnar Lodbrok ('Ragnar of the Shaggy Breeches'). Regner is the central, quasi-mythical figure in Book Nine of Saxo Grammaticus.

As noted above (see Landgartha) Regner, king of Denmark, invades Norway to avenge his grandfather and, with Lathgertha's help, defeats Frø. He then pursues, woos and wins Lathgertha, killing the bear and the hound which she has set to guard her chastity. He lives peacefully with her for three years; they have a son (Friedlef) and two daughters. Regner then falls in love with Thora, daughter of the king of Sweden, divorces Lathgertha, and wins Thora by killing the monstrous snakes she keeps: the protective trousers he wears for the task earn him the name 'Lodbrok'. When Harrald Klak (see below) raises a rebellion against Regner, Lathgertha comes to his aid and together they defeat him. On Thora's death, Regner goes on to father further children and marry a third wife. He defeats resistance at home, including a rebellion by his son Ubbi and brings good laws to Denmark. He also wages a series of raids and campaigns abroad, including the defeat and capture of Dublin, eventually dying in a snake-pit at the hands of King Ælla of Northumbria (*HD*, I, pp 279–93, II, pp 150–5). Alternative and amplified versions of the life of Regner/Ragnar and his sons are found in the Icelandic prose works *Ragnars Saga and Páttr of Ragnars Sonum* and in the two poems *Krákumál* and Ragnar's *Death Lay*. Lathgertha does not appear in these other sources; instead Ragnar marries Aslaug (also known as Aslög, Kraka, Kráka, Randalin), the disguised daughter of Sigurd and Brynhildr. In Burnell's allegory, Reyner is identified as English and more particularly may be read as a controversial figure for Charles I.

Valdemar: Invented character. His name is taken from two kings of Denmark who feature in Saxo Grammaticus: Valdemar I (1131–82) and his son Valdemar II (1170–1241) to whom the Preface is addressed. The first, also known as Valdemar the Great, rebuilt Denmark after a long period of civil war; the second, also know as Valdemar the Victorious, is credited with a Golden Age of Danish expansion (*HD*, I, p. 6, II, pp 20–1). Burnell's Valdemar figures the role of good – though often spurned – advisor. He also, as devisor of the Masque in Act 3, suggests a writer/historian figure such as Saxo Grammaticus, or indeed Burnell himself.

Inguar and *Hubba*: Invented characters. Though Burnell's sympathetic and entertaining characters are very different, the names Inguar and Hubba invoke Ragnar's legendary sons Ivar/Hynguar/Ingwar Ragnarson (Ivar the Boneless) and Ubbi/Ubbe Ragnarson. In Saxo Grammaticus, Ivar is the son of Thora and Ubbi of the high-born woman, with whom Ragnar lodges, disguised as a maidservant. Ubbi leads a rebellion against his father whom he disrespects because of the circumstances of his birth. Once reconciled, both sons accompany their father on his expedition to Dublin. Ivar later leads an expedition to England to avenge his father's death in the snakepit at the hands of King Ælla of Northumbria. Their exploits are elaborated further in the *Ragnars Saga*, where they are the sons of Ragnar and Aslaug. According to Abbo of Fleury's account of the passion of St Edmund, Ivar the Boneless was responsible for the martyrdom of King Edmund of East Anglia (869 AD). Ubbi is also associated with this expedition. Ivar is also identified in the *Annals of Ulster* with Ímar, founder of the Uí Ímair, the Viking dynasty who ruled the Kingdom of Dublin throughout the ninth century and died in 873 (*HD*, I, pp 286–92, II, pp 153–4, 156–7). A character named Hubba appears in the intriguing play *Locrine* (*c*.1591), variously attributed in the past to Shakespeare, Greene and Peele and influenced by Spenser. The play, based on Geoffrey of Monmouth's Brutus myth, tells of Brutus's son and inheritor Locrine. Hubba is the son of the Scythian King Humber who leads an – entirely fictional – invasion of Britain; Hubba's mother, in defeat, becomes Locrine's secret lover.

Cowsell and *Radgee*: Invented characters with no obvious source: Cowsell, as his name suggests, is the rural cousin; Radgee (diminutive of Radger – also used in text) is more used to court life. The Oxford English Dictionary lists a 1665 use of the world Radgee for Raja, meaning maharaja.

Rolfo: Invented character. Rolf/Hrolf Krake, the sixth-century Danish king, appears in Saxo Grammaticus and in Anglo-Saxon sources (*HD*, I, pp 38–9, II, pp 43–50).

Harrold: Harald 'Klak' Halfdansson (*c.*785–*c.*852) ruled in Jutland twice, *c.*812–14 and *c.*819–27. On being expelled a second time from Denmark, he famously travelled to Mainz to ask Louis the Pious for support and was baptized a Christian. In Saxo Grammaticus Lathgertha's assistance is pivotal in Regner's defeat of Harald Klak's rebellion (*HD,* I, pp 282–4, 290–1, 294, II, pp 154–5). He also appears in Belleforest (*HT,* 869). Burnell brings forward the date of Harrold's conversion making him Christian at his first appearance in the play.

Eric: Saxo Grammaticus briefly mentions 'Erik, the brother of Harald' who invades Denmark after the death of Regner and Thora's son, Sivard III (also known as Snake in the Eye). This Erik is quickly deposed and killed and Erik I, Sivard III's young son (thus Regner's grandson), takes back the throne. He first persecutes, later promotes, Christianity, building a church at Hedeby. Erik I's direct descendants include Gorm II ('the Englishman') and Harald III (Æthelred of England) (*HD,* I, pp 293, 294, II, p. 162). Burnell seems to fuse the two Eriks in the Angel's prophecy (5. 390–404) when the links of the progeny of Eric with England are foretold.

Lothaire: Lothair (or Lothar) I (795–855), eldest son of Emperor Louis the Pious. He ruled alongside his father from 817–40 and then as sole emperor until his death. He does not appear in Saxo Grammaticus or Belleforest.

Vraca: In Saxo Grammaticus, Regner's second wife is Thora; in Belleforest, she is nameless. The name Vraca does however invoke Kraka, one of the names for Ragnar Lodbrok's wife Aslaug in the saga sources. Burnell's allegory names Vraca as Frollo's daughter and thus identifies her with Scotland.